R. Joseph Ponniah · Sathyaraj Venkatesan
Editors

The Idea and Practice of Reading

 Springer

Editors
R. Joseph Ponniah
Department of Humanities and Social
  Sciences
National Institute of Technology
Tiruchirappalli, Tamil Nadu
India

Sathyaraj Venkatesan
Department of Humanities and Social
  Sciences
National Institute of Technology
Tiruchirappalli, Tamil Nadu
India

ISBN 978-981-10-8571-0   ISBN 978-981-10-8572-7   (eBook)
https://doi.org/10.1007/978-981-10-8572-7

Library of Congress Control Number: 2018934940

© Springer Nature Singapore Pte Ltd. 2018
This work is subject to copyright. All rights are reserved by the Publisher, whether the whole or part of the material is concerned, specifically the rights of translation, reprinting, reuse of illustrations, recitation, broadcasting, reproduction on microfilms or in any other physical way, and transmission or information storage and retrieval, electronic adaptation, computer software, or by similar or dissimilar methodology now known or hereafter developed.
The use of general descriptive names, registered names, trademarks, service marks, etc. in this publication does not imply, even in the absence of a specific statement, that such names are exempt from the relevant protective laws and regulations and therefore free for general use.
The publisher, the authors and the editors are safe to assume that the advice and information in this book are believed to be true and accurate at the date of publication. Neither the publisher nor the authors or the editors give a warranty, express or implied, with respect to the material contained herein or for any errors or omissions that may have been made. The publisher remains neutral with regard to jurisdictional claims in published maps and institutional affiliations.

Printed on acid-free paper

This Springer imprint is published by the registered company Springer Nature Singapore Pte Ltd. part of Springer Nature
The registered company address is: 152 Beach Road, #21-01/04 Gateway East, Singapore 189721, Singapore

*Dedicated to
Jessica Josephene
Joshua Benedict
and
Taran Sathyaraj*

Acknowledgements

We wish to thank our contributors, not only for waiting patiently throughout the process but also for making this book possible. Our thanks to Gurumurthy Neelakantan, Professor of English, Indian Institute of Technology, Kanpur for advising us to submit our book prospectus to Springer. We wish to extend our thanks to our many friends and acquaintance who provided constant support and encouragement.

Our warmest appreciation to the faculty of the Department of Humanities and Social Sciences, National Institute of Technology, Trichy. We also wish to thank Shinjini Chatterjee and Priya Vyas for their valuable assistance and editorial work throughout the process. They are devoted professionals.

Our families. They are special to us.

R. Joseph Ponniah
Sathyaraj Venkatesan

Contents

1. **The Idea, Practice and Power of Reading** 1
   R. Joseph Ponniah and Sathyaraj Venkatesan

2. **Twenty-First-Century Second Language Literacy Development in Universities** 11
   Hazel L. W. Chiu

3. **Extensive Reading and Vocabulary Acquisition** 25
   Nina Daskalovska

4. **Acquisition of Writing by Reading and Its Impact on Cognition** 41
   J. Mary Jennifer and R. Joseph Ponniah

5. **Blending Cognitive and Socio-constructive Pedagogies: Building Autonomous Readers in the ESL Classroom** 57
   Kshema Jose

6. **Using L1 Reading Strategies to Develop L2 Reading** 85
   Mahananda Pathak

7. **First-Language Reading Promotes Second-Language Reading and Acquisition: Towards a Biolinguistic Approach** 113
   R. Joseph Ponniah

8. **Genetics of Reading Ability and Its Role in Solving Reading Difficulties** 125
   Radhakrishnan Sriganesh, D. R. Rahul and R. Joseph Ponniah

9. **Reading Comprehension in ESL Contexts: An Applied Cognitive Semantics Perspective** 141
   N. P. Sudharshana

10	**Perspectives from the Art and Science of Reading** 163
	C. E. Veni Madhavan and C. N. Ajit
11	**Cognitive Load Theory, Redundancy Effect and Language Learning** 177
	Carlos Machado and Pedro Luis Luchini

Editors and Contributors

About the Editors

R. Joseph Ponniah, Ph.D., is Associate Professor of English in the Department of Humanities and Social Sciences at the National Institute of Technology, Tiruchirappalli. His current research and teaching interest include Biolinguistics, Reading, English Language Teaching and Second Language Acquisition. He is widely published in peer-reviewed international journals, such as *The International Journal of Foreign Language Teaching*, *The Reading Matrix*, *Journal of Asia TEFL* and *Journal on Educational Psychology*. He has delivered keynote addresses and invited talks in conferences and workshops and has also mentored ESL teachers in Orientation and Training Programmes.

Sathyaraj Venkatesan is Associate Professor of English in the Department of Humanities and Social Sciences at the National Institute of Technology, Tiruchirappalli. He received his Ph.D. from the Indian Institute of Technology (IIT) Kanpur and was a Fellow at the School of Criticism and Theory at Cornell University, New York. He is currently a Senior International Field Bibliographer with the Publications of Modern Language Association of America (PMLA). He is the author of *Edgar Allan Poe: Tales and Other Writings* (2017, Orient BlackSwan), *AIDS in Cultural Bodies: Scripting the Absent Subject (1980–2010)* (2016, Cambridge Scholars Publishing) with Gokulnath Ammanathil, and *Mapping the Margins: A Study of Ethnic Feminist Consciousness in Toni Morrison's Novels* (2011). He has published over 50 research papers in peer-reviewed international journals.

Contributors

C. N. Ajit obtained his BE and M.Tech. degrees from the Indian Institute of Science (IISc), Bangalore and Indian Institute of Technology, Bombay. He joined the R&D wing of ITI Ltd. in 1974, and has subsequently moved to CDAC, Kolkata and a number of other companies to head the R&D function. He has many publications and presentations in national and international forums. His work has been recognized by awards for outstanding R&D performance (1993) and excellence in indigenous development (1996). He is currently working at the Society for Innovation and Development at the Indian Institute of Science with responsibility in the areas of Industry–Academia Interaction and Entrepreneurship. His current research interests lie in interdisciplinary areas.

Hazel L. W. Chiu received her Ph.D. degree from the Institute of Education, University of London. She has taught English language and linguistics courses at the Hong Kong Polytechnic University and the Open University of Hong Kong. Her professional/research interests include reading and writing, grammar teaching and learning, task-based language teaching, the use of language arts materials for language teaching, and independent language learning. She has published articles on extensive reading, university writing and independent language learning.

Nina Daskalovska is Associate Professor at Goce Delcev University, Republic of Macedonia. She obtained her M.A. degree in applied linguistics and English language teaching from the University of Nottingham, UK, and her Ph.D. from Sts. Cyril and Methodius University in the Republic of Macedonia. Her areas of interest include English language teaching methodology, vocabulary acquisition, extensive reading and computer-assisted language learning.

J. Mary Jennifer is pursuing a Ph.D. at the National Institute of Technology, Department of Humanities and Social Sciences, Tiruchirappalli, India. Her research interests include reading and cognition, reading–writing relationships and promoting extensive reading in second-language contexts.

Kshema Jose is Assistant Professor of English at the Department for Training and Development in EFLU, Hyderabad. She received her Ph.D. from the Central Institute of English and Foreign Languages, Hyderabad in the area of hypertext reading. She specializes in digital literacy and new literacies, and has conducted national and international teacher training programmes in the use of technology in the ESL classroom. She has authored, co-authored and edited textbooks for English teaching and teacher training (*Reading Module*, 2000) for the District Centre Scheme; *Fast Tracks II—A Multi-skill course in English* (2010), Cambridge University Press; and *The English Express. A skill-based Interactive Series* (2013), DC Books.

Pedro Luis Luchini is an English language trainer who graduated from the Universidad Nacional de Mar del Plata (UNMdP), Argentina. He has an M.A. in ELT and Applied Linguistics from King's College, University of London, UK and a Doctorate in Letters from UNMdP. He is a Fulbright scholar. He has taught Spanish as a foreign language at the College of DuPage, Illinois, USA and English as a foreign language at the Shanghai Normal University, China. He won the Faculty Enrichment Program Scholarship to visit Concordia University, Montreal, Canada, and a Doctoral Research Award Scholarship to Concordia University. He is currently a teacher-researcher and full-time Adjunct Professor for the English Teacher Training Program, Humanities Division, UNMdP and co-director of research group *"Cuestiones del Lenguaje"*, UNMDP. His areas of interest are: English language development, English applied phonology and cognition.

Carlos Machado holds an English teaching degree from the Universidad Nacional de Mar del Plata (UNMdP), and a Master's degree in applied linguistics from Universidad Cervantes, Spain. Currently, he is a Ph.D. candidate at the Universidad Nacional del Sur, Argentina. Carlos is a writing instructor at UNMdP and at tertiary institutions where he also teaches English grammar and research. He is a member of the research group *Cuestiones del Lenguaje* at UNMdP. His main areas of interests are writing, reading, language acquisition and cognition.

C. E. Veni Madhavan obtained his BE and ME in Electrical Engineering from the College of Engineering, Madras and BITS Pilani, respectively, and his Ph.D. in mathematical control theory from IISc. He joined the Computer Science and Automation Department of IISc in 1983 and retired formally in August 2014 as a Senior Professor. He has held many senior, scientific leadership positions at IISc and with the Indian government. He has published over 80 papers in refereed journals and conferences, delivered many invited talks, guided several theses, and worked on numerous R&D projects. He is the co-author of a book on public-key cryptography. In 2001 he obtained an award for distinguished services to mathematics education and research, and in 2011 received an award from IISc for excellence in research in engineering. He is presently working at IISc on R&D projects in the areas of cryptography and natural language processing and on technical activities spanning policy preparation, academic counselling and research mentorship.

Mahananda Pathak is Assistant Professor in the Department of Materials Development, Testing and Evaluation at the English and Foreign Languages University (EFLU), Hyderabad. Prior to joining EFLU, he was Assistant Professor of English at GITAM University, Hyderabad; Teaching Associate at the Tata Institute of Social Sciences (TISS), Hyderabad; an adjunct faculty in the English Language Teaching Centre (ELTC), University of Hyderabad; and a teacher trainer in Aizawl (Mizoram). His publications include "Using the 'Can Do' Self-Assessment Grid across Languages to Develop Academic Reading and Writing Skills: A Case Study", *Languaging* (October 2014); and "Maximized L1 to maximally enable L2: Why?" *Rajasthan ELTI Journal* (March 2012). His very recent publication includes a chapter in *Multilingual Education in India: The Case for English* (Viva Books, New Delhi, 2016). He enjoys working with learners from regional-medium backgrounds and has a special interest in developing bi/multilingual instructional materials for them.

D. R. Rahul is a Junior Research Fellow in the Department of Humanities and Social Sciences, National Institute of Technology, Tiruchirappalli, India. His area of interest is English language teaching (ELT) and his current research concentrates on biolinguistics with a focus on genetics of language and language disabilities. He has also worked as an assistant professor for two years in India.

N. P. Sudharshana is Assistant Professor of English in the Department of Humanities and Social Sciences at IIT Kanpur. His main research area is applying cognitive linguistics to teaching and learning English as a second language. His doctoral thesis was on the role of general cognition and language-specific patterns in encoding motion events and topological relations in English as a second language. Currently, he is working on designing a cognitive linguistics motivated task-based framework for grammatical and reading instruction in English as a second language (ESL) contexts. Previously, he worked on school curriculum projects in the states of Rajasthan and Haryana.

Radhakrishnan Sriganesh is a Junior Research Fellow in the Department of Humanities and Social Sciences, National Institute of Technology, Tiruchirappalli, India. His areas of research are the genetics of language acquisition and language disabilities. He has served as a soft skills trainer for two years (2014–2016) in KG Information Systems Private Limited Coimbatore, India and also worked as a credit analyst at Fido Telecom Services in Toronto, ON (Canada).

Chapter 1
The Idea, Practice and Power of Reading

R. Joseph Ponniah and Sathyaraj Venkatesan

Abstract This introductory chapter reviews the essays presented in this volume in the light of recent theories on reading. The chapter, while charting the paradigm shift occasioned by cognitivism and biolinguistics, emphasizes the multiple benefits of reading over explicit instruction. In particular, it states the centrality of cognition in the acquisition of all aspects of language such as vocabulary, syntax and grammar. Further, this foreword cum introductory essay illustrates global reading and literacy practices, and engages the potentials of general reading with a focus on meaning such as pleasure reading, extensive reading, free voluntary reading, etc. This essay also shows how general reading both promotes and facilitates academic reading. Finally, while reviewing and theoretically contextualizing the essays in this volume, this chapter not only attests to the centrality of reading and cognition but also to the critical role of reading in the acquisition of the properties of a language.

Keywords Cognition · Pleasure reading · Biolinguistics · Academic reading
Incidental acquisition of language

Preface to Reading and Language Practices

Second-language teaching and learning has witnessed a paradigm shift from behaviourism to cognitivism. Behaviourism, which was a dominant psychological theory between the two world wars, emphasized the role of environment and treated language as a set of rigid rules and habits. Further, behaviourism believed in training learners through tedious drills and exercises using tasks that reinforce

---

R. J. Ponniah (✉) · S. Venkatesan
Department of Humanities and Social Sciences, National Institute of Technology Tiruchirappalli, Tiruchirappalli, Tamil Nadu, India
e-mail: joseph@nitt.edu

© Springer Nature Singapore Pte Ltd. 2018
R. Joseph Ponniah and S. Venkatesan (eds.), *The Idea and Practice of Reading*,
https://doi.org/10.1007/978-981-10-8572-7_1

responses from learners for the acquisition of language. During the 1950s and later this was challenged by cognitivism, which emphasized the innate ability of human beings and the role of the mind in the acquisition of language. More importantly, cognitivists consider language as acquired through active engagement with meaning in the form of reading and listening. Human beings, after all, have an innate propensity to construct meaning as they use knowledge gained through prior experience and acquired knowledge to comprehend unfamiliar patterns and structures by associating new information with previous knowledge.

This shows not only how reading helps in generating new ideas but also how in the course of generating ideas readers incidentally acquire aspects of language such as vocabulary, syntax and grammar. Every time readers read unfamiliar words, they acquire partial meaning of words and repeated exposure to words resulting in the acquisition of complete meaning, which indicates that they acquire the grammar of words in addition to their meaning. Vocabulary knowledge is correlated with the amount of reading and this is the reason we find increasing differences in the vocabulary knowledge of readers and non-readers. Named the Matthew Effect, this phenomenon explains how readers become high achievers and non-readers become low achievers in terms of language acquisition.[1] In fact, readers acquire more meaning than the meaning given in dictionaries. For instance, the word 'rose' in Robert Burns' famous line 'My love is like a red, red rose' symbolically represents love but typically dictionaries do not give extended meanings of words. The inadequacy of dictionary meaning is discussed by Chomsky (2007). He explains that even in the best-studied languages, dictionaries and grammar books scratch only the basic properties of language. For instance, Chomsky, analysing a simple sentence, "John is painting the house brown", argues that we apparently know that John is not actually painting the complete concrete structure called house but only the external surface of walls. Put differently, dictionaries do not give such deeper-level meaning of words, but such meaning can be acquired by exposure to language by reading.

Language properties such as vocabulary, syntax and grammar do not exist in isolation and they complement each other to give complete meaning. Therefore, learning properties of language in isolation cannot help acquire language. Every linguistic element contains meaning and learners assign meaning to linguistic properties when they are exposed to such elements in contexts. Language contains both content words and functional words. However, teaching practices associate meaning only with the content words and not with the functional words. This is the reason linguistic elements are divided into two broad categories, grammar and vocabulary, in ESL textbooks. This compels teachers to teach vocabulary and grammar by decontextualizing language properties. Since learners consciously learn the meaning of words in isolation, the word meaning learnt explicitly fades away

---

[1]Coined by Keith Stanovich, a psychologist, the Matthew Effect refers to how regular readers become high achievers while below average readers become low achievers.

over a period of time, leaving the recall of such words poor. Further, learners experience difficulty using consciously learnt grammar rules in actual contexts.

In fact, reading helps in the incidental acquisition of grammatical properties of language and the meaning associated with them. When readers experience a new language structure, they assign some meaning to the structure using the current language and the mind stores the structure for future use. If similar kinds of structures appear in different contexts, the mind adds some more meaning to the partially acquired structures. The brain uses the acquired structures to generate a number of new structures. The generation of new structures happens when readers analyse, synthesize and evaluate the comprehended ideas to generate new ideas. The impact of reading on language and content improves composing/writing skills by positively affecting cognitive capabilities, as writing is a cognitive-linguistic process.

Despite consistent evidence supporting the claim that reading results in the acquisition of all aspects of language, teaching reading to students has been a challenging task for ESL teachers. This may be because reading is an unpleasant experience for novice and non-readers. Creating a positive attitude towards reading is necessary because this influences reading behaviour and beliefs about reading and compels readers to be involved in the content while reading. Providing books with themes that give pleasure will motivate a reader to read for pleasure because the brain seeks the path of pleasure to fulfil the innate propensity to grow. This implies that reading is more a 'psychological issue' than a 'language issue'. Studies over decades (Wurr, 2003; Carroll & Snowling, 2004; Nation, Clarke, & Snowling, 2002) have analysed and attributed reading difficulties to language problems but little research has been done to analyse the psychological problems involved in reading. Evidence (McEwen, Eiland, Hunter, & Miller, 2011; Blicher, Feingold, & Shany, 2017; Hewitt & Stephenson, 2012; Knickerbocker, Johnson, & Altarriba, 2015) from biology points out that negative emotions such as stress and anxiety are found to be detrimental, through genetic processes, to any learning, providing support to the claim that a reading problem is indeed a 'psychological problem'.

Studies of language transfer also claim that readers should have a threshold level of language competence in L2 for the transfer of L1 linguistic knowledge. Linguistic competence can enhance comprehension but cannot create an innate desire to read because the brain seeks pleasure from an activity and if reading is an unpleasant experience the brain will not allow a person to continue reading. This shows that competence in second language alone cannot promote reading but learners need conditions that support and fuel the intrinsic motivation to learn. Pleasure is a crucial ingredient that can support reading in both L1 and L2. If a learner has a pleasure reading habit in L1, he/she can easily be motivated to read an L2 text if the L2 text has a similar theme to L1 texts. The pleasure extracted from L1 reading will create a positive attitude towards L2 reading because it will intrinsically motivate a person to read. Such reading helps transfer both conceptual and linguistic knowledge to L2. Further, a wide range of cognitive abilities developed by reading L1 text can positively affect L2 reading and moreover, reading strategies acquired subconsciously in L1 can be used while reading L2 texts because there are common underlying principles that govern both L1 and L2.

Pleasure reading results in the acquisition of proficiency in general language and it makes academic reading more comprehensible and easier. Despite the benefits of reading, cramming and rote learning are given prime importance in academia to help students score well on tests. However, this approach to learning may be detrimental to thinking skills. In order for students to be analytical, critical and creative, they must be motivated to do more deep/academic reading. This not only improves performance on high-stakes standardized tests but also aids the acquisition of skills and deep knowledge in a specific discipline.

Academic reading is deep reading that strongly affects higher-order thinking skills, as it prompts readers to relate one idea to other ideas, to categorize and reorganize them in novel ways to come up with new ideas, and to relate them to personal experiences for further insights into theories, facts and concepts. This kind of critical reading results in the acquisition of domain knowledge and specific language in addition to the development of a wide range of cognitive abilities.

Loading additional tasks onto readers while reading burdens them with a heavy cognitive overload and makes the learning environment anxious. Instructional designs that push learners to split their attention will make learning ineffective and will negatively affect reading comprehension. Comprehension is a complex cognitive process and it cannot be boiled down to the mere process of accessing the meaning of words and combining them with grammatical items. Readers resort to cognitive procedures such as retrieving information from long-term memory to assign meaning, relating different ideas to predict the conveyed meaning. If they are burdened with more information, it will not facilitate language acquisition but will in fact make acquisition tedious.

Also helps in strengthening The cognitivist position on language acquisition, which suggests that it is a complex cognitive-linguistic process enabled by a different set of human genes, is strengthened by considering reading from a biological perspective. A favourable expression of those genes enables a neural network in the brain that corresponds to effective reading. Also, reading as a biologically enabled skill has a reciprocal relationship with emotion and cognition. Despite this, in-class reading often disregards the importance of emotion in learning and tends to focus on cognitive aspects, which in turn can increase anxiety. The identification of genes associated with reading, the accompanying neural network and the environmental effect on reading push the boundaries of reading pedagogies to consider these aspects of a reader for novel and effective teaching of reading.

Human communication is theoretically constituted along the axis of listening, speaking, reading and writing. While there is considerable scholarship on listening, speaking and writing and a definitive surge of interest in reading techniques (for instance, skimming, scanning and prediction), there is a glaring lack of established critical scholarship on its relationship to cognition, emotion, second-language acquisition, vocabulary and, specifically, the incidental role of reading in convalescing speaking and writing. While this book on reading demonstrates the inevitability and prominence of reading for academic inquiry, it also illustrates the cognitive and curative affordances of reading. In so doing, it provides theoretical and empirical tools not only to further research on reading but also to illustrate the determinative role of reading in shaping *cognition* itself.

Synthesizing Research Perspectives on Reading

The first essay, by Hazel L. W. Chiu, titled "Twenty-First-Century Second Language Literacy Development in Universities" (Chap. 2) examines the role and importance of reading and writing in the development of literacy in twenty-first-century universities. Treating reading/writing as "the foundational skills for education and language development", Chiu contends that the development of technology has made literacy a complex issue. Accordingly, reading and writing today involve multimodal materials, multifarious genres and multiple communicative demands requiring highly sophisticated skills and abilities, as well as a good understanding of context. Drawing instances from universities in Hong Kong, Chiu argues that where English is often used as a second language and as a medium of instruction, it has become increasingly challenging for students to develop literacy skills both for work and study, and to fulfil the various curriculum targets such as the development of critical thinking skills, creativity, independent and lifelong learning. However, only a small number of studies have been conducted in universities in Hong Kong on supporting or facilitating the development of literacy skills. Taking these cues, the chapter discusses the major types of research effort: (i) supporting literacy development in independent language learning centres; (ii) supporting literacy development in university curricula; (iii) making use of technology to facilitate literacy development; and (iv) investigating students' literary concepts and practice to improve understanding and develop appropriate strategies to develop literacy skills. Further, the author is convinced that the nature of thinking inculcated by literacy skills determines several and varied aspects of the future society and the role of writing, reading and technology within such a framework. Although technology has enhanced literacy skills, Chiu stresses the "need to maintain an appropriate balance between the conventional and the novel" to realize the inclusive goals of the modern literacy environment. In so doing, this topical essay maps the complex interplay of second-language reading literacy, university and the role of technology in the twenty-first century as it calls for continuous efforts to utilize the new affordances for enhanced learning experiences.

One of the important aspects of learning a foreign language is vocabulary acquisition. Taking this cue, Nina Daskalovska's "Extensive Reading and Vocabulary Acquisition" (Chap. 3) explains how extensive reading for language development enables incidental acquisition of vocabulary. Confirming extant theories on vocabulary and identifying vocabulary knowledge as a critical determinant for reading, Dakslovsky demonstrates the synergetic relationship between vocabulary knowledge and reading. Reviews of L1 and L2 studies on vocabulary confirm that most of a learner's vocabulary knowledge is acquired from reading with a focus on meaning. In particular, a number of studies have demonstrated that foreign language learners can acquire vocabulary through reading. In fact, language learning programmes that include extensive reading are more effective than explicit learning of vocabulary through decontextualized exercises. Instead of blatantly dismissing explicit vocabulary learning Dakslovsky argues for a balanced programme that offers opportunities for both explicit and implicit learning of vocabulary. According to the author, such an approach is the best option for learners to enrich their vocabulary and to develop a vocabulary size necessary for successful communication and use the target language in various contexts and situations. By way of conclusion, the essay delineates salient features of successful extensive reading programmes, selection of reading materials and implications for teaching.

J. Mary Jennifer and R. Joseph Ponniah's chapter titled "Acquisition of Writing by Reading and Its Impact on Cognition" (Chap. 4) treats reading as an effective tool that impacts writing skills such as content, vocabulary, spelling and syntax. The study investigated by these authors presents the effects of reading on adult ESL rural students at an arts and science college in India. The data collected from the subjects using a pre-test and a post-test, as well as through a questionnaire, reports significant improvement in writing performance. Further, the results confirm how reading accounts for the improvement of writing skills, and other aspects of language. The chapter also assesses the relationship between reading self-efficacy and writing performance. Overall results show that reading self-efficacy beliefs had a positive influence on writing performance. In addition, long-term reading exposure makes the composing process easier as it reduces writing apprehensions. This study has profound implications in its illustration of the positive impact of reading on the development of cognitive capabilities.

Kshema Jose's chapter "Blending Cognitive and Socio-constructive Pedagogies: Building Autonomous Readers in the ESL Classroom" (Chap. 5) extensively reviews how autonomy in L2 reading can be promoted in ESL reading classes using cognitive and socio-cognitive approaches. Educators now realize that autonomy, adaptability and self-reliance in developing reading competence need to be the focus of twenty-first-century pedagogy. Working within the cognitive-constructivist domain, the essay investigates the effects of a strategy training programme on developing reading competence in ESL readers. The cognitive approach to reading involves selection, acquisition, construction, and integration of information which in turn helps readers to record information and to subconsciously acquire language properties. On the other hand, the socio-constructive approach considers readers' learning ability and intelligence as dynamic space arising out of collaborated responses to specific situations. Here learning is facilitated through social interaction mediated by tools like teamwork and dialogue which in turn determines cognitive abilities. Blending cognitive and socio-constructive approaches, this experimental study attempts to promote the habit of reading among learners. Furthermore, the author develops a strategy training programme to test the efficacy of the hypothesis that providing exposure to alternative strategies through a programme that precedes collaborative learning activities with personal cognitive development activities might encourage learners to achieve independence in reading. Accordingly, the author chooses ten adult ESL learners at varying levels of proficiency and deploys tools such as comprehension tasks, think aloud, strategy questionnaires, aids for prompting metacognition, retrospective and introspective interviews, and group think to gain access to reader strategies and allow exposure to peer strategies. Her study reveals that all learners develop fluency in demonstration and discussion of strategies. The results of the study show an increase in the comprehension performance of all participants and that all of them either adopted or adapted strategies from peers. The findings demonstrate how awareness of strategy use does not necessarily promote autonomous reading but rather, the author proposes, alternative strategies are used to solve comprehension problems for continued reading.

Mahananda Pathak's (Chap. 6) thought-provoking chapter titled "Using L1 Reading Strategies to Develop L2 Reading" explores how reading capabilities developed in one 'enabled' language could be transferred to another language with the help of carefully developed instruction. The essay is significant in that existing studies have not paid much attention to the previous reading experiences of an individual in the context of teaching reading in ESL classrooms. Taking children studying in Assamese (the official state language of Assam, one of the north-eastern states of India) as a case study, Pathak frames reading as an abstract assemblage of capabilities that could be transferred from L1 (here Assamese) to L2 (here English) through planned instruction. The underlying premise is that the reading capabilities and strategies that exist in the more enabled language or 'own language' (Cook, 2010) can be transferred and exploited to develop reading capabilities in the second language. By introducing Assamese-English texts/tasks and activating the reading strategies of Assamese class VI students, Pathak demonstrates the role of L1 in enhancing and enabling reading skills in English. The study confirms that using the reading comprehension ability of the first language enables the subjects to transfer that ability to the second language. Further, the results show that children were able to infer the meaning of words and sentences in context using L1 language/world knowledge. Such an exploration becomes essential in the context of Indian bi/multilingualism where children live with, and more importantly, very often function in at least two languages with considerable ease. Although the present ethnographic study is limited to Assamese-speaking regional-medium children, the model, if adopted and followed, has clear pedagogical implications in any context where "bilingualism" is a social/linguistic reality.

R. Joseph Ponniah's "First-Language Reading Promotes Second-Language Reading and Acquisition: Towards a Biolinguistic Approach" (Chap. 7) explores the possible transfer of L1 pleasure reading habits to L2 and the consequent acquisition of a second language by reading L2 texts from a biolinguistic perspective. His argumentative arc is premised on the fact that human beings, facilitated by supportive environmental conditions, have an inherent disposition to learn. Within this biological truism, the author conducts a study on a subject who evinces a keen interest in learning Business English. Although the author initially instructed her to read a few historical novels in L2, the subject expressed difficulty in reading them as the themes did not interest her. Biologically interpreted, the brain does not sustain interest in any activity that does not give pleasure to it. Later, when she was exposed to English novels having similar themes to those in L1 which she often read for pleasure, the subject was found to be using reading strategies imbibed subconsciously while reading L1 texts. By way of conclusion, Ponniah confirms that the pleasure extracted from L2 reading provides compelling input for the acquisition of the English language and such an acquired language is used for the specific purpose. Melding biology and a case study in ELT, the author affirms that the brain has the capacity to generate language using current language knowledge.

Sriganesh et al.'s "Genetics of Reading Ability and Its Role in Solving Reading Difficulties" (Chap. 8) frames reading as a heritable aptitude. The authors argue that reading is a heritable and biologically endowed ability that is enabled by the exaptation of genetic subskills that are readily available as language and object recognition abilities. The significant role of genes in biological processes such as formation and plasticity of the specialized neural networks that accompany reading, the role of epigenetic modification of genes in reading and the reciprocal effects of emotion and cognition in reading are discussed in this interesting essay. With due consideration of the genetic make-up of individuals, its effect on formation of neural circuits corresponding to reading and the gene–environment interaction, the article proposes that knowledge of these aspects of a reader is pertinent to providing effective pedagogical solutions.

Framing 'cognitive semantics' as an umbrella term applied to several streams of research sharing the common premise that language and general cognition are interrelated and interdependent, N. P. Sudharshana's "Reading Comprehension in ESL Contexts: An Applied Cognitive Semantics Perspective" (Chap. 9) presents a cognitivist turn in the context of reading. Accordingly, he derives the following principles which are relevant for language pedagogy: all linguistic elements have a conceptualization dimension and thus they are 'meaningful'; all linguistic elements are abstracted from their real-life usage contexts; discourse, just like individual linguistic elements, is highly structured and rooted in usage contexts; metaphoric and metonymic concepts prevail in our thought process; and linguistic elements represent categorization in human cognition based on perceived commonalities and motivated extensions. While the first part of the article briefly sketches the salient principles, the second part elaborates on the implications of these principles for reading in ESL contexts by illustrating the application of cognitive semantics principles with a sample text. Extending some current cognitive semantics-based practices to other areas of pedagogy, the chapter argues that cognitive semantics can facilitate in-depth reading comprehension in ESL contexts mainly by offering tools for detailed linguistic analyses and reconstruction of meaning.

C. E. Veni Madhavan and C. N. Ajit in "Perspectives from the Art and Science of Reading" (Chap. 10) explore "the synergistic roles of reading general material versus specialized (or academic) reading" from two principal directions: (a) the art of reading to cover subjective perspectives about reading, and (b) the science of reading to analyse and discuss all that is considered objective. Classifying the enterprise of reading as 'art' and 'science' at one and the same time and experimenting the potential of reading from a student population, Madhavan and Ajit formulate a theoretical model. Specifically, they develop empirical arguments towards a principal hypothesis that reading collateral or sidestream material accentuates the understanding of subsequent reading of mainstream material. Anchored in the biological and mathematical sciences and drawing upon extant theories from linguistics, cognitive psychology, cognitive neuroscience and computational modelling to examine this intuitively plausible hypothesis, these authors demonstrate how general reading facilitates and vastly improves comprehension in academic reading. The strength of the essay lies not only in the authors' deployment of various methodologies and transdisciplinary tools but in the way they establish the dynamic and synergetic relationship between general and academic reading, which have often been considered as two separate activities.

The last chapter, by Carlos Machado and Pedro Luis Luchini, titled "Cognitive Load Theory, Redundancy Effect and Language Learning", uses the cognitive load theory to illustrate the power of reading comprehensible texts as the predictor for successful language learning. Instead of using a dual mode which invokes both reading and listening, the authors underscore the potency of a single mode of instruction, that is, "reading alone". In the dual mode of learning, information is processed using multiple forms, which eventually distracts learners from understanding the content by increasing cognitive load. Against this theoretical background, the chapter investigates the extent to which the "redundancy effect" influences the L2 reading comprehension skills of two groups of young learners with different proficiency levels in a middle school in Argentina.[2] The study found that the students who worked with the single mode of instruction obtained better scores in the task set than the other group. The results of the experimental study support the hypothesis that the subjects who devoted their time to reading alone performed better than the subjects who spent their time reading and listening. The authors also share some pedagogical implications and provide recommendations for the teaching of L2 reading comprehension.

These insightful chapters representing and illustrating global reading practices not only attest to the centrality of reading but also its critical role in determining the acquisition of the properties of a language and its impact on cognition. The chapters clearly demonstrate the multiple stakes of engaging in reading: pragmatic, cognitive, practical, analytic and genetic. They experimentally and theoretically prove that reading provides comprehensible input which in turn facilitates the subconscious acquisition of any language and also makes possible the use of language in various contexts. Specifically, the pleasure component in reading motivates learners to be immersed in the meaning with compelling attention, which further eases the acquisition of language. The key take away is how L1 pleasure reading habits and the subconsciously acquired L1 reading strategies can easily be transferred to L2.

---

[2]Redundancy effect refers to "the phenomenon in instruction where learning is hindered when additional information is presented to learners compared to the presentation of less information" (Jin, 2012).

Academic reading also has cognitive consequences as it involves selection, acquisition, construction and integration of ideas which in turn positively affects academic writing. As the chapters in this volume demonstrate; reading has wide-ranging pedagogical implications for the learning environment. Significant ones include: (a) reading must be integrated into the curriculum by conducting customized programmes; (b) students should have access to a variety of books in order to be encouraged to read; (c) students must be made aware that reading results in acquisition of all measures of language competence; and (d) pleasure reading improves the effectiveness of learning.

References

Blicher, S., Feingold, L., & Shany, M. (2017). The role of trait anxiety and preoccupation with reading disabilities of children and their mothers in predicting children's reading comprehension. *Journal of Learning Disabilities, 50*(3), 309–321. https://doi.org/10.1177/0022219415624101.
Carroll, J. M., & Snowling, M. J. (2004). Language and phonological skills in children at high risk of reading difficulties. *Journal of Child Psychology and Psychiatry, 45*(3), 631–640. https://doi.org/10.1111/j.1469-7610.2004.00252.x.
Cook, G. (2010). *Translation in language teaching: An argument for reassessment.* Oxford: OUP.
Chomsky, N. (2007). *New horizons in the study of language and mind.* Cambridge: Cambridge University Press.
Hewitt, E., & Stephenson, J. (2012). Foreign language anxiety and oral exam performance: A replication of Phillips's MLJ study. *The Modern Language Journal, 96*(2), 170–189. https://doi.org/10.1111/j.1540-4781.2011.01174.x.
Jin, P. (2012). Redundancy effect. In *Encyclopedia of the sciences of learning* (pp. 2787–2788). US: Springer.
Knickerbocker, H., Johnson, R. L., & Altarriba, J. (2015). Emotion effects during reading: Influence of an emotion target word on eye movements and processing. *Cognition and Emotion, 29*(5), 1–23. https://doi.org/10.1080/02699931.2014.938023.
McEwen, B. S., Eiland, L., Hunter, R. G., & Miller, M. M. (2011). Stress and anxiety: Structural plasticity and epigenetic regulation as a consequence of stress. *Neuropharmacology, 62*(1), 3–12. https://doi.org/10.1016/j.neuropharm.2011.07.014.
Nation, K., Clarke, P., & Snowling, M. J. (2002). General cognitive ability in children with reading comprehension difficulties. *British Journal of Educational Psychology, 72*(4), 549–560. https://doi.org/10.1348/00070990260377604.
Wurr, A. J. (2003). Reading in a second language: A reading problem or a language problem? *Journal of College Reading and Learning, 33*(2), 37–41. https://doi.org/10.1080/10790195.2003.10850146.

Chapter 2
Twenty-First-Century Second Language Literacy Development in Universities

Hazel L. W. Chiu

Abstract The literacy skills of reading and writing are important foundation skills for learning. The two skills of reading and writing have often been connected in the exploration of literacy development. A great deal of research has been undertaken on instructional strategies and other means of supporting the development of reading skills, both for young learners and for learners at higher educational levels. Literacy has become a complex issue in the twenty-first century because of the development of technology. Reading and writing today involve multimodal materials, multifarious genres and multiple communicative demands brought by the development of technology and the use of the internet. This requires highly sophisticated skills and abilities, as well as a good understanding of context. In universities in Hong Kong where English is often used as a second language and a medium of instruction, it has become increasingly challenging for students to develop literacy skills both for work and study, and to fulfil the various curriculum targets such as the development of critical thinking skills, creativity, independent and lifelong learning. A number of studies have been conducted in universities in Hong Kong on supporting or facilitating the development of literacy skills (particularly reading skills). This chapter discusses research efforts exploring the benefits of self-directed language learning (such as extensive reading), as well as the role of technological support and curriculum design in enhancing literacy development. Investigating students' literary concepts and practice also helps to improve understanding and develop appropriate strategies to support the development of literacy skills.

Keywords Literacy · Academic literacy · Reading and writing Technology · Self-directed language learning

---

H. L. W. Chiu (✉)
University of London, London, UK
e-mail: hazelchiu@hotmail.com

Introduction

The concept of 'literacy' has often been considered as connected to printed texts and how they are produced and used. As suggested by Barton and Hamilton (2000), literacy can be best understood as a set of social practices consisting of observable events which are mediated by written texts. The term 'literacy', therefore, involves the ways in which people interact with texts, and with one another, through the use of texts. It is mainly associated with the activity or ability of 'reading and writing'.

As reading and writing are the foundation skills for education and language development, literacy has always received a great deal of attention in school and university curricula. According to Paxton and Frith (2014), reading and writing are central to the process of learning in any discipline and need to be taken into consideration when planning curricula for different subjects.

A number of studies have been conducted on supporting the development of literacy skills in primary and secondary schools. Some researchers have emphasized the important role of literacy in the school curriculum. Kitson (2015), for example, highlights the importance of developing literacy capabilities for reading comprehension in the curriculum. Raisanen and Korkeamaki's (2015) study also shows the importance of the teacher's constant attention and a reflective attitude in the implementation of the new literacy curriculum in attending to interests which differ from traditional practices.

Literacy has also received a great deal of attention in the university curriculum. Langer (2011) stresses the importance of helping students to develop "academic literacy", that is, the ability to acquire, think and communicate about knowledge in different disciplines, such as building an understanding, bolstering an argument, creating a proof, analysing data and offering evidence. Studies have shown that academic literacy is a great challenge for university students, and needs to be given emphasis in the curriculum (Mkandawire & Walubita, 2015; Pessoa et al., 2014).

In recent years, literacy has been receiving increasing attention because of monumental changes in contemporary literacy practices due to technological advancement. Because of the erosion of the printed text as a medium of communication in modern society due to the development of new technologies, the term 'literacy' has taken on more complex meanings in the twenty-first century. As suggested by Kress (2003), although language-as-speech will remain a major mode of communication, language-as-writing will increasingly be displaced by image in many domains of public communication. The mode of image and the medium of the screen will produce profound changes in the forms and functions of writing.

Warschauer (2007) also asserts that today, literacy no longer means just reading and writing in print forms or on paper. I It may involve other aspects of text-related interaction, such as (a) computer literacy: comfort and fluency in using hardware and software; (b) information literacy: the ability to find, analyse, and critique information available online; (c) multimedia literacy: the ability to interpret and produce documents combining texts, sounds, graphics, and video; and

(d) computer-mediated communication literacy: the mastery of the pragmatics of synchronous and asynchronous CMC.

Vacca, Vacca, and Mraz (2014, p. 12) describes this new literacy as "a synthesis of language, thinking, and contextual practices through which people make and communicate meaning" in ways "complex and multidimensional". Knoll (2003, p. 1) believes that this complexity has been intensified by the phenomenon known as globalization and the "Internet Revolution". To communicate in the contemporary literacy arena "requires a fluency that goes beyond the spoken language and embraces a variety of uses of the written language as well". It also requires a good understanding of social, institutional, and cultural relationships (Lankshear & Knobel, 2003).

A number of studies have also shown the important role of technology in supporting literacy curricula in schools. Leu et al. (2011), for example, argue that the teaching of online reading comprehension skills should be integrated into school reading curricula. Other studies have also shown that multimodal strategies (such as the use of visual art to facilitate reading and writing instruction) are beneficial for the development of literacy skills, as they provide opportunities for making and representing meaning creatively (Barton, 2015; Barton & Baguley, 2014; Butti, 2015; Shaw, 2014).

Aside from conventional academic literacy skills, the continuous development of literacy at university has become an increasingly complex issue because of the increasingly important role of digital communication in society. As suggested by Carr (2014, p. 438) in his discussion on university composition, there is a growing tendency for university writing to be involved in various types of "making" or "doing", as in digital composition or multimodal essays which join written text with aural and visual resources, and involve different means of presentation. These new developments in literacy concepts and practices have eroded conventional literacy standards and expectations and produced additional demands on students in developing the types of literacy skills that suit increasingly complex contexts of social, academic and professional communication.

Types of Reading and Writing Demands at University

University students need to master various different genres for social, academic and professional communication. In places where English as a second language is the medium of instruction, such as in the universities in Hong Kong, literacy challenges for students are greater than those who use English as both a first language and a medium of instruction.

The two major types of reading and writing skills Hong Kong students need to master are academic English and workplace/professionally related English. The former involves the common types of essays, reports, academic papers/articles in books/journals which university students are expected to read and write during their studies, or afterwards if they continue working in academia. The latter involves materials they will have to handle in the workplace, such as business correspondence, workplace reports and other discipline-specific materials such as computer manuals, laboratory reports and progress reports for architectural projects. In additional to the fundamental reading and writing skills students need to master to complete their studies, many universities also include in the language curriculum the types of reading and writing skills they need to use in their discipline, which will help them to function effectively in their professional workplace later.

Literacy development has become increasingly demanding at universities today, as there is a wide array of curriculum targets which students are expected to accomplish. These often impose additional demands on the development of literacy skills. Aside from acquiring subject knowledge in specific disciplines, students are expected to become rounded, well educated members of society with good general knowledge, critical thinking, creativity, collaborative, independent and lifelong learning skills. As curriculum targets become more divergent, the types of demands on literacy skills also become more challenging.

At the University of Hong Kong, a conventional university with a long history, language enhancement courses start with "Core University English", academic English for all first-year students; this is followed by subjected-related academic or workplace courses in the second year (Centre for Applied English Studies, 2016). The situation is similar in another more technically oriented university, Kong Polytechnic University. In addition to academic or workplace/professionally related courses, there are other language-related courses with specific focuses, such as those related to popular culture or common interest topics like films, fiction, and globalization (English Language Centre, 2016).

In another university offering both face-to-face and distance-learning courses without a language centre to oversee the language enhancement courses for the whole university, the language courses being offered do not seem to be very different either. Sometimes academic or workplace English seem to emerge in the general language enhancement courses entitled "Effective Use of English" or "Effective Communication", such as those offered in language studies or language education, and business administration (School of Education and Languages, 2016; The Open University of Hong Kong, 2016). In other subjects, like translation, university language courses focusing on writing and speaking receive particular attention (School of Arts and Social Sciences, 2016).

Differences in academic and workplace genres are a major source of confusion. While academic genres are for a general academic audience, workplace genres are for a specific audience in a particular profession. The difference in communication style is most obvious in more technical subjects such as science, computing and engineering. Communication in these subjects often involves more technical terminology, and there are institutional constraints on communication for specific communities of practice in terms of style and procedures. Very often, the mode of general academic communication may be quite different from these types of workplace communication. This poses another type of learning demand on students who need to distinguish between these different modes of communication and decide when to make use of which mode of communication strategies.

The need for university students to make use of a wide array of communication genres competently is a also a great challenge for them. Sometimes the different genres students are exposed to may cause interference and confuse students about specific or typical genre features. One of the difficulties is distinguishing the different styles of written and spoken communication. While students are expected to write in formal academic style in written assignments such as essays and reports, in academic spoken communication, such as oral presentation and seminar discussion, they can make use of conversational features similar to those they use in their social communication. These formal and informal features of academic reading and writing on the one hand, and academic listening and speaking on the other, are a source of confusion and often hinder students from producing different types of academic genre to the appropriate standard.

Related to the difficulty in distinguishing between written and spoken genres are the differences between academic genres and everyday communication genres, which is another major source of confusion. In Hong Kong where English is used as a second language, Cantonese or Mandarin Chinese is most commonly used as the language for social interaction. However, English is sometimes also used in social interaction, as university students may make friends with foreigners and mainland Chinese speaking different dialects, when they will need to use English a medium of communication. The need to adjust to different social contexts with different expectations of style and formality deviating from those of academic communication is a great challenge for university students.

The Impact of Technology on Literacy Development

Literacy has become an increasingly complex issue in the twenty-first century because of the development of technology. With the popularity of social media and mobile applications like WhatsApp, written and spoken communication genres often merge and become indistinguishable. As suggested by Tagg (2012), text and talk merge in modern communication. With the immediacy of communication enabled by technology, the distinction between formal, pre-planned written communication and the more casual, immediate spoken communication is eroded, whether in social or workplace contexts. The difference in language style between the two modes of communication has also become less conspicuous. Text messages on mobile devices and social media are basically a kind of written communication. However, because of the immediacy of the communication, they have assumed characteristics of spoken communication, such as more casual/informal communication style, with less emphasis on planning and less compliance with typical genre features. Features of spoken communication can often be found in these written texts which are in fact a type of textual spoken communication.

This type of modern text-talk is often multimodal, involving not just texts as a medium of communication, but also other forms of audio-visual material such as pictures, photos, audio and visual recordings. There is no longer a need to adhere to typical genre features of some specific written genres, nor even the possibility of doing so, as the use of multimodal materials to fulfil multiple communicative demands often obliterates these specific genre features, and new communication genres also emerge to fulfil changing needs. This multifarious situation results in confusion and mingling of/in communication styles and adherence to genre features, as well as problems in observing standards. Various transgressions in genre features, such as the use of formal/informal language, the use of textual or audio-visual material, and code-switching or code-mixing of different languages have now become increasingly unavoidable or even acceptable.

Communication nowadays is more immediate and more oriented towards individuals. There is wider scope for individuals to express their views and gain information without restriction on the internet. This has certainly fostered a stronger sense of individual autonomy. The freedom of the individual, however, is restricted by how they are expected to behave within different communicative contexts, or communities of practice. While individual freedom seems to have increased, the individual's communicative behaviour is also more subject to public surveillance. Individuals are also expected to take into consideration other people's communicative behaviour and collaborate with others in communication (Tagg, 2012). The two opposing/driving forces of individual autonomy and collaboration in communities of practice is a major feature of modern communication.

Recent Research on Facilitating the Development of Literacy Skills at University

University students have gone beyond the stage of basic literacy development. They are expected to have general competence in reading and writing. However, today's university students are said to have declining skills in reading and writing, as university education becomes popularized, and literacy skills become multifarious in a technology-driven world where literacy standards are being eroded as different genre features mingle and interact with one another. Reading and writing in English are particularly demanding tasks for university students who learn English as a second or foreign language. These students need to handle the conflicting demands of literacy in more than one language, which creates another dimension of challenge in using English appropriately in various different contexts.

A number of studies on supporting/facilitating the development of literacy skills have been conducted in universities in different parts of the world where English is used as a second or foreign language. There are four main types of research effort. One type deals with the development of literacy skills beyond the formal curriculum as a kind of self-directed learning motivation fostered by independent language learning centres often established in universities where English is learned as a second or foreign language. Another type of research study focuses on facilitating the development of literacy skills within the formal curriculum, either the subject or the language curriculum. The third type deals with the use of technology in facilitating the development of literacy skills. There is also a small body of research which aims to investigate students' literary concepts and practice so as to improve understanding and develop appropriate strategies to develop literacy skills.

Support for Literacy Development in Independent Language Learning Centres

A great deal of research has been undertaken in recent decades to show the benefits of extensive reading for language acquisition, particularly at an elementary or intermediate level of learning English as a second language. Some of the studies have focused on adolescent readers. These studies have demonstrated a strong positive relationship between leisure reading and academic success (Allington & McGill-Franzen, 2003; Mokhtari & Sheorey, 1994). Others are related to specific areas of language acquisition, such as those conducted by Gardner (2004) and Kweon and Kim (2008) on vocabulary learning, Bell (2001) and Iwahori (2008) on reading fluency/ability, and Wu (2000) on writing development.

Independent language learning centres are language resource centres which provide different types of learning materials for self-learning. These materials facilitate enhancement of different language skills, and are particularly useful for extensive reading. In some of these learning centres, activities are sometimes organized to encourage extensive reading. A small-scale action research study by Chiu (2015a) conducted guided reading sessions in an independent language learning centre of a university in Hong Kong and aimed to help students access extensive reading materials targeted at general first-language readers. Students were guided to read a short extract from popular fiction or non-fiction material and responded to comprehension questions. They then had a short discussion on what they had read, and reflected on their learning experience. Results seemed to indicate potential for these reading support sessions to develop students' interest and ability in extensive reading. The procedures and support materials developed for these sessions can be easily replicated on different books for use in similar independent language learning centres. Although the books used in the study were slightly above the language level of most of the students, who are L2 learners of English, there is evidence that students were able to be involved and contributed useful ideas in the discussions with teacher guidance. Students felt that they had gained a better understanding of the book by the end of the reading sessions and some of them indicated that they would be interested in reading the book later or watching the film adapted from the book.

Studies have also investigated the use of writing conferences in helping students develop their writing skills, very often as an additional support beyond the classroom. These studies have shown the benefits of writing conferences in enhancing students' attitudes, abilities, or strategies in writing (Eodice, 1998; Haneda, 2004; Lambert, 1999; Stemper, 2002; Strauss & Xiang, 2006).

At universities, this type of writing conference often occurs in independent language learning centres, which provide both language learning resources and additional language support for students' voluntary independent learning. One study by Chiu (2012) reports the use of one-to-one writing conferences to support the development of writing skills in an independent language learning centre. These learner-centred writing sessions offered assistance to suit the various writing needs of university students, such as: (a) assignments for different subjects (term papers, project reports, theses); (b) various types of applications (for jobs, postgraduate studies, exchange programmes, internships, scholarships); (c) public exam skills development [IELTS, Use of English exam (public pre-university matriculation examination in Hong Kong which some students need to re-take)]; and (d) students' own writing practices for various purposes to develop their writing skills and ability.

The development of good writing skills and extensive reading habits requires self-directed learning efforts. However, these are difficult to develop without initial teacher support. These one-to-one writing conferences are a kind of awareness-building learning session to help students develop the skills to identify problems in their writing and do useful revision on their own. In other words, the consultation sessions are a kind of model reflective exercise for students to imitate in order to improve their writing on their own.

Findings from the study show that students had positive attitudes towards this type of writing conference. A recurring theme in student feedback was the usefulness of teacher guidance to suit individual needs in terms of writing development, and in specific areas such as language, connection of ideas and logical thinking. Some students also felt that the conference sessions were interesting.

Support for Literacy Development in University Curricula

A number of studies investigate the development of literacy skills within the formal university curriculum (Marshall, Zhou, Gervan, & Wiebe, 2012; Olivier & Olivier, 2013; Tribble & Wingate, 2013). Improving or adjusting the curriculum to facilitate the development of literacy skills can take place either in the language curriculum or within the curriculum of a different discipline.

A study by Chiu (2014) reports an attempt at using more unconventional journalistic and literary genres in designing elective (reading and) writing courses for the new language curriculum in response to the university curriculum reform in Hong Kong, which was extended from three years to four years, with more emphasis on the development of generic and literacy skills (The Hong Kong Polytechnic University, 2013).

Data were collected from a pilot course to examine whether these unconventional genres help to scaffold the writing ability of students and cultivate their interest in reading and writing. Results indicate that the use of the unconventional genres of journalistic and literary writing helped to engage students' interest in extensive reading of works other than the formal academic writing they were expected to learn well at university. Students also benefited from the use of a genre-based writing pedagogy in developing their writing skills. Guiding students to analyse writing models helped to scaffold their ability and model their writing for unfamiliar genres. Students also felt that making use of more personal and creative writing strategies was motivating; the writing skills they learned from these unconventional genres were useful for their day-to-day communication and future writing development.

Another study by Cheng et al. (2014) is a writing-across-the-curriculum project which aims to integrate writing activities in courses from different subject areas. In this study, discipline-specific scaffolding activities were designed to facilitate the good use of writing skills in learning and assignments for different subjects across ten academic departments in the university. To support the development of their writing ability, students were given guidance on reading effectively to extract relevant information, and on improving their use of vocabulary and expressions to refine their writing. Findings indicate the benefits of identifying resources and developing activities for supporting the development of writing skills across different disciplines. The sharing of the experience of designing and implementing language activities to facilitate learning in different subject areas was also useful for non-language subject teachers.

Technological Support for Literacy Development

The third type of research deals with the use of technology in facilitating the development of literacy skills. A number of research studies have shown that web-based learning, such as the use of CMC (Cheng, Chen, & Brown, 2012; Li, 2013), blogs (Arslan & Sahin-Kizil, 2010; Sun & Chang, 2012; Vurdien, 2013), and wikis (Aydin & Yildiz, 2014; Liou & Lee, 2011), has the potential to facilitate the development of reading and writing skills.

The study by Chiu (2015b) examines the experience of implementing web-work activities for an English for Academic Purposes (EAP) course in a university in Hong Kong. The course covered academic writing and presentation skills using a blended mode of face-to-face classroom teaching and web learning. Aside from classroom learning and conventional assignments, students on this course were required to complete 6 hours of self-learning each week and attain a minimum score of 60% in order to pass the course. These web-based activities included objective web exercises, as well as activities making use of social networking tools such as blogs, wikis and discussion forums for students to share ideas.

A good variety of multimodal materials aimed at attending to a wide range of learning needs have been used for web activities, showing a good effort to enhance motivational engagement. Of the five types of educational materials (narrative, interactive, adaptive, communicative, and productive) described by Laurillard (2002), at least three are prominently featured in the e-learn materials. These include audio-visual narrative materials, communicative media materials in the forms of blogs, forums and wikis, and materials for adaptive and productive media.

Data were collected and analysed from the pilot of web-based materials in an EAP course. Results indicate that more meaningful and motivating activities with clear purposes, such as the social networking activities, were more welcomed by students, with a higher participation rate than those activities which are mechanical, or too demanding and time-consuming.

The findings point to several major considerations for effective e-learn materials design. The first is integration of purposeful materials to achieve clear learning purposes. The second is the use of a variety of multimodal, interesting and meaningful materials and activities for enhancing motivational and cognitive engagement. Lastly, it is important to provide students with a supportive learning environment to empower them to fulfil their own learning needs or targets autonomously.

Investigating Literacy Concepts and Practice

Research on academic literacy has shown that it is a great challenge for university students, especially for those who are starting their university studies and finding that the literacy skills and abilities they need are very different from those they learned at school (Marshall et al., 2012; Olivier & Olivier, 2013; Tribble & Wingate, 2013). There is a need to find ways of facilitating the development of academic literacy skills within the language and subject curricula, and even beyond them, to involve self-directed learning efforts. More research efforts are needed to investigate students' literary concepts and practice, improve understanding of appropriate strategies to develop literacy skills, and support students' literacy development.

One study by Chiu (2015c) explores the literacy concepts and practices of students in English Language Education in a university in Hong Kong. Data were collected by a small-scale questionnaire survey and a small-group interview, and by analysing students' essay-writing assignments. Findings indicate that students' habits and interest in reading and writing differ greatly in some aspects, but are similar in others.

In the questionnaire, students were asked to indicate their level of agreement (on a Likert scale of 1 to 5) with eight statements about their habits and interest in reading and writing. There was a great difference between individual students' average ratings of the eight statements, with the highest at 4.50 and the lowest at 2.38. This indicates that students' reading and writing habits and interests may differ greatly.

The data collected were quite homogeneous in terms of the frequency of the types of materials students usually read and write for their studies, as well as for entertainment/personal or social purposes. However, there seems to be a wider variety in the actual types of materials students read and write for their studies, as well as those they read for entertainment/personal or social purposes. There is relatively less variety in the types of materials students write for entertainment/personal or social purposes.

Analysis of their writing shows that students seem to have quite a satisfactory command of academic literacy. They can make quite a clear distinction of literacy demands between communicating academically on the one hand, and communicating for personal and social purposes on the other. Although they cannot make use of all the academic features perfectly, it is clear that they understand the main features and grasp the major differences from social/digital writing style. The variety of social/digital writing features they demonstrated in their writing also show a potency in this new writing medium for creative and interesting communication.

Findings from the interview seem to indicate that although students can make good use of the digital media for social and personal communication, and they also read web materials for their studies, they may not be in favour of more extensive use of digital materials for their academic assignments. For example, they are against the idea of having the multimodal essay as an assignment. Time and convenience seems to be their major consideration for different types of communication. Their negative views of this aspect of digital development for academic studies need to be explored further.

Discussion and Conclusion

The twenty-first-century literacy arena is multi-faceted, particularly at university. It is a colourful picture to exploit for learning, which calls for the use of a variety of skills to meet multiple learning demands and outcomes. Such an environment provides exciting opportunities for making use of higher-order skills in the process of reading and writing development.

The digital medium is a useful means to enhance reading exposure and opportunities, as well as motivation in reading and writing. Research has shown that it can be beneficial not only for enhancing the development of literacy skills, but also in facilitating the use of creativity and critical thinking skills.

Alongside the benefits, the new literacy environment also brings increasing demands on university students. With the erosion of conventional genres and the emergence of new reading and writing genres, literacy expectations are hard to define and are evolving continually. Literary standards are increasingly context dependent and hard for students to grasp. There are no clearly defined rules and models to follow which can facilitate the learning process, while at the same time there are expectations that university students will be versatile in making use of a variety of reading and writing strategies.

The challenge of literacy development in the twenty-first century is that there is a need to maintain an appropriate balance between the conventional and the novel. There is a need to observe certain literacy standards in academia, while allowing scope for creative and unconventional use of the language in reading and writing in line with the inclusive modern literacy environment. In such a complex literacy arena, there is also a need for useful strategies to support the development of different types of literacy skills to help university students function as competent members of academia and the educated public.

There is also a need for further research on university students' literacy concepts and practices to inform curriculum planning to suit modern digital developments. The findings will also be useful for working out useful strategies to support and facilitate students' literacy development.

References

Allington, R., & McGill-Franzen, A. (2003). The impact of summer setback on the reading achievement gap. *Phi Delta Kappan, 85*(1), 68–75.

Arslan, R. S., & Sahin-Kizil, A. (2010). How can the use of blog software facilitate the writing process of English. *Computer Assisted Language Learning, 23*(3), 183–197.

Aydin, Z., & Yildiz, S. (2014). Using wikis to promote collaborative EFL writing. *Language Learning and Technology, 18*(1), 160–180.

Barton, G. (2015). Literacy in the middle years visual arts classroom: A 'functional' approach. *Literacy Learning: The Middle Years, 23*(2), 40–52.

Barton, G., & Baguley, M. (2014). Learning through story: A collaborative, multimodal arts approach. *English Teaching, 13*(2), 93–112.

Barton, D., & Hamilton, M. (Eds.). (2000). *Situated literacies: Reading and writing in context.* London and New York: Routledge.

Bell, T. I. (2001). Extensive reading: Speed and comprehension. *Reading Matrix: An International Online Journal, 1*(1).

Butti, L. (2015). Whose literacy is it, anyway? *English Journal, 104*(6), 14–16/*29*(3), 435–441.

Carr, J. F. (2014). Composition, English, and the university. *PMLA, 1.*

Centre for Applied English Studies. (2016). Undergraduates (4-year curriculum). Retrieved January 16, 2016 from http://caes.hku.hk/home/english-courses/undergraduates-4-year/.

Cheng, J., Chen, C., & Brown, K. L. (2012). The effects of authentic audience on English as a second language (ESL) writers: A task-based, computer-mediated approach. *Computer Assisted Language Learning, 25*(5), 435–454.

Cheng, W., Chan, M., Chiu, H., Kwok, A., Lam, K. H., & Lam, K. M. (2014). *Enhancing students' professional competence and generic qualities through writing in English across the curriculum.* Hong Kong: The Hong Kong Polytechnic University.

Chiu, H. (2012). Supporting the development of autonomous learning skills in reading and writing in an independent language learning centre. *Studies in Self-Access Learning Journal, 3*(3), 266–290.

Chiu, H. (2014). Using unconventional genres for university writing courses. In *Proceedings for the 4th Centre for English Language Communication Symposium 2013* (pp. 98–106). Singapore: National University of Singapore.

Chiu, H. (2015a). Supporting extensive reading in a university where English is used as a second language and a medium of instruction. *The Reading Matrix, 15*(1), 234–251.

Chiu, H. (2015b). Materials design and pedagogy for technology-enhanced language learning. *International Journal of Computer-Assisted Language Learning and Teaching, 5*(1), 22–34.

Chiu, H. (2015c). Contemporary literacy concepts and practices in English Language Education. *International Journal of Arts and Sciences, 8*(6), 213–228.

English Language Centre. (2016). Language and communication requirement (LCR) subjects. Retrieved January 16, 2016, from http://elc.polyu.edu.hk/subjects/#LCR.

Eodice, M. (1998). Telling teacher talk: Sociolinguistic features of writing conferences. *Research and Teaching in Developmental Education, 15*(1), 13.

Gardner, D. (2004). Vocabulary input through extensive reading: A comparison of words found in children's narrative and expository reading materials. *Applied Linguistics, 25*(1), 1–37.

Haneda, M. (2004). The joint construction of meaning in writing conferences. *Applied Linguistics, 25*(2), 178–219.

Iwahori, Y. (2008). Developing reading fluency: A study of extensive reading in EFL. *Reading in a Foreign Language, 20*(1), 70–79.

Kitson, L. (2015). Building literacy capabilities for comprehension in the curriculum: A framework for teachers. *Literacy Learning: The Middle Years, 23*(1), 54–65.

Knoll, B. (Ed.). (2003). *Exploring the dynamics of second language writing*. Cambridge: Cambridge University Press.

Kress, G. (2003). *Literacy in the new media age*. London: Routledge.

Kweon, S.-O., & Kim, H.-R. (2008). Beyond raw frequency: Incidental vocabulary acquisition in extensive reading. *Reading in a Foreign Language, 20*(2), 191–215.

Lambert, G. M. S. (1999). *Helping 12th grade honors English students improve writing skills through conferencing*. Unpublished M.Sc. thesis, Nova Southeastern University.

Langer, J. A. (2011). *Envisioning knowledge: Building literacy in the academic disciplines*. New York and London: Teachers College Press.

Lankshear, C., & Knobel, M. (2003). *New literacies: Changing knowledge and classroom learning*. Buckingham and Philadelphia: Open University Press.

Laurillard, D. (2002). *Rethinking university teaching: A conversational framework for the effective use of learning technologies* (2nd ed.). London and New York: RoutledgeFalmer.

Leu, D. J., McVerry, J. G., O'Byrne, W. L., Kiili, C., Zawilinski, L., Everett-Cacopardo, H., et al. (2011). The new literacies of online reading comprehension: Expanding the literacy and learning Curriculum. *Journal of Adolescent & Adult Literacy, 55*(1), 5–14.

Li, J. (2013). Synchronous text-based computer-mediated communication tasks and the development of L2 academic literacy. *International Journal of Computer-Assisted Language Learning and Teaching, 3*(1), 16–32.

Liou, H.-C., & Lee, S.-L. (2011). How wiki-based writing influences college students' collaborative and individual composing products, processes, and learners' perceptions. *International Journal of Computer-Assisted Language Learning and Teaching, 1*(1), 45–61.

Marshall, S., Zhou, M., Gervan, T., & Wiebe, S. (2012). Sense of belonging and first-year academic literacy. *Canadian Journal of Higher Education, 12*(3), 116–142.

Mkandawire, M. T., & Walubita, G. (2015). Feedback study on developing critical literacy among Malawian and Zambian undergraduate university students using a freirean praxis. *Journal of Education and Training Studies, 3*(2), 150–159.

Mokhtari, K., & Sheorey, R. (1994). Reading habits of university ESL students at different levels of English proficiency and education. *Journal of Research in Reading, 17*(1), 46–61.

Olivier, L., & Olivier, J. (2013). The influence of affective variables on the acquisition of academic literacy. *Per Linguam, 29*(2), 56–71.

Paxton, M., & Frith, V. (2014). Implications of academic literacies research for knowledge making and curriculum design. *Higher Education, 67*(2), 171–183.

Pessoa, S., Miller, R. T., & Kaufer, D. (2014). Students' challenges and development in the transition to academic writing at an English-medium university in Qatar. *International Review of Applied Linguistics in Language Teaching, 52*(2), 127–157.

Raisanen, S., & Korkeamaki, R.-L. (2015). Implementing the Finnish literacy curriculum in a first-grade classroom. *Classroom Discourse, 6*(2), 143–158.

School of Arts and Social Sciences. (2016). Programme structure. Retrieved January 16, 2016, from http://www.ouhk.edu.hk/wcsprd/Satellite?pagename=OUHK/tcSchWeb2014&l=C_CFTS&lid=1385167531355&c=C_CFTS&cid=191170029800&lang=eng&sch=ASS&mid=0.

School of Education and Languages. (2016). Programme structure and curriculum. Retrieved January 16, 2016, from http://www.ouhk.edu.hk/wcsprd/Satellite?pagename=OUHK/tcSchWeb2014&l=C_EL&lid=191128000600&c=C_EL&cid=191129000800&lang=eng&sch=EL&mid=6.

Shaw, L. J. (2014). Breaking with tradition: Multimodal literacy learning. *New England Reading Association Journal, 50*(1), 19–27.

Stemper, J. (2002). *Enhancing student revising and editing skills through writing conferences and peer editing.* Unpublished M.A. thesis, Saint Xavier University, Chicago, IL.

Strauss, S., & Xiang, X. (2006). The writing conference as a locus of emergent agency. *Written Communication, 23*(4), 355–396.

Sun, Y.-C., & Chang, Y.-J. (2012). Blogging to learn: Becoming EFL academic writers through collaborative dialogues. *Language Learning and Technology, 16*(1), 43–61.

Tagg, C. (2012). Digital English. In D. Allington & B. Mayor (Eds.), *Communicating in English: Text, talk and technology* (pp. 307–341). London: The Open University and Routledge.

The Hong Kong Polytechnic University. (2013). 4-year undergraduate curriculum structure. Retrieved May 30, 2013, from http://4yc.polyu.edu.hk/curriculum.html.

The Open University of Hong Kong (2016). Programme information for new students. Retrieved January 16, 2016, from http://www.ouhk.edu.hk/wcsprd/Satellite?pagename=OUHK/tcGenericPage2010&lang=eng&status=1&c=C_ETPU&cid=191153051400.

Tribble, C., & Wingate, U. (2013). From text to corpus: A genre-based approach to academic literacy instruction. *System, 41,* 307–321.

Vacca, R. T., Vacca, J. A. L., & Mraz, M. (2014). *Content area reading: Literacy and learning across the curriculum.* NJ: Pearson Education.

Vurdien, R. (2013). Enhancing writing skills through blogging in an advanced English as a Foreign Language class in Spain. *Computer Assisted Language Learning, 26*(2), 126–143.

Warschauer, M. (2007). Technology and writing. In C. Davison & J. Cummins (Eds.), *The international handbook of English language teaching* (pp. 907–912). Norwell, MA: Springer.

Wu, S. R. (2000). *Journal writing in university pleasure-reading activities.* Taiwan: Center for General Education, National Yang-Ming University.

Chapter 3
Extensive Reading and Vocabulary Acquisition

Nina Daskalovska

Abstract One of the important aspects of learning a foreign language is vocabulary acquisition. Many scholars agree that even though direct instruction can contribute to learning vocabulary, the greatest part of vocabulary growth happens while learners are exposed to the target language. As studies have shown that the range of vocabulary in spoken language is much smaller than that in written texts, it is believed that the main factor that influences vocabulary development is the quantity of texts that learners read. A number of studies have demonstrated that foreign language learners can acquire vocabulary through reading and that language learning programmes that include extensive reading are more effective than only explicit learning of vocabulary through decontextualized exercises. Therefore, language instruction should include explicit vocabulary learning as well as vocabulary learning strategies and reading strategies, but it should also provide opportunities for incidental vocabulary learning through extensive reading, as it is one of the best ways of developing vocabulary knowledge and reading skills. The chapter elaborates on the importance of extensive reading for language development with a focus on vocabulary acquisition. It includes studies on the effects of reading on learning vocabulary. The last section is devoted to the characteristics of successful extensive reading programmes, selection of reading materials and implications for teaching.

Keywords Extensive reading · Vocabulary acquisition · Explicit vocabulary learning · Incidental vocabulary learning · Vocabulary size

N. Daskalovska (✉)
Goce Delcev University, Stip, Republic of Macedonia
e-mail: nina.daskalovska@ugd.edu.mk

© Springer Nature Singapore Pte Ltd. 2018
R. Joseph Ponniah and S. Venkatesan (eds.), *The Idea and Practice of Reading*,
https://doi.org/10.1007/978-981-10-8572-7_3

Introduction

Many language learners regard reading as the most important skill, especially in foreign language contexts where learners are exposed to the target language mostly in its written form as the opportunities for oral communication are fewer than in second-language contexts. In order to read fluently and with understanding, learners need to develop a number of sub-skills such as decoding letters and words, activating their previous knowledge, guessing the meaning of words they are not familiar with, predicting the content of the text, getting the main idea, identifying the text structure, using reading strategies, and so on. Even though many aspects of the reading process are still not well understood, Hirsh suggests that reading comprehension largely depends on three factors: reading fluency, breadth of vocabulary, and domain knowledge (2003: 12).

Many linguists agree that there is a correlation between reading speed and the level of text comprehension because the person who reads quickly pays more attention to the meaning of the text rather than the reading processes which he performs automatically (Grabe & Stoller, 2001; Hirsh, 2003; Stanovich, 1998). Slow reading and focusing on individual words hinders the construction of meaning and text comprehension (Day & Bamford, 1998). Fry claims that good readers read 350 words per minute while slow readers read 150 words per minute (qtd. in Bell, 2001).

Apart from fluency, Hirsh points out that reading comprehension is closely related to vocabulary knowledge (16). He quotes a study by Hart and Risley which shows that the vocabulary size of high-achieving first-grade students is twice that of low achievers, and that this difference constantly increases, so that by 12th grade these students know four times more words than the low-achieving students. Cunningham and Stanovich explain this phenomenon with the so-called Matthew Effect (1998: 137). Namely, when the word-recognition process takes up a large part of the cognitive capacities, there are fewer cognitive resources for text understanding and integration. As reading without understanding is not a pleasant experience, it leads to avoiding reading activities, which in turn leads to fewer opportunities for developing automaticity of word recognition. It results in developing negative emotions towards reading and school in general. On the other hand, students who have developed automaticity of word recognition enjoy reading because they can focus on meaning, so that they read more and more which results in the development of reading skills and other cognitive abilities.

However, in addition to vocabulary knowledge, in order to understand the text, the reader also needs to have domain knowledge: "While word knowledge speeds up word recognition and thus the process of reading, world knowledge speeds up comprehension of textual meaning by offering a foundation for making inferences" (Hirsh, 2003: 12). Hirsh explains that because many words have multiple meanings, the reader needs to have knowledge of the topic in order to determine the meaning of the words in that particular context. He also needs to make inferences based on his previous knowledge because understanding requires active construction of meaning through supplying the missing information in the text (17). For example, irony and metaphor are literary devices which do not express meaning explicitly, so that in order to understand them readers need to activate the relevant general knowledge which is not given in the text.

Thus, text comprehension depends on many factors, but even though all of them have some influence, it seems that the crucial factor for foreign language learners, as has been demonstrated by many studies on reading comprehension, is vocabulary knowledge. Laufer and Sim found that in interpreting texts, students consider words as the main indicators of meaning, they use their background knowledge to a lesser degree and they do not pay any attention to syntax (Laufer, 1997: 21). Laufer concludes that using the reading strategies developed while learning to read in their mother tongue does not help foreign language learners unless they have acquired considerable vocabulary size so that the automatic recognition of a large number of words in the text would free the cognitive resources needed to infer the meaning of unknown words and to interpret the global meaning of the text (23). In order to understand a text and to be able to infer the meaning of unfamiliar words, readers need to know at least 95% of all the words, which according to Hirsh and Nation is the first threshold "where there is one unknown word in every two lines", while the second threshold is 97–98% coverage which enables much better text comprehension (1992: 690). Whereas the first threshold, which implies knowledge of about 3,000 words, may be sufficient for understanding general texts and guessing the meaning of 60–80% of the unknown words (Clarke & Nation, 1980: 212), it appears that the second threshold is necessary for reading academic texts which requires knowledge of 5,000 word families (Coady, 1997; Hirsh & Nation, 1992). However, as Hu and Nation point out, "the relationship between vocabulary knowledge and reading comprehension is complex and dynamic", meaning that when learners start learning to read they use their vocabulary knowledge to understand the text, but after they have developed their reading skills, reading texts become the source for acquiring new vocabulary (2000: 403).

Many studies have confirmed the positive effects of reading on vocabulary development. A study conducted by Carol Chomsky revealed that elementary school children who read and were read to more than the other children scored higher on vocabulary, syntax, and reading comprehension tests (Chall, 14). What is more, the highest scores were achieved by the children who read and had read to them books that were at a higher readability level than their current linguistic development. The results of this study were confirmed in other studies which showed that reading harder books contributed to better vocabulary knowledge and reading comprehension, while reading books below the learners' current reading level did not have that effect.

This and other studies that will be presented in the following section show that one of the positive effects of reading is vocabulary development.

The Effects of Reading on Vocabulary Acquisition

Most scholars agree that even though direct vocabulary learning is an effective way of increasing one's vocabulary knowledge, the best part of vocabulary acquisition happens through exposure to the language rather than through direct learning. Moreover, the main factor in the different vocabulary size of learners is the "reading volume rather than oral language"; analysis of the vocabulary used in written texts and speech showed that compared to written language, speech is "lexically impoverished" (Cunningham & Stanovich, 1998: 138–139). Ellis (1995) also claims that reading is the ideal method for vocabulary acquisition because less frequent words occur more often in written texts than in speech. In addition, reading allows learners to analyse the context, to test hypotheses and to discover the meaning of unknown words as they can read at their own pace and can go back and forth, which is impossible with speech.

The term *extensive reading* was first introduced by Palmer (1968: 165, 1921: 111) who described it as reading a large amount of text "rapidly and carelessly" and focusing on the meaning rather than the language. He contrasted it to *'intensive reading'* which involves studying a text "line by line, referring at every moment to our dictionary and our grammar, comparing, analysing, translating, and retaining every expression that it contains". He believed that both types of reading are important for language learning. In his view, extensive reading could be used both for language study and for pleasure and information: "real-world reading but for a pedagogical purpose" (Day & Bamford, 1998: 5). The methodology of extensive reading was later developed by Michael West who called it *supplementary reading*, where the aim was developing reading skills in a foreign language, consolidating previously acquired vocabulary, learning new vocabulary, and motivating learners to continue to learn the language (Nation & Wang, 1999: 357).

One of the greatest promoters of the idea that language can be easily acquired through extensive reading is Krashen (1987, 1989, 1993, 2004a), who claims that language development happens when learners are involved in processing comprehensible input which enables the integration of the new forms into their existing language system through establishing connections between form and meaning. There is no doubt that extensive reading can be a valuable source of language input. It enables learners to encounter words in different natural contexts and to acquire the different aspects of word knowledge such as meaning, collocation, register, style, grammar, etc. Moreover, reading gives learners opportunities to learn less frequent words which are not usually used in speech but are important for developing their lexicon. Nation (2001) points out that learning vocabulary through reading has several benefits. First, as reading is an individual activity, learners with different language proficiency can read and learn the language according to their own level. Second, it can increase learners' motivation for learning the language by allowing them to choose reading materials based on their own interests. And third, it enables learners to learn outside the classroom (151).

In the following section we will present first- and second-language studies on the acquisition of vocabulary through reading.

Overview of Research on Vocabulary Acquisition Through Reading

The usual procedure in studies on vocabulary acquisition through reading is as follows: the participants read a text followed by a test to determine the knowledge of the target words. In order to establish the knowledge of the target words prior to the experiment, there is usually a pre-test. However, as the pre-test could turn the participants' attention to the target words during reading, instead of a pre-test in some studies the target words are replaced with non-existent words.

These studies differ in many respects. One of them is the number and characteristics of the participants. There are participants of different ages and proficiency levels, and their number ranges from one to several hundred. Another difference is the type and length of texts. Most of the studies use simplified texts, but in some of the studies the participants read authentic texts. The length of the texts ranges from several pages to a large number of books. The number of target words is also different and it ranges from six to 100 and more. Regarding the type of testing instruments, multiple-choice tests are the most often used type of tests. Other instruments include word-recognition tests, translation, interviews, and so on. Most of the studies focus on one aspect of word knowledge, usually meaning. The participants are usually tested immediately after the reading treatment, and very few studies investigate the long-term effect of reading on vocabulary development. The factors that influence vocabulary acquisition include word frequency, the participants' vocabulary size, contextual factors, and so on. The results of these studies are quite different and show acquisition of 6–96% of the target words.

First-Language Studies on Vocabulary Acquisition

One of the most cited studies on vocabulary acquisition through reading is the study conducted by Saragi, Nation, and Meister (1978) whose aim was to determine if there was a relationship between word frequency in the text and word acquisition. The participants were 20 adult native English speakers who read the book *A Clockwork Orange* by Anthony Burgess which contains 241 'nadsat' words which were invented by the author. Their frequency in the text ranged from one to 209 times. Several days after reading the book the participants were tested on their knowledge of the meaning of 90 target words. The results showed that on average they managed to learn the meaning of 76% of the words. The conclusion of the study was that a lot of words can be acquired incidentally from reading and that the frequency of the words in the text affects their acquisition, even though there are other factors in play such as the context or the similarity to words from their mother tongue.

Another study that investigated the role of frequency is the study by Jenkins, Stein, and Wysocki (1984) in which the participants were 112 fifth-grade pupils divided into three groups according to the number of times they encountered the target words through reading. The testing instruments included giving definition of the target words, choosing the correct definition, completing sentences containing the target words, and understanding a paragraph containing the target words. The participants who encountered the words ten times demonstrated superior results compared with the other two groups and the acquisition rate ranged from 16 to 27%. The authors concluded that increasing the number of encounters resulted in greater gains and that more than two encounters are needed for word acquisition to happen. The results also showed that the more proficient learners had better results than the less proficient learners.

In a study conducted by Nagy, Herman, and Anderson (1985) 57 eighth-grade students read one of two authentic texts containing 1,000 words, in each of which fifteen more difficult words were selected as target words. After the reading, the participants were tested on the knowledge of all 30 words. The testing instruments included an interview and a multiple-choice test containing definitions of the target words. The results showed that the participants managed to learn two-three words from the text they read. On the basis of these results, the authors concluded that the probability of recognizing the correct definition of a previously unknown word after only one encounter was one out of ten.

In a follow-up study (Nagy, Anderson, & Herman, 1987), 352 students from third, fifth and seventh grade read one of two texts containing 1,300 words, of which 35 words were chosen and target words. One week after the reading treatment, the participants were tested on their knowledge of all 70 words with a multiple-choice test containing definitions of the target words. The results in this study were lower and the probability of recognizing the correct definition of a previously unknown word after only one encounter was one out of 20. The authors suggested that the difference was due to the time between the reading treatment and the post-test, as in the first study the participants were tested immediately while in the second study the post-test was conducted one week after the reading. The study also showed that the conceptual difficulty of the words was the only variable that significantly affected the acquisition of the words.

Second-Language Studies on Vocabulary Acquisition

The first published study on second-language vocabulary acquisition through reading conducted by Pitts, White, and Krashen (2015) was a partial replication of Saragi et al.'s study. The participants were 35 adult language learners who read two chapters of the novel *A Clockwork Orange*. The treatment lasted an hour, after which the participants were given a multiple-choice test in order to determine the acquisition of 30 'nadsat' words that were encountered from one to 27 times in the text. The results of the experimental group were compared to those of the control group and they showed that the experimental group learned 6.4% or 1.81 of the target words. The authors conducted another experiment including sixteen participants who received information about the novel and watched two scenes of the film based on the book. In the second experiment the participants learned 8.1% or 2.42 target words. The authors pointed out that the book was difficult for the participants so that more than 50% did not manage to read the whole text. Moreover, the participants in the original study had the advantage of reading the whole novel, encountering the words more times and understanding the novel better than the participants in their study.

In a real reading extensive conditions experiment (Cho & Krashen, 1994), four participants aged from 21 to 35 read books of their own choice from a reading programme for young native speakers. Three of the participants were asked to underline the new words when they encountered them for the first time, but they were given no further instructions as the researchers wanted to see which strategies they would use and whether the strategies would change during the experiment. Two of them used a dictionary and wrote the new words in a notebook, but they did not revise them later. The third participant used a dictionary only for the first four books. The fourth participant did not use a dictionary at all. All participants enjoyed reading and they read between ten and 23 books in less than a month. In order to determine the effect of reading, they were given a test which contained the words they had underlined and they had to give either a synonym or a definition. The number of tested words ranged from 165 to 535 words. The results showed that the participants learned from 56 to 80% of the previously unknown words. They believed that reading improved their speaking skills and comprehension skills as well as their grammar knowledge.

Horst, Cobb, and Meara (1998) conducted an experiment in which the participants were 34 language learners who read and listened to the simplified version of the novel *The Mayor of Casterbridge* which contains 21,232 words. After the reading treatment they were tested on their knowledge of 45 target words with different frequency. The testing instrument consisted of a multiple-choice test and a word-association test which were also administered as pre-tests before the reading treatment. In order to investigate the role of the participants' vocabulary size, Nation's (1990) Vocabulary Levels Test was administered before the treatment. The results of the multiple-choice test showed that the participants learned the meaning of 4.62 out of 23 or 20% of the unknown words. The word-association test showed a lower gain of 1.18 words or 16%. The correlation between the word frequency and the learning gains was 0.49. The authors concluded that the possibility of learning words through reading was greater for words encountered eight times or more. Regarding the relationship between vocabulary size and learning gains, the study demonstrated that vocabulary size is an important factor that influences the rate of acquisition of vocabulary from reading.

The role of frequency was also investigated by Rott (1999) who found out that four encounters did not result in much greater gains than two encounters, while six encounters contributed to significantly greater receptive and productive knowledge of previously unknown words.

Zahar, Cobb, and Spada (2001) investigated the acquisition of vocabulary by 144 seventh-grade learners in Canada who read the text *The Golden Fleece* which is an authentic text categorized for learners at an intermediate level of language proficiency. The participants were divided into five groups on the basis of their language proficiency and were given the Vocabulary Levels Test in order to analyse the difference between the five groups. They were tested on their knowledge of 30 target words thirteen days before the treatment and two days after the treatment. The pre-test showed that the participants already knew 19.66 of the target words, while the post-test showed an increase of 2.16 words. The correlation between the word frequency and the learning gains was 0.36, and the biggest effect was seen for the participants with lower vocabulary size. In addition, this study examined the role of contextual clues, and the analysis showed that its effect was lower than that of the frequency of the words in the text. The authors concluded that authentic texts can be a valuable source for vocabulary learning, but beginning learners need to encounter words more often in order to be able to acquire them.

In order to investigate the effect of reading more books, Pigada and Schmitt (2006) conducted an experiment in which an adult learner who was learning French as a foreign language read four simplified books with a total of 228 pages in the course of one month. The authors selected 133 target words of which 70 were nouns and 63 were verbs. They interviewed the learner before and after the reading treatment checking spelling, meaning and grammatical knowledge. The results showed that the knowledge of spelling increased by 23%, the knowledge of meaning increased by 15.4%, while the grammatical knowledge increased by 30% for the nouns and 16.6% for the verbs. The authors also investigated partial knowledge and found that the participant demonstrated some knowledge of 65.4% of the target words. The study demonstrated that reading can contribute to significant knowledge of the written form of the words and that two to three encounters can help learners gain some knowledge of the words which increases significantly after ten encounters. However, it also showed that word frequency is only one of the factors that influence vocabulary acquisition from reading.

Another study which demonstrated that reading can lead to incidental acquisition of meaning and grammatical knowledge of words is the study conducted by Ponniah (2011) with 49 first-year undergraduate students in India. The participants in the experimental group read the text *The Chinese Statue,* in which 51 words were selected as target words. The control group was asked to study the dictionary meaning of the target words. After the treatment, both groups were tested on their knowledge of the words by giving the meaning of the words and using them in sentences. The scores of the experimental group were superior to those of the control group on both tests. The author concluded that reading can help learners gain knowledge of meaning and grammar of previously unknown words.

The aim of Brown, Waring, and Donkaewbua's (2008) study was to investigate vocabulary acquisition from three input modes: reading only, reading and listening, and listening only. For that purpose the authors used three stories from simplified books. After the reading treatment the participants were tested on their knowledge of 84 target words which were substituted with non-existent words. In order to test different aspects of word knowledge, two types of test were used: a multiple-choice test and a translation test which were administered three times—immediately after the treatment, after one week and after three months. The first post-test showed that the participants who read and listened to the text at the same time learned the meaning of 48% of the target words, those who only read the text learned 45% while those who only listened to the text learned 29% of the target words. The translation test showed lower results of 16, 15, and 2% respectively. The results of the multiple-choice test persisted after three months, while the results of the translation test significantly decreased during this period. In relation to the role of frequency, the study showed that the more frequent words could be learned and remembered better than the less frequent words.

In order to investigate the rate of acquisition of three aspects of word knowledge through reading, Daskalovska (2016) conducted a study in which 122 participants read an authentic novel. The measuring instruments consisted of two tests: a spelling test and a test on meanings and collocations which included 100 words with different frequency. The first test measured productive knowledge of spelling, while the second test measured receptive knowledge of meanings and collocations. The tests were conducted before and after the treatment. At the end of the experiment, the participants were asked to complete a questionnaire. Apart from investigating the effects of reading an authentic novel on the acquisition of three aspects of word knowledge—spelling, meaning and collocation—the study also focused on the influence of reading on the acquisition of partial and deeper knowledge of the words, and the relationship between word frequency and learning gains. The results show that there was significant improvement in all three aspects of word knowledge. Namely, the participants learned the collocations of 26.44% of the target words, the meaning of 25.97%, and the spelling of 24.23% of the words. The measuring instrument detected greater partial than deeper knowledge gains in word meanings and collocations. In relation to frequency, the greatest learning gains in all three aspects of word knowledge were demonstrated for the words that occurred between eleven and 20 times in the text. The author concludes that incorporation of extensive reading into language learning programmes can contribute to significant improvement of learners' vocabulary knowledge.

There are many other studies on vocabulary acquisition from reading, but it is impossible to present all of them here. However, the above-mentioned studies show that extensive reading can help language learners increase their vocabulary size and acquire different aspects of word knowledge at the same time, which is not always possible with other ways of learning vocabulary.

Implication for Teaching

Some linguists believe that explicit learning of vocabulary is more efficient as learners can learn more words in a shorter time and that the effect of such learning is more long-lasting. On the other hand, research has shown that the number of words that can be learned through explicit learning in the classroom is only a few hundred words a year (Nagy et al. 1987) and that explicit instruction cannot provide opportunities for acquisition of all word knowledge aspects such as collocations, word associations, register, etc. as these can only be acquired after multiple encounters in context.

In addition, it is believed that communicative language teaching which involves various activities that enable learners to use the language in situations that resemble real-life situations can help them enrich their vocabularies. However, a study conducted by Lightbown et al. (1999) demonstrated that there were very small differences between the quantity and quality of input in audio-lingual and communicative language-teaching classrooms. Therefore, they suggest that we cannot expect to see natural vocabulary development only through communicative teaching.

The more recent literature suggests that in the beginning stages of learning, instruction should focus on explicit learning of vocabulary by using techniques for direct vocabulary learning, which in the later stages should be replaced by learning vocabulary from context (Coady, 1997; Meara, 1997). A good language programme should be a combination of explicit vocabulary learning and activities that enable incidental learning of vocabulary. Moreover, learners should be encouraged to read outside the classroom.

Nuttall points out that in English language teaching texts are usually used to present and practice language items, which is not "an authentic use of a text" (1982: 19). Even though reading can contribute to enriching one's language, real-life reading has other purposes, such as reading for pleasure, reading for learning some new information, etc. Therefore, we have to differentiate between *intensive* and *extensive* reading, or as Brumfit labels them, *reading for accuracy* and *reading for fluency* (qtd. in Nuttall 23). The aim of intensive reading is arriving "at a profound and detailed understanding of the text: not only of what it means, but also of how the meaning is produced" (ibid.). Thus, intensive reading helps learners increase their understanding and learn the language better by seeing language items used in context, as well as learning how to use reading strategies. However, the limited time in the classroom does not enable learners to develop their reading skills and to achieve accuracy and fluency effectively. Therefore, what is needed is an extensive reading programme which would help learners develop their reading skills and learn the language outside the classroom as well. Eskey and Grabe also emphasize that language knowledge and reading skills can only be developed by reading extensively: "Classroom work can point the way but cannot substitute for the act itself: people learn to read by reading, not by doing exercises" (1998: 228). Many other scholars agree that extensive reading is the key to achieving automaticity in recognizing words and phrases and developing reading skills (Bamford & Day, 1997; Carrell & Eisterhold, 1988; Wallace, 1992). Discussing the question of how much the teacher should intervene, Eskey and Grabe state that regardless of learners' age, proficiency, educational needs and the available time, there are three constants which are independent from other factors: the quantity of reading, the appropriate materials, and the judgement of the teacher (1998: 228). It is obvious that in order to achieve the aims of a reading programme, learners need to read a lot and that the reading materials should be enjoyable and should correspond to their needs and interests. Even though the teacher is not usually present while learners read, his/her role, according to Eskey and Grabe, is crucial as it is the teacher who can stimulate interest in reading, to motivate learners and to show them the value of reading. In addition, the teacher should help the learner choose appropriate materials and teach them reading strategies in order to enable them to cope with unfamiliar language and to learn to read effectively, as well as to give feedback that will provide further help and encouragement to read extensively.

Waring maintains that extensive reading should not be seen as an additional or optional, but an essential and integral part of language learning programmes (2009: 93). He does not deny the benefits of using language textbooks and explicit instruction, but claims that they cannot enable acquisition of the different meanings and use of thousands of words and phrases as well as the numerous grammatical rules and their applications. He says that textbooks usually present new material such as vocabulary, grammar, reading strategies or pronunciation rules and provide minimal practice of these elements, but they do not provide enough revision and recycling, which is the essential condition for gaining deeper knowledge and mastering the knowledge and skills, and the only way to achieve this is through extensive reading. In his view, the knowledge that learners gain in the classroom is abstract and cannot be used for productive purposes. Extensive reading would enable learners to encounter the new language elements in authentic contexts and to see how they function so that they can develop both accuracy and fluency in using the language.

Characteristics of Extensive Reading Programmes

Extensive reading means reading large quantities of reading materials according to learners' interest and proficiency level. Day and Bamford give the following ten most important characteristics of successful extensive reading programmes (1998: 7–8):

1. Students read as much as possible.
2. A variety of materials on a wide range of topics is available.
3. Students select what they want to read.
4. The purposes of reading are usually related to pleasure, information and general understanding.
5. Reading is its own reward.
6. Reading materials are well within the linguistic competence of the students.
7. Reading is individual and silent.
8. Reading speed is usually faster rather than slower.
9. Teachers orient students to the goals of the programme, explain the methodology, keep track of what each student reads, and guide students in getting the most of the programme.
10. The teacher is a role model of a reader for students.

Hill (1997) points out that in order for an extensive reading programme to be successful, it should be a programme that would involve the whole school and that would continue to function for a long time. The programme may start with fewer books, but the number of books should constantly increase in order to answer the needs of all the students in the school. It is necessary to establish a library system with all the typical library operations, to prepare a methodology for the reading programme, to set goals, and to monitor and assess the success of the programme. The extensive reading programme can be integrated in the regular language learning programme or as an extra-curricular activity and the students should be required to read a specific number of books during a school term (Day & Bamford, 1998: 41). Day and Bamford suggest giving points for reading which would count towards the final grade, for example, for fifteen books read in a term the student can get 15 points or 15% of the grade. If the reading programme cannot be integrated into the regular programme, then it can function as an optional activity. In this case, the teacher needs to explain the benefits of reading and to encourage learners to read on their own, but points can still be given for the books the students have read during the term. A third possibility the authors suggest is establishing a readers' club which would function as an extra-curricular activity. The members can meet once a week and discuss the books they have read. They can also write a few sentences about the book they have read, their opinions, feelings and reactions, and the teacher can give feedback or ask questions. It is important that the teacher shares his/her enthusiasm for reading with their students and takes part in the discussions. The activities after reading are beneficial for students because they will give them opportunities to use the language they have encountered in the books. Swain (1999) points out that while receiving large quantities of comprehensible input is essential, it is not enough for mastering the language and it has to be supplemented by output in spoken or written form.

Another way of improving the language is 'narrow reading', which means reading several books by the same author or on the same topic. Krashen (2004b: 17) claims that this kind of reading is beneficial for two reasons. First, as every author has his own distinctive style and favourite expressions and every topic is characterized by special vocabulary or type of discourse, this type of reading will enable recycling of the same vocabulary and structures. Second, since the knowledge of the topic and the general knowledge enable better understanding of the text, the more you read on the same topic, the more you learn about it and at the same time improve the language.

Selection of Reading Materials

When deciding on the reading materials for a particular group of students, teachers need to have in mind students' age and language proficiency, but above all they should think about students' interests. As Davies points out, the key words are "quantity and variety, rather than quality", which means that the literary merit of the reading materials is not so important as its attractiveness and relevance for the students (1995: 329). Day and Bamford suggest that higher-proficiency students can enjoy reading carefully selected authentic books, popular magazines and newspapers, whereas lower-proficiency students can read books and magazines written for children and young native speakers as they are shorter, contain illustrations, and are easier for reading, but for beginners the most suitable books would be simplified books written for foreign language learners (1998: 53–60). Simplified books are written and adapted for language learners by limiting the vocabulary and the grammatical structures which help beginners to consolidate the knowledge they have gained during lessons, develop their reading skills and enjoy reading. According to Nation and Wang, the biggest argument in favour of simplified books is that without them they cannot experience reading in a foreign language that corresponds to their proficiency level (1999: 356).

Communicative approaches to language teaching emphasize the use of authentic materials because simplified books lack the characteristics of authentic books and thus do not adequately prepare learners for using the language in the real world. However, in order to be able to read with understanding, learners need to know at least 95–98% of the words, which means knowing 3,000–5,000 words (Hirsh & Nation, 1992: 690). Therefore, many linguists suggest that until they have acquired a substantial vocabulary size, language learners should read simplified books and books for young native speakers. Reading difficult books will not help students develop a desire for reading and for developing their reading skills. Therefore, learners should be given the freedom to choose the reading materials according to their interest and proficiency level, to avoid using a dictionary and try to guess the meaning of the unknown words, and if the book is too difficult or boring they should not hesitate to stop reading it and find something more suitable for reading. This is the way we read in real life, so if the teachers explain to their students that they should adopt the same approach to reading in English, they can understand the nature and the aim of the extensive reading programme better, which would certainly have an effect on their attitude and motivation to read in English.

From what has been said so far, we can draw the following conclusions and implications regarding extensive reading:

1. In order to be successful, learners need to read a large amount of comprehensible texts regularly. It seems that two to three graded readers a month and five to nine books at one level would be enough to provide enough encounters of the vocabulary at that level.
2. Learners should have various materials at their disposal, so that they can choose the reading texts according to their interests and language competence.
3. Reading should not be connected with tests and grades as the books should be read for pleasure and enjoyment and reading should be an aim in itself.
4. Reading can be accompanied by discussions, exercises and activities in order to increase the effects of reading.

5. Teachers should motivate learners to read, explain the benefits of reading, help them develop reading strategies, reading habits and a love of reading, and help them choose appropriate reading materials.
6. Teachers need to set goals for reading and to keep a record of what the learners have read over a period of time.
7. Teachers should serve as a role model for reading and should discuss the books they read with their students.

Bearing in mind that the aim of language learning is to enable learners to use the language in the real world, and the fact that vocabulary has an essential role in language use, teachers should pay a great deal of attention to learning vocabulary and developing learners' vocabulary size. One of the best ways to achieve that aim is to incorporate extensive reading into language learning programmes.

References

Bamford, J., & Day, R. (1997). Extensive reading: What is it? Why bother? *The Language Teacher Online, 21*(5). Retrieved September 7, 2015.

Bell, T. (2001). Extensive reading: Speed and comprehension. *The Reading Matrix, 1*(1). Retrieved September 7, 2015.

Brown, R., Waring, R., & Donkaewbua, S. (2008). Incidental vocabulary acquisition from reading, reading-while-listening, and listening to stories. *Reading in a Foreign Language, 20*(2), 136–163.

Carrell, P. L., & Eisterhold, J. C. (1988). Schema theory and ESL reading pedagogy. In P. L. Carrell, J. Devine, & D. E. Eskey (Eds.), *Interactive approaches to second language reading* (pp. 73–92). Cambridge: Cambridge University Press.

Cho, K.-S., & Krashen, S. D. (1994). Acquisition of vocabulary from Sweet Valley Kids Series: Adult ESL acquisition. *Journal of Reading, 37*, 662–667.

Clarke, D. F., & Nation, I. S. P. (1980). Guessing the meanings of words from context: Strategy and techniques. *System, 8*, 211–220.

Coady, J. (1997). L2 vocabulary acquisition: A synthesis of research. In J. Coady & T. Huckin (Eds.), *Second language vocabulary acquisition: A rationale for pedagogy* (pp. 237–290). New York: Cambridge University Press.

Cunningham, A. E., & Stanovich, K. E. (1998). What reading does for the mind. *American Educator, 22*, 8–15.

Daskalovska, N. (2016). Acquisition of three word knowledge aspects through reading. *The Journal of Educational Research, 109*(1), 68–80.

Davis, C. (1995). Extensive reading: An expensive extravagance? *ELT Journal, 49*(4), 329–336.

Day, R., & Bamford, J. (1998). *Extensive reading in the second language classroom*. Cambridge: Cambridge University Press.

Ellis, N. C. (1995). The psychology of foreign language vocabulary acquisition: Implications for CALL. *Computer Assisted Language Learning, 8*(2&3), 103–128.

Eskey, D. E., & Grabe, W. (1998). Interactive models for second language reading. In P. L. Carrell, J. Devine, & D. E. Eskey (Eds.), *Interactive approaches to second language reading* (pp. 223–238). Cambridge: Cambridge University Press.

Grabe, W., & Stoller, F. L. (2001). *Teaching and researching reading*. Harlow, Essex: Pearson ESL.

Hill, D. (1997). Setting up an extensive reading program: Practical tips. *The Language Teacher, 21*(5), 17–20.

Hirsh, E. D. (2003). Reading comprehension requires knowledge of words and the world. *American Educator, 27*(1), 10–13.

Hirsh, D., & Nation, P. (1992). What vocabulary size is needed to read unsimplified texts for pleasure? *Reading in a Foreign Language, 8*(2), 689–696. Retrieved September 8, 2015.

Horst, M., Cobb, T., & Meara, P. (1998). Beyond A Clockwork Orange: Acquiring second language vocabulary through reading. *Reading in a Foreign Language, 11*(2), 207–223. Retrieved September 8, 2015.

Hu, M., & Nation, P. (2000). Unknown vocabulary density and reading comprehension. *Reading in a Foreign Language, 13*(1), 403–430. Retrieved September 8, 2015.

Jenkins, J. R., Stein, M. L., & Wysocki, K. (1984). Learning vocabulary through reading. *American Educational Research Journal, 21*(4), 767–787.

Krashen, S. D. (1987). *Principles and practice in second language acquisition*. Hertfordshire: Prentice Hall International.

Krashen, S. D. (1989). We acquire vocabulary and spelling by reading: Additional evidence for the input hypothesis. *The Modern Language Journal, 73*(4), 440–464. Print.

Krashen, S. D. (1993). The case for free voluntary reading. *The Canadian Modern Language Review, 50*(1), 72–82.

Krashen, S. D. (2004a). *The power of reading: Insights from the research* (2nd ed.). Portsmouth: Heinemann.

Krashen, S. D. (2004b). The case for narrow reading. *Language Magazine, 3*(5), 17–19.

Laufer, B. (1997). The lexical plight in second language reading. In J. Coady & T. Huckin (Eds.), *Second language vocabulary acquisition: A rationale for pedagogy*. Cambridge: Cambridge University Press.

Lightbown, P. M., Meara, P., & Halter, R. (1999). Contrasting patterns in classroom lexical environments. In A. Dorte, B. Henriksen, I. Mees, & Erik Poulsen (Eds.), *Perspectives on foreign and second language pedagogy*. Odense: Odense University Press.

Meara, P. (1997). Models of vocabulary acquisition. In N. Schmitt & M. McCarthy (Eds.), *Vocabulary: Description, acquisition and pedagogy*. Cambridge: Cambridge University Press.

Nagy, W. E., Anderson, R. C., & Herman, P. A. (1987). Learning word meanings from context during normal reading. *American Educational Research Journal, 2*(2), 237–270.

Nagy, W. E., Herman, P. A., & Anderson, R. C. (1985). Learning words from context. *Reading Research Quarterly, 20*(2), 233–253.

Nation, P. (1990). *Teaching and learning vocabulary*. Rowley, MA: Newbury House.

Nation, P. (2001). *Learning vocabulary in another language*. Cambridge: Cambridge University Press.

Nation, P., & Wang, K. (1999). Graded readers and vocabulary. *Reading in a Foreign Language, 12*(2), 355–380.

Nuttall, C. (1982). *Teaching reading skills in a foreign language*. Oxford: Heinemann International.

Palmer, H. E. (1921). *The principles of language study*. New York: World Book Company.

Palmer, H. E. (1968). *The scientific study and teaching of languages*. Oxford: Oxford University Press.

Pigada, M., & Schmitt, N. (2006). Vocabulary acquisition from extensive reading: A case study. *Reading in a Foreign Language, 18*(1), 1–28.

Pitts, M., White, H., & Krashen, S. (2015). Acquiring second language vocabulary through reading: A replication of the Clockwork Orange study using second language acquirers. *Reading in a Foreign Language, 5*(2), 271–275. Retrieved September 7, 2015.

Ponniah, J. R. (2011). Incidental acquisition of vocabulary by reading. *The Reading Matrix, 11*(2), 135–139. Retrieved September 7, 2015.

Rott, S. (1999). The effect of exposure frequency on intermediate language learners' incidental vocabulary acquisition and retention through reading. *SSLA, 21*(4), 589–619.

Saragi, T., Nation, P., & Meister, G. F. (1978). Vocabulary learning and reading. *System, 6*(2), 72–78.

Stanovich, K. E. (1998). Twenty-five years of research on the reading process: The grand synthesis and what it means for our field. *National Reading Conference Yearbook, 47*, 44–58.

Swain, M. (1999). Integrating language and content teaching through collaborative tasks. In W. Christopher & W. Renandya (Eds.), *New insights for the language teacher* (pp. 125–147). Singapore: SEAMEO Regional Language Centre.
Wallace, K. (1992). *Reading*. Oxford: Oxford University Press.
Waring, R. (2009). The inescapable case for extensive reading. In A. Cirocki (Ed.), *Extensive reading in English language teaching* (pp. 93–111). Munich, Germany: Lincom.
Zahar, R., Cobb, T., & Spada, N. (2001). Acquiring vocabulary through reading: Effects of frequency and contextual richness. *The Canadian Modern Language Review, 57*(4), 541–572.

Chapter 4
Acquisition of Writing by Reading and Its Impact on Cognition

J. Mary Jennifer and R. Joseph Ponniah

Abstract Reading is an effective tool that contributes to the development of language with a strong impact on writing skills such as content, vocabulary, spelling, syntax and mechanics. The study investigated the effects of reading on adult ESL rural students of an arts and science college in India. The data were collected using pre- and post-test and also based on a questionnaire. The results reported statistically significant improvement in writing performance as well as improvement of language aspects. Further, the present study assessed the relationship between reading self-efficacy beliefs and writing performance. Overall results showed that reading self-efficacy beliefs had a positive influence on writing performance. In addition, long-term reading exposure makes the composing process easier and minimizes writing apprehensions and block. The profound implication of this study is that reading has a positive impact on the development of certain cognitive capabilities.

Keywords Cognition · Reading motivation · Reading–writing relationship
Self-efficacy · Writing apprehensions

Research on reading postulates that reading is an essential factor in the promotion of compositional skills through its positive effect on writing abilities (Carson, 1993; Ferris & Hedgecock, 2005; Krashen, 1984, 2004; Lee & Hsu, 2009; Smith, 2004). Reading expands knowledge of content, spelling, vocabulary, syntax and grammar. The extended knowledge in all dimensions scaffolds the writing process as there is reciprocal facilitation of reading and writing (Tierney & Shanahan, 1991). Evidence from research also suggests that both reading and writing rely on common cognitive resources (Carretti, Re, & Arfé, 2013), procedural knowledge (Prat-Sala & Redford, 2010) and affective schemata (Shell, Murphy, & Bruning, 1989). The cognitive resources of reading and writing require similar thought processes in meaning

---

J. Mary Jennifer · R. J. Ponniah (✉)
Department of Humanities and Social Sciences, National Institute of Technology Tiruchirappalli, Tiruchirappalli, Tamil Nadu, India
e-mail: joseph@nitt.edu

construction (Pearson, 1985; Spivey, 1990; Stotsky, 1983), which include activation of prior knowledge and accessing the appropriate information from memory and linguistic structures. Procedural knowledge such as planning, aligning and drafting enables readers and writers to set goals and purposes, and to develop a narrative thread in order to infer and convey ideas by involving cognition. Similarly, affective schemata comprise the affective variables such as attitude and motivation, which have a significant impact on reading and writing abilities as both competencies involve self-regulated behaviour.

The cognitive system has to be strengthened to attain conceptual and linguistic knowledge through continual exposure to reading. Evidence suggests that the cognitive benefits of reading such as pattern recognition, attention and text comprehension support writing by deepening the thinking process. Studies have also suggested that reading facilitates the composing process, and writing improves reading skills, and there is an undeniable connection between reading and writing (Willingham, 2017) as cognitive sub-processes are mutually facilitative (Grabe & Kaplan, 1996; Stotsky, 1982; Tierney & Shanahan, 1991; Zamel, 1992). In fact, studies conducted to improve writing by reading have proved that writing on what one has read enhances the comprehension of text through various processes including connecting relevant ideas, analysing and reviewing which have an indirect influence on reading skills. It is found that writing practices increase knowledge of spelling, phonology and syntax (Graham & Hebert, 2011; Tierney & Shanahan, 1991; Weiser & Mathes, 2011). Classroom studies on extensive reading have also demonstrated statistically significant improvement in writing skills (Elley, 1991; Elley & Mangubhai, 1983; Hafiz & Tudor, 1990; Lai, 1993; Lee & Hsu, 2009; Mason & Krashen, 1997; Mermelstein, 2015; Tsang, 1996; Tudor & Hafiz, 1989). The study conducted by Lee and Hsu (2009) reported remarkable gains in all key areas required for writing such as content, vocabulary, organization, language use, spelling/mechanics and fluency. Hafiz and Tudor (1989, 1990) and Tsang (1996) found significant improvement in the syntax and semantics of their participants' written language. Hafiz and Tudor (1989, 1990) and Lai (1993) confirmed that vocabulary and fluency are developed in writing. Hafiz and Tudor (1990) observed a variety of diction in their participants' writing after extensive reading sessions.

Learners who received longer exposure to reading had greater gains in overall writing scores (Lee & Hsu, 2009). In particular, readers who started to read in their early stages develop reading comprehension skills, verbal ability, and reading fluency in their later years (Cunningham and Stanovich, 1997). These skills had a significant impact on their writing and as a result, their syntactic structures were better formed than those of the infrequent readers (Stotsky, 1983). Further, reading in volumes had a positive influence on writing scores (Al-Rajhi, 2004; Constantino, 1995; Hafiz & Tudor, 1990; Janopoulos, 1986; Kaplan & Palhinda, 1981; Polak & Krashen, 1988; Salyer, 1987; Tudor & Hafiz, 1989). Kirin (2010) found that abundant reading was one of the determinants improving the writing ability of lower-level EFL learners. However, some researchers report that reading will benefit readers only in the long run (Lee & Hsu, 2009; Mermelstein, 2015). In line with this view, short-term studies on reading with limited reading materials benefit only some of the writing aspects and have also found that participants' writing scores in some of the key areas are not statistically significant (Hafiz & Tudor, 1990; Tsang, 1996).

Longer reading exposure not only results in the acquisition of writing competence but also positively affects cognitive capabilities. Reading contributes to the composing proficiency by shaping the readers' cognition. In addition, studies have found an overall positive correlation between cognition and composing skills (Parodi, 2007; Shanahan, 1984; Shanahan & Lomax, 1986; Stotsky, 1983). Deciphering meaning from the composed idea helps readers to subconsciously absorb the nuances of writing style coupled with domain knowledge (Lee & Hsu, 2009). Tsang (1996) has also argued that reading in large amounts provided readers with an "appropriate model of the target language at an appropriate level..., improved general knowledge and thus helped develop content in writing...[and] exposed students to appropriate models of construction, agreement, tense, number, and word order/function" (p. 228). Moreover, as writing is a cognitive-linguistic activity (Deane et al., 2008), the learner must be cognitively competent to develop the compositional skill. Accessing more reading materials enables the learner to be efficient in cognitive competence and also to be aware of multiple functions of written language as reading provides a functional model for writing (Brooke, 1988; Eckhoff, 1983). Reading not only serves as a model but also encompasses various levels of cognitive processes (Kendeou & Trevors, 2012; van den Broek & Espin, 2012; van den Broek, Rapp, & Kendeou, 2005), such as decoding (Perfetti, 1985), retention of vocabulary knowledge (Nagy, Herman, & Anderson, 1985) and reading frequency (Fuchs, Fuchs, Hosp, & Jenkins, 2001) which are considered to be lower-level cognitive processes that help readers translate the written code into meaningful language structures (Kendeou, van den Broek, Helder, & Karlsson, 2014). The higher-level cognitive processes entail three functions: inference making, executive function and comprehension monitoring. Inference making activates prior knowledge to connect different parts of the text (van den Broek, 1997); executive function helps a reader to organize and reflect on the whole concept with the help of schemata (Cain, Oakhill, & Bryant, 2004; Kendeou et al., 2014; Sesma, Mahone, Levine, Eason, & Cutting, 2009); and the comprehension-monitoring function helps identify redundant, non-important information and organize the supporting details into a holistic network, eventually constructing the core idea of the text (Marzec-Stawiarska, 2016; Oakhill, Hartt, & Samols, 2005). Similarly, cognition in writing involves generating and organizing relevant ideas using linguistic knowledge with appropriate grammar and punctuation in a tone appropriate to convey those ideas to the audience. Thus, both reading and writing involve cognitive functions such as intelligence, attention, perception, memory, comparing and contrasting, differentiating, categorizing, analysing, synthesizing, and creativity (Stone, Silliman, Ehren, & Apel, 2004). In this way, reading develops cognitive efficiency and cognitive capabilities, eventually leading to the growth of proficient writing skills.

Despite plausible evidence supporting the claim that readers acquire writing skills by activating cognitive abilities, it is difficult to motivate non-readers to create an interest in reading. It is because they either have difficulty in comprehending a text or negative attitudes towards reading. Text comprehension requires a reader to be lexically aware and familiar with the prior knowledge during the reading process. Indeed, comprehension is predicted by cognitive flexibility which requires longer duration of reading (Cole, Duncan, & Blaye 2014). Lack of long-term and repeated reading experiences delay automaticity in word recognition and text integration (Cunningham & Stanovich, 1997). Inflexible cognitive support results in negative reading experiences which may build up unfavourable attitudes towards reading and in turn lead to less involvement in reading-related activities, whereas possession of rich background knowledge and linguistic skills facilitates avid readers to read proficiently and frequently as they enjoy reading. As a result, avid readers become richer and poor readers become poorer and this phenomenon is called Matthew effect (Cunningham & Stanovich, 1998). In fact, readers of lower ability tend to view reading as "schoolwork" (Bondy, 1990) that requires disciplined effort and hard work and which in fact is "a serious, difficult process" (Elley, 1992, p. 77). Students of higher reading ability, on the other hand, take a meaning-centred approach (Devine, 1984). For them reading is a "pleasant, imaginative activity" (Elley, 1992, p. 77). Further, the cognitive flexibility of higher-ability readers motivates subsequent pleasure reading experiences which help them to develop favourable reading attitudes. Further, involving students in shared reading induces an interest that leads to the growth of receptive and expressive language (Wesseling, Christmann, & Lachmann, 2017). Accordingly, Ro and Chen (2014) found that students possessing positive reading attitudes had higher frequencies in reading. Grabe (1991) claims "Longer concentrated periods of silent reading build vocabulary and structural awareness, develop automaticity, enhance background knowledge, improve comprehension skills, and promote confidence and motivation" (p. 396).

Cognitive ability is influenced by linguistic proficiency, critical thinking and inferencing skills but non-cognitive elements such as affective variables play an essential role in processing cognition (Kahneman, Slovic, & Tversky, 1982). Positive emotional classroom climate is crucial in developing positive reading and writing behaviour (Hidi & Boscolo, 2006). Yamashita (2015) pointed out that "greater affective involvement stimulates cognitive processes such as focused attention and facilitates comprehension" (p. 172) as the affective variables have a mediating effect on cognition. For instance, unpleasant emotions such as anxiety and shame may not directly affect cognitive capacity but those negative emotions indirectly distort the brain functioning by interrupting the recall from memory while inferencing or comprehending a text (Bryan, Burstein & Ergul, 2004; Grills-Taquechel, Fletcher, Vaughn & Stuebing, 2012; Tobias, 1979). In the same way, while composing, negative emotion cripples the thought process and causes aversion towards writing (Brand & Powell, 1986). Learners with lower self-esteem and self-efficacy beliefs develop negative schema which leads to unsuccessful reading experiences. On the other hand, learners with higher self-esteem are intrinsically motivated as they experience positive emotions such as joy and excitement which influence them to sustain positive reading behaviour. In other words, intrinsic motivation is positively correlated to reading for enjoyment and reading in volumes (Becker, McElvany, & Kortenbruck, 2010; Lau, 2009). Formation of positive reading behaviour in the early stages builds self-concept as readers and, in turn, this self-concept significantly predicts subsequent reading performance and attainment (Chapman, Tunmer, & Prochnow, 2000). Likewise, writers with positive self-esteem are enriched through increased reading and writing achievements (Shell, Colvin, & Bruning, 1995). Prat-Sala and Redford (2010) examined the relationship between variables such as self-efficacy in reading, self-efficacy in writing and writing performance of first- and second-year undergraduates. The results reported that self-efficacy beliefs in reading and writing were found to be correlated with writing performance for both groups, which implies that self-concept beliefs in reading and writing support writing performance. In line with this view, Kush, Marley, and Brookhart (2005) posit that reading attitudes impact the generative process of writing and it has been confirmed that positive attitudes towards reading influence writing (Carson, Carrell, Silberstein, Kroll, & Kuehn, 1990).

Positive reading behaviour is an outcome of positive reading experiences that result from reading engagement and reading attainment. Reading engagement can also be associated with reading for pleasure or reading for enjoyment (Cremin, Mottram, Powell, Collins, & Safford, 2014). Engagement in reading results in successful meaning construction and total involvement in reading activity provides satisfaction for readers. This occurs only when the text is well within the linguistic competence of the reader along with pleasurable content, because linguistically challenging texts require cognitive effort which slows down the reading process and extinguishes pleasure in reading, negatively affecting motivation (Stoller, 2015). When reading experience is successful, the act of reading itself motivates a reader to continue reading. The pleasure element in reading along with successful reading experience facilitates more reading and motivates intrinsically. Intrinsically motivated readers are often engaged in reading behaviourally, emotionally and cognitively (Fredricks, Blumenfeld, & Paris, 2004). The involvement and attention in reading contribute to the amount of voluntary reading which in turn leads to better comprehension. When reading becomes pleasurable, the learners are familiar with the content which relieves stress in the writing situation and this leads to pleasurable writing as well (Clark, 2013; Park & Ro, 2015).

Reading motivation is indispensable to conditioning the reading process. Lack of motivation can mitigate reading to a great extent even when the texts are comprehensible and interesting. Reading motivation can be defined as "the enduring readiness of a person to initiate reading activities" (Schaffner, Philipp, & Schiefele, 2014). It also represents the internal engagement one has to persist with the reading activity. Reading motivation is associated with the amount of time that readers engage in reading (Becker et al., 2010; Schaffner, Schiefele, & Ulferts, 2013; Schaffner et al., 2014). Such readers are intrinsically motivated and they read broadly, choosing challenging texts with persistence. Indeed, intrinsic reading motivation was found to be a positive predictor of reading amount and reading comprehension while extrinsic motivation was a non-significant or negative predictor of reading achievement (Andreassen & Braten, 2010; Guthrie, Wigfield,

Metsala, & Cox, 1999; Park, 2011; Schiefele, Schaffener, Moller, & Wigfield, 2012), because readers with intrinsic motivation are self-regulated and become engaged in reading while readers with extrinsic motivation perform reading for rewards and recognition. Park (2011) found that extrinsic motivation is detrimental when the students are less intrinsically motivated which is also consistent with the finding of Lin, McKeachie, and Kim (2003). However, moderate level of extrinsic motivation predicted higher reading performance with medium or high levels of intrinsic motivation (Park, 2011). Moreover, readers with higher levels of extrinsic motivation fail to persist in the activity further when the environment cannot provide favourable conditions.

Participants

The participants in this study were eighteen female freshmen of an Arts and Science College aged 17–18. They had completed secondary education in rural schools where the medium of instruction was Tamil. They did not have any exposure to reading in English language apart from the textbooks prescribed for their English course. In order to score higher grades on tests, they memorized essays provided by the teachers before appearing for tests. Hence, their exposure to English language was limited and so was their language proficiency. These students had enrolled for a Bachelor of Arts degree in English Literature which demands a good deal of reading and only a few had the habit of reading.

Aim of the Study

1. To prove that continual exposure to reading strengthens the composing process.
2. To identify the relationship between reading self-efficacy beliefs and writing performance.

Procedure

A pre-test was administered prior to the reading programme in order to assess the language ability of the participants. The questions included:

1. Describe your hometown. (descriptive)
2. Narrate the following:
   (a) What would you do if you have a million dollars?
   (or)

(b) Write about a happy moment in your life. (narrative)
3. Today, there are more and more reality shows on television. Do these shows make good television? Why or why not? Explain your answers using specific reasons and examples. (argumentative)
4. What is your all-time favourite movie and why?
5. Write an essay persuading readers to watch this film. (persuasive)

During the treatment period, the participants read the provided materials for three hours per week and they continued to read for 45 days. The reading materials included informative passages and summaries of novels. The number of words in reading texts was about 800–900. In the beginning, the participants were less motivated as they found the reading materials uninteresting. In order to raise their level of motivation and interest, materials such as short stories, summaries of movies and recipes were introduced based on the suggestions given by the participants themselves. The given simplified reading materials provided comprehensible input and therefore, their reading experiences were pleasurable. When they could comprehend the text, it increased their level of interest and motivation which is proportionate to the level of comprehension.

In order to motivate students to share the reading material with peers, participants were allowed to discuss in groups once a week. During the discussion sessions, participants were encouraged to summarize the text they had read. At the end of each hour, the instructor checked whether the participants had completed their reading tasks. At times, the instructor facilitated free writing to reduce writing apprehensions.

The participants were asked to respond to a questionnaire which was structured in three parts: pleasure reading habits (e.g., time spent on pleasure reading, reading purposes); opinions about the reading programme (e.g., whether reading materials are comprehensible and pleasurable); reading continuity (e.g., how often they read, whether persisting reading activities after the reading programme); and reading self-efficacy beliefs (e.g., reading confidence and motivation). The questionnaire was based on a five-point Likert response scale ranging from 1 (strongly disagree) to 5 (strongly agree). Higher scores indicated better reading parameters. Participants who scored above the mean were categorized as frequent readers and others as infrequent readers. This categorization was further validated using their pre-test scores. Cronbach's alpha test was conducted to check internal consistency. The value of Cronbach's alpha, 0.87, indicates that the data is reliable and consistent.

Results

Table 4.1 presents the mean scores for the participants on the pre- and the post-test. The results show that there is a statistically significant difference between pre-and post-test writing mean scores on all the sub-scales. According to Cohen (1988), an effect size of 0.2 indicates a small effect; 0.5, a medium effect; and 0.8,

Table 4.1 Mean scores, pre- and the post-test

	Pre-test		Post-test		Mean difference	Effect size
	Mean	SD	Mean	SD		
Content	5.00	2.91	8.20	5.01	3.20	0.78
Vocabulary	1.18	0.53	2.31	1.47	1.12	1.01
Organization	1.13	0.64	1.76	0.98	0.63	0.76
Language use	1.30	0.69	2.30	1.54	1.00	0.83
Mechanics	1.16	0.60	1.35	0.44	0.19	0.36

Table 4.2 Paired sample t-test results

	Pre-test		Post-test			95% CI for mean difference				
Outcome	M	SD	M	SD	N		R	T	df	p
	9.99	5.00	19.92	9.49	18	−13.17, −6.69	0.76	−6.46	17	0.000

Note: *CI* confidence interval

Table 4.3 Reading and writing scores, frequent and infrequent readers

Frequent readers					
	N	Minimum %	Maximum %	Mean	SD
Pre-test	11	20	50	12.89	4.00
Post-test	11	35	85	25.72	6.34
Reading score	11	74.28	97	60.64	5.60
Infrequent readers					
Pre-test	7	7.5	20	5.43	2.11
Post-test	7	15	42.5	10.79	5.37
Reading score	7	35.7	71	35.71	9.69

a large effect. The results show almost a large effect size for all the parameters except mechanics. Especially, substantial effect is found for language use which reflects the improved writing after experiencing more reading.

Table 4.2 shows the outcome of paired sample *t*-test. The results indicate that there is a statistically significant difference between the pre-test and the post-test scores.

Table 4.3 illustrates the reading and writing scores of frequent and infrequent readers. The mean scores imply that students who read frequently perform better in writing and also confirm that infrequent reading results in lower writing scores.

Table 4.4 presents the Pearson correlation between reading self-efficacy beliefs and writing performance of frequent and infrequent readers. The results reveal that

Table 4.4 Pearson correlation of reading self-efficacy beliefs and writing performance

			WP
FR	RS	Pearson correlation	0.835**
		Sig. (2-tailed)	0.001
		N	11
			WP
IFR	RS	Pearson correlation	0.373
		Sig. (2-tailed)	0.410
		N	7

**Correlation is significant at the 0.01 level (2-tailed) for frequent readers
FR frequent readers; *IFR* infrequent readers; *RS* reading self-efficacy; *WP* writing performance

reading self-efficacy beliefs of frequent readers are significantly correlated with writing performance ($r = 0.835$, $n = 7$, $p < 0.001$). There is no stronger relationship between self-efficacy beliefs and writing performance of infrequent readers ($r = 0.373$, $n = 7$, $p = 0.410$).

Discussion

The results confirm that the writing score of frequent readers is proportionate to the reading score. The correlational analyses of the questionnaire indicated that positive experiences in reading for a longer period not only contribute to acquiring the language properties, but also to the development of self-concepts in reading and writing performances. This finding is consistent with Pajares and Johnson (1994), Shell et al. (1989), and Prat-Sala and Redford (2010). The wide background knowledge, cognitive activation and reading enjoyment determine the high frequencies in reading. Moreover, results from the questionnaire infer that there is a positive correlation between reading continuity and pleasure that the readers derive from the act of reading. Thus, the frequency increases when the reading experience turns out to be rewarding and it decreases when reading experience is not pleasurable.

The results confirm that the improvement in writing skills is in correlation with the amount of reading of comprehensible texts. This is the reason why the participants who experienced more comprehensible input (frequent readers) performed better than the participants (infrequent readers) whose reading does not fall within their linguistic competence. Frequent readers had greater gains as the reading experience was more pleasurable and enjoyable for them. In the early stages of the reading programme, infrequent readers experienced difficulty in decoding meaning from the text. Further, the reading experience was not rewarding and compelling for infrequent readers because of the delay in automaticity and word recognition

(Cunningham & Stanovich, 2001). However, their language acquisition was proportionate to the comprehensible input they received.

The study corroborates that reading results in the acquisition of skills required for writing, confirming that writing ability is the result of the increased amount of reading that provides understandable content. Moreover, this kind of reading lowers writing apprehensions and motivates readers to do free writing (Lee, 2005). In fact, writing is a composing process that requires synthesis and the development of ideas using current knowledge. The participants were able to write better on the post-test, indicating that reading enabled them to generate new ideas which could be the contribution of activated cognition. In particular, students who had better comprehension produced quality written constructs. This indicated that their thinking skills had also improved. More precisely, reading contributes to the development of the complex skills required for writing with a strong impact on comprehension, and there are enormous implications that it affects cognitive capabilities as well.

The analysis of pre- and post-test test scores confirmed that readers performed better on all the sub-scales which include content, organization, vocabulary, language use and mechanics; they also showed improvement in comprehension, cognition, writing style and fluency. Reading provides compelling input in an anxiety-free environment that makes language acquisition easier and enjoyable. This indeed is consistent with comprehension hypothesis and affective filter hypothesis (Krashen, 2003) which state that language acquisition will be high only when the reading materials are comprehensible and pleasurable. The participants enjoyed reading, as the materials assigned for reading were interesting, and therefore they immersed themselves in the content. Furthermore, the participants expressed that reading short stories is more enjoyable than the informative texts provided because the theme is interesting and the language is within their comfort zone, and this motivated them to engage with meaning which, in fact, had a positive effect on thinking.

The pre-test answers indicate that the participants experienced writing apprehensions and therefore could not write the required content with precision. Moreover, the erroneous assumption that they should focus on form to improve writing inhibited them from writing the appropriate content (Lee, 2005). A question on the pre-test asked the participants to write about their home town. Instead of writing about their home town, many wrote about their family and neighbours (see Sample 1), confirming that they experienced writer's block presenting their intended meaning.

Sample 1: "*I love my family and my parents and I love my younger sister, neighbours. My house is very beautiful, my father native place.*" (Pre-test write-up)

The above example confirmed that the subject failed to convey the intended meaning; what she wrote was not relevant to the context. But the same subject was able to describe the village on the post-test (Sample 2).

Sample 2: *"My village has five beautiful ponds. And it is surrounded by mountains and gardens and it is shadowed with coconut trees. Also, it is called as lemon-city. Agriculture is the occupation. And it is a cool place."* (Post-test write-up)

This indicates reading helps students to organize and present their intended meaning clearly and precisely supported by cognitive abilities. The post-test answers confirmed that the students were able to write their ideas appropriately as they gained exposure to reading. Most of the students wrote about the special features of their hometown which include landscapes, climate, famous temples, shops etc. on the post-test. This confirms that reading bridges the gap between the intended and the conveyed meaning and helps to come up with appropriate content. This is consistent with the study that reading in volumes is the determinant of reading comprehension, language acquisition and improved cognitive flexibility (Cunningham & Stanovich, 2003).

Reading showed a strong impact on the growth of vocabulary knowledge and this is consistent with studies on incidental acquisition (Pigada & Schmitt, 2006; Ponniah, 2011) of vocabulary showing that readers acquire meaning of words incidentally and use the acquired words when writing. Furthermore, exposure to words in contexts will result in better use of vocabulary as well as increased knowledge of lexis and syntax, indicating that they have acquired grammar of the words in addition to meaning (Ponniah, 2011). This kind of vocabulary knowledge is more powerful than intentional learning (Lee & Hsu, 2009) because it is more difficult to use the consciously learned words in sentences. Further, the students developed a good deal of semantic knowledge in comparison with all other linguistic measures. The students acquired verbal awareness not only by reading but also through discussions. They also attempted to incorporate the words elicited through such discussions while composing. This is consistent with the view that shared reading promotes receptive and expressive vocabulary (Wesseling et al., 2017; Sénéchal & LeFevre, 2002, 2014). The following samples are from pre- and post-tests. Subject 1, Pre-test: *My father arranged a birthday cake for me. First time I cut the cake. I am very surprise.*

Post-test: *The day before my birthday, my roommates arranged a cake for me. I was very surprised.*
Subject 2, Pre-test: *It has lots of twists and turns.*
Post-test: *There are many twists and turns in this movie which makes us really spell-bound.*
Subject 3, Pre-test: *Behind my house there was a river. The river was look like black and the water is very impured.*
Post-test: *There is a river behind my house. The river was very dirty.*

Additionally, these shared reading experiences provided opportunities to verbalize thoughts in a stress-free situation, enabling the participants to acquire vocabulary incidentally, and motivated the participants to read more because sharing itself gives pleasure and this makes the learning environment pleasurable. In fact, it helped participants to choose the books that interest them, and sharing makes reading easier and comprehensible as they get information from peers about the book before they read. The social interactions also contribute to the increased level of reading motivation and confidence.

This study also confirms that reading improves comprehension abilities, which facilitates language acquisition, affecting both writing and cognition of readers. It is also proved that reading and writing are interconnected activities and cognition is the base which stimulates the process of comprehension and composing. Through reading, cognition is enhanced and in effect thinking is shaped, eventually fostering a significant improvement on the skills required for writing. Nevertheless, motivational aspects have to be considered to raise the level of self-efficacy beliefs with the assistance of positive reading and writing experiences. The developmental self-efficacy beliefs assist students to set goals and to persevere with their goals and aspirations. Research also reports that students who have high self-efficacy are less anxious and highly comfortable in performing the tasks. Therefore, raising self-efficacy modulates self-regulated behaviour, in addition to increased enjoyment of reading and writing.

References

Al-Rajhi, A. (2004). *Joining the online literacy club: Internet reading among Saudi EFL learners*. Ph.D. dissertation. Pennsylvania: Indiana University of Pennsylvania. Retrieved from ProQuest Digital Dissertations database (UMI Publication No. AAT 3149714).

Andreassen, R., & Braten, I. (2010). Examining the prediction of reading comprehension on different multiple-choice tests. *Journal of Research in Reading, 33*(3), 263–283. https://doi.org/10.1111/j.1467-9817.2009.01413.x.

Becker, M., McElvany, N., & Kortenbruck, M. (2010). Intrinsic and extrinsic reading motivation as predictors of reading literacy: A longitudinal study. *Journal of Educational Psychology, 102*(4), 773–785. https://doi.org/10.1037/a0020584.

Bondy, E. (1990). Seeing it their way: What children's definitions of reading tell about us improving teacher education. *Journal of Teacher Education, 41*(5), 33–45.

Brand, A. G., & Powell, J. L. (1986). Emotions and the writing process: A description of apprentice writers. *Journal of Educational Research, 79*(5), 280–285.

Brooke, R. (1988). Modeling a writer's identity: Reading and imitation in the writing classroom. *College Composition and Communication, 39*, 23–41.

Bryan, T., Burstein, K., & Ergul, C. (2004). The social-emotional side of learning disabilities: A science based presentation of the state of the art. *Learning Disability Quarterly, 27*, 45–52. https://doi.org/10.2307/1593631.

Cain, K., Oakhill, J., & Bryant, P. (2004). Children's reading comprehension ability: Concurrent prediction by working memory, verbal ability, and component skills. *Journal of Educational Psychology, 96*(1), 31–42.

Carretti, B., Re, A. M., & Arfé, B. (2013). Reading comprehension and expressive writing: A comparison between good and poor comprehenders. *Journal of Learning Disabilities, 46*, 87–96.

Carson, J. (1993). Reading for writing: Cognitive perspectives. In J. Carson & I. Leki (Eds.), *Reading in the composition classroom: Second language perspectives* (pp. 85–104). Boston: Heinle and Heinle Publishers.

Carson, J., Carrell, P., Silberstein, S., Kroll, B., & Kuehn, P. (1990). Reading-writing relationships in first and second language. *TESOL Quarterly, 24*(2), 2.

Chapman, J. W., Tunmer, William E., & Prochnow, J. E. (2000). Early reading-related skills and performance, reading self-concept, and the development of academic self-concept: A longitudinal study. *Journal of Educational Psychology, 92*, 703–708.

Clark, C. (2013). *Children's and young people's reading in 2012.* London: National Literacy Trust.

Cohen, J. (1988). *Statistical power analysis for the behavioral sciences* (2nd ed.). Hillsdale, NJ: Lawrence Earlbaum Associates.

Cole, P., Duncan, L. G., & Blaye, A. (2014). Cognitive flexibility predicts early reading skills. *Frontiers in Psychology, 5*, 1–8.

Constantino, R. (1995). Learning to read in a second language doesn't have to hurt: The effect of pleasure reading. *Journal of Adolescent and Adult Literacy, 39*, 68–69.

Cremin, T., Mottram, M., Powell, S., Collins, R., & Safford, K. (2014). *Building communities of engaged readers: Reading for pleasure.* London: Routledge.

Cunningham, A. E., & Stanovich, K. E. (1997). Early reading acquisition and its relation to reading experience and ability 10 years later. *Developmental Psychology, 33*, 934–945.

Cunningham, A. E., & Stanovich, K. E. (1998). What reading does for the mind. *American Educator, 22*(1 & 2), 8–15.

Cunningham, A. E., & Stanovich, K. E. (2001). What reading does for the mind? *Journal of Direct Instruction, 1*, 137–149.

Cunningham, A. E., & Stanovich, K. E. (2003). Reading matters: How reading engagement influences cognition. In J. Flood, D. Lapp, J. Squire, & J. Jensen (Eds.), *Handbook of research on teaching the English language arts* (2nd ed., pp. 666–675). Mahwah, NJ: Lawrence Erlbaum Associates.

Deane, P., Odendahl, N., Quilan, T., Fowles, M., Welsh, C., & Bivens-Tatum, J. (2008). *Cognitive models of writing: Writing proficiency as a complex integrated skill (RR-08-55).* Princeton, NJ: Educational Testing Service.

Devine, J. (1984). ESL readers' internalized models of the reading process. In J. Handscombe, R. A. Orem, & B. P. Taylor (Eds.), *On TESOL '83. Ed. The question of control* (pp. 95–108). Washington, DC: TESOL.

Eckhoff, B. (1983). How reading affects children's writing. *Language Arts, 60*(6), 607–616.

Elley, W. (1991). Acquiring literacy in a second language: The effects of book-based programs. *Language Learning, 41,* 375–411. https://doi.org/10.1111/j.1467-1770.1991.tb00611.x.

Elley, W. B. (1992). *How in the world do students read? IEA study of reading literacy.* New York: International Association for the Evaluation of Educational Achievement.

Elley, W. B., & Mangubhai, F. (1983). The impact of reading on second language learning. *Reading Research Quarterly, 9*(1), 53–67.

Ferris, D., & Hedgecock, J. (2005). *Teaching ESL composition: Purpose, process, and practice* (2nd ed.). Mahwah, NJ: Erlbaum.

Fredricks, J. A., Blumenfeld, P. C., & Paris, A. (2004). School engagement: Potential of the concept: State of the evidence. *Review of Educational Research, 74,* 59–119. https://doi.org/10.3102/00346543074001059.

Fuchs, L. S., Fuchs, D., Hosp, M. K., & Jenkins, J. R. (2001). Oral reading fluency as an indicator of reading competence: A theoretical, empirical, and historical analysis. *Scientific Studies of Reading, 5*(3), 239–256.

Grabe, W. (1991). Current developments in second language reading research. *TESOL Quarterly, 25*(3), 375–406.

Grabe, W., & Kaplan, R. B. (1996). *Theory and practice of writing.* London, UK: Longman.

Graham, S., & Hebert, M. (2011). Writing to read: A meta-analysis of the impact of writing and writing instruction on reading. *Harvard Educational Review, 81*(4), 710–744.

Grills-Taquechel, A. E., Fletcher, J. M., Vaughn, S. R., & Stuebing, K. K. (2012). Anxiety and reading difficulties in early elementary school: Evidence for unidirectional- or bi-directional relations? *Child Psychiatry and Human Development, 43*, 35–47. https://doi.org/10.1007/s10578-011-0246-1.

Guthrie, J. T., Wigfield, A., Metsala, J. L., & Cox, K. E. (1999). Motivational and cognitive predictors of text comprehension and reading amount. *Scientific Studies of Reading, 3*(3), 231–256. https://doi.org/10.1207/sl532799xssr0303_3.

Hafiz, F. M., & Tudor, I. (1989). Extensive reading and the development of language skills. *English Language Teaching Journal, 43*, 4–11.

Hafiz, F. M., & Tudor, I. (1990). Graded readers as an input medium in L2 learning. *System, 18*, 31–42.

Hidi, S., & Boscolo, P. (2006). Motivation and writing. In C. A. MacArthur, S. Graham, & J. Fitzgerald (Eds.), *Handbook of writing research* (pp. 144–170). New York: Guilford Press.

Janopoulos, M. (1986). The relationship of pleasure reading and second language writing proficiency. *TESOL Quarterly, 20*, 763–768.

Kahneman, D., Slovic, P., & Tversky, A. (1982). *Judgment under uncertainty: Heuristics and biases*. Cambridge: Cambridge University Press.

Kaplan, J., & Palhinda, E. (1981). Non-native speakers of English and their composition abilities: A review and analysis. In W. Frawley (Ed.), *Linguistics and literacy* (pp. 425–457). NY: Plenum Press.

Kendeou, P., & Trevors, G. (2012). Learning from texts we read: What does it take? In M. J. Lawson & J. R. Kirby (Eds.), *The quality of learning* (pp. 251–275). Cambridge, UK: Cambridge University Press.

Kendeou, P., van den Broek, P., Helder, A., & Karlsson, J. (2014). A cognitive view of reading comprehension: Implications for reading difficulties. *Learning Disability Research & Practice, 29*, 10–16. https://doi.org/10.1111/ldrp.12025.

Kirin, W. (2010). Effects of extensive reading on students' writing ability in an EFL class. *The Journal of Asia TEFL, 7*(1), 285–308.

Kush, J. C., Marley, W. W., & Brookhart, S. M. (2005). The temporal-interactive influence of reading on achievement and reading attitude. *Educational Research and Evaluation, 11*(1), 29–44.

Krashen, S. (1984). *Writing: Research, theory and applications*. Oxford: Pergamon Institute of English.

Krashen, S. (2003). *Explorations in language acquisition and use: The Taipei lectures*. Portsmouth, NH: Heinemann.

Krashen, S. (2004). *The power of reading* (2nd ed.). Englewood, CO: Libraries Unlimited.

Lai, F. K. (1993). The effect of a summer reading course on reading and writing skills. *System, 21*, 87–100. https://doi.org/10.1016/0346-251X(93)90009-6.

Lau, K. L. (2009). Reading motivation, perceptions of reading instruction and reading amount: A comparison of junior and senior secondary school students in Hong Kong. *Journal of Research in Reading, 32*(4), 366–382.

Lee, S. Y. (2005). Facilitating and inhibiting factors in English as a foreign language writing performance: A model testing with structural equation modeling. *Language Learning, 55*(2), 335–374.

Lee, S. Y., & Hsu, Y. (2009). Determining the crucial characteristics of extensive reading programs: The impact of extensive reading of EFL writing. *The International Journal of Foreign Language Teaching, Summer*, 12–20.

Lin, Y., McKeachie, W. J., & Kim, Y. C. (2003). College student intrinsic and/or extrinsic motivation and learning. *Learning and Individual Differences, 13*, 251–258.

Marzec-Stawiarska, M. (2016). The influence of summary writing on the development of reading skills in a foreign language. *System, 59*, 90–99. https://doi.org/10.1016/j.system.2016.04.006.

Mason, B., & Krashen, S. (1997). Extensive reading in English as a foreign language. *System, 25*, 91–102. https://doi.org/10.1016/S0346-251X(96)00063-2.

Mermelstein, A. (2015). Improving EFL writing through enhanced extensive reading. *Reading in a Foreign Language, 27*(2), 182–198.

Nagy, W. E., Herman, P. A., & Anderson, R. C. (1985). Learning words from context. *Reading Research Quarterly, 20*(2), 233–253.
Oakhill, J., Hartt, J., & Samols, D. (2005). Levels of comprehension monitoring and working memory in good and poor comprehenders. *Reading and Writing, 18*(7–9), 657–686.
Pajares, F., & Johnson, M. (1994). Confidence and competence in writing: The role of self-efficacy, outcome expectancy, and apprehension. *Research in the Teaching of English, 28*, 313–331.
Park, J., & Ro, E. (2015). The core principles of extensive reading in an EAP writing context. *Reading in a Foreign Language, 27*(2), 308–313.
Park, Y. (2011). How motivational constructs interact to predict elementary students' reading performance: Examples from attitudes and self-concept in reading. *Learning and Individual Differences, 21*(4), 347–358. https://doi.org/10.1016/j.lindif.2011.02.009.
Parodi, G. (2007). Reading–writing connections: Discourse-oriented research. *Reading and Writing, 20*(3), 225–250. https://doi.org/10.1007/s11145-006-9029-7.
Pearson, P. D. (1985). Changing the face of reading comprehension instruction. *The Reading Teacher, 38*(8), 724–738.
Perfetti, C. A. (1985). *Reading ability*. New York: Oxford University Press.
Pigada, M., & Schmitt, N. (2006). Vocabulary acquisition from extensive reading: A case study. *Reading in a Foreign Language, 18*(1), 1–28.
Polak, J., & Krashen, S. (1988). Do we need to teach spelling? The relationship between spelling and vocabulary reading among community college ESL students. *TESOL Quarterly, 22*, 141–146.
Ponniah, R. J. (2011). Incidental acquisition of vocabulary by reading. *The Reading Matrix, 11*(2), 135–139.
Prat-Sala, M., & Redford, P. (2010). The interplay between motivation, self-efficacy and approaches to studying. *British Journal of Educational Psychology, 80*, 283–305.
Ro, E., & Chen, C. (2014). Pleasure reading behavior and attitude of non-academic ESL students: A replication study. *Reading in a Foreign Language, 26*, 49–72.
Salyer, M. (1987). A comparison of the learning characteristics of good and poor ESL writers. *Applied Linguistics Interest Section Newsletter, TESOL, 8*, 2–3.
Schaffner, E., Philipp, M., & Schiefele, U. (2014). Reciprocal effects between intrinsic reading motivation and reading competence? A cross-lagged panel model for academic track and nonacademic track students. *Journal of Research in Reading*, 1–18. https://doi.org/10.1111/1467-9817.12027.
Schaffner, E., Schiefele, U., & Ulferts, H. (2013). Reading amount as a mediator of the effects of intrinsic and extrinsic reading motivation on reading comprehension. *Reading Research Quarterly, 48*, 369–385.
Schiefele, U., Schaffner, E., Möller, J., & Wigfield, A. (2012). Dimensions of reading motivation and their relation to reading behaviour and competence. *Reading Research Quarterly, 47*(4), 427–463.
Sénéchal, M., & LeFevre, J. (2002). Parental involvement in the development of children's reading skill: A 5-year longitudinal study. *Child Development, 73*, 445–460.
Sénéchal, M., & LeFevre, J. (2014). Continuity and change in the home literacy environment as predictors of growth in vocabulary and reading. *Child Development*. Advance online publication. https://doi.org/10.1111/cdev.12222.
Sesma, H. W., Mahone, E. M., Levine, T., Eason, S. H., & Cutting, L. E. (2009). The contribution of executive skills to reading comprehension. *Child Neuropsychology, 15*(3), 232–246.
Shanahan, T. (1984). Nature of the reading–writing relation: An exploratory multivariate analysis. *Journal of Educational Psychology, 76*, 466–477.
Shanahan, T., & Lomax, R. (1986). An analysis and comparison of theoretical models of the reading–writing relationship. *Journal of Educational Psychology, 78*, 116–123.
Shell, D. F., Colvin, C., & Burning, R. H. (1995). Self-efficacy, attributions and outcome expectancy mechanisms in reading and writing achievement: Grade-level and achievement level differences. *Journal of Educational Psychology, 87*, 386–398.

Shell, D. F., Murphy, C. C., & Bruning, R. H. (1989). Self-efficacy and outcome expectancy mechanisms in reading and writing achievement. *Journal of Educational Psychology, 81,* 91–100.

Smith, F. (2004). *Understanding reading: A psycholinguistic analysis of reading and learning to read* (6th ed.). Hillsdale, NJ: Erlbaum.

Spivey, N. N. (1990). Transforming texts: Constructive processes in reading and writing. *Written Communication, 7*(2), 256–287. https://doi.org/10.1177/0741088390007002004.

Stoller, F. L. (2015). Viewing extensive reading from different vantage points. *Reading in a Foreign Language, 27,* 152–159.

Stone, C. A., Sillian, E. R., Ehren, B. J., & Apel, K. (2004). *Handbook of language and literacy.* New York: The Guilford Press.

Stotsky, S. (1982). The role of writing in developmental reading. *Journal of Reading, 25*(4), 330–340.

Stotsky, S. (1983). Research on reading/writing relationships: A synthesis and suggested directions. *Language Arts, 60,* 627–642.

Tierney, R. J., & Shanahan, T. (1991). Research on the reading-writing relationship: Interactions, transactions, and outcomes. In R. Barr, M. L. Kamil, P. Mosenthal, & P. D. Pearson (Eds.), *Handbook of reading research* (pp. 246–280). Hillsdale, NJ: Erlbaum.

Tobias, S. (1979). Anxiety research in educational psychology. *Journal of Educational Psychology, 71*(5), 573–582.

Tsang, W. K. (1996). Comparing the effects of reading and writing on writing performance. *Applied Linguistics, 17,* 210–233. https://doi.org/10.1093/applin/17.2.210.

Tudor, I., & Hafiz, F. (1989). Extensive reading as a means of input to L2 Learning. *Journal of Research in Reading, 12,* 164–178.

van den Broek, P. (1997). Discovering the cement of the universe: The development of event comprehension from childhood to adulthood. In P. van den Broek, P. W. Bauer, & T. Bourg (Eds.), *Developmental spans in event comprehension and representation* (pp. 321–342). Mahwah, NJ: Lawrence Erlbaum Associates.

van den Broek, P., & Espin, C. A. (2012). Connecting cognitive theory and assessment: Measuring individual differences in reading comprehension. *School Psychology Review, 41,* 315–325.

van den Broek, P., Rapp, D., & Kendeou, P. (2005). Integrating memory based and constructionist processes in accounts of reading comprehension. *Discourse Processes, 39*(2), 299–316.

Weiser, B., & Mathes, P. (2011). Using encoding instruction to improve the reading and spelling performance of elementary students at risk for literacy difficulties: A best-evidence synthesis. *Review of Educational Research, 81,* 170–200.

Wesseling, P. B. C., Christmann, C. A., & Lachmann, T. (2017). Shared book reading promotes not only language development, but also grapheme awareness in German kindergarten children. *Frontiers in Psychology, 8,* 364. https://doi.org/10.3389/fpsyg.2017.00364.

Willingham, D. T. (2017). *The Reading Mind: A cognitive approach to understanding how the mind reads.* San Francisco, CA: Jossey-Bass.

Yamashita, J. (2015). In search of the nature of extensive reading in L2: Cognitive, affective, and pedagogical perspectives. *Reading in a Foreign Language, 27,* 168–181.

Zamel, V. (1992). Writing one's way into reading. *TESOL Quarterly, 26*(3), 463–485. https://doi.org/10.2307/3587174.

Chapter 5
Blending Cognitive and Socio-constructive Pedagogies: Building Autonomous Readers in the ESL Classroom

Kshema Jose

Abstract The dynamicity of technology used to present information and the resultant fluidity in text forms have led educators to concede that autonomy in reading and adaptability to changing forms of texts need to form the core of any reading instruction that aims to develop independent and/or lifelong readers. Working with a cognitive/socio-constructivist perspective, this chapter discusses the effects of a strategy training programme on reading competence of adult ESL readers. Viewing reading as a social process, the strategy programme conceived by the researcher harnessed the power of distributed cognition available in group interactions to empower individuals in the group to reach beyond their current levels of reading competence. The strategy training programme was designed based on two factors: (i) that interpersonal strategy development opportunities might facilitate intrapersonal strategy development; and (ii) that individual cognitive awareness needs to precede social interactions if collaboration was to have any learning effect. The strategy training programme reported in this paper therefore provided scope to develop in readers an awareness of strategies they used, and also opportunities to view and learn reading strategies used by peers. Results of the study showed that all learners demonstrated an increase in their reading comprehension performance—a consequence of increase in their reading strategies repertoire and the retention of newly acquired reading strategies, both contributive factors to independent reading comprehension.

Keywords Reading strategies · Reader autonomy · Lifelong skills
Cognitivism · Socio-constructivism · Strategy training

K. Jose (✉)
Department for Training and Development, EFLU, Hyderabad, India
e-mail: kshema@efluniversity.ac.in

© Springer Nature Singapore Pte Ltd. 2018
R. Joseph Ponniah and S. Venkatesan (eds.), *The Idea and Practice of Reading*,
https://doi.org/10.1007/978-981-10-8572-7_5

Introduction

Reading as a skill needs no selling introduction; it is a universally acknowledged basic life skill. Grouping it with other life skills like swimming, drives home the point that reading is a skill essential for survival. Termed variously a *lifelong skill*, a *gate skill*, a successful *workforce skill* and an essential *workplace skill* by agencies as varied as UNESCO and the European Universities Association, reading is not only essential for academic growth, but also for success in the world outside since level of reading skill becomes a determiner of one's level of information literacy, i.e., one's ability to search, access, evaluate and use information—a capability essential for professional success.

Reading helps development of our other capacities as well. It throws open a broad spectrum of language and body knowledge that widens one's learning, and cultivates and advances one's oral and written communications. It makes one a more well-informed citizen by developing higher-order reasoning and promoting critical thinking ("To read or not to read", 2007). "The Rose Review" (2008) contends that reading is also a source of personal entertainment that paves the way for personal growth through emotional development.

It is no wonder then that teaching to read still forms the crux of most reading instruction in schools. However, literacy no longer being a static construct complicates and compounds the fact that teaching reading is also one of the most challenging areas of education. Our students cannot be taught to meet all their future reading requirements while at school precisely because all their future reading requirements cannot be predicted or anticipated while they are at school. We teach our learners to read the printed word, and once out of classrooms they are required to adapt their reading skills to suit newer reading environments like wikis, social media posts, hypertexts, visual texts, discussion blogs and short messages. Evidently, literacy is deictic (Coiro, 2003); as texts get increasingly multimodal, the nature of literacy changes from a monolithic construct to one that encompasses multiple literacies or multiliteracies (Leu, O'Byrn, Zawilinski, McVerry, & Everett-Cacopardo, 2009).

Factoring in the dynamicity of texts, educators now realize that in an information-laden society one's potential to learn continually and independently, and to adapt to the changing demands of literacy, nature of texts and reading purposes, forms a significant indicator of one's success, and that the primary focus of reading instruction should therefore be on nurturing reader autonomy, adaptability and self-reliance in developing one's competency as a reader.

Developing independent reading habits thus assumes a prime role in the pedagogies of the twenty-first century.

Autonomy in Reading

Autonomy in learning helps learners control their process of learning to suit their needs and styles thereby making learning more focused and purposeful (Holec, 1981). In an information-rich society like the current, one's ability to gain, receive, send and exchange information in English is a prime variable that determines success in personal, social, educational and professional activities. Autonomous readers are context adaptable to requirements of multiple information environments and are capable of utilizing and exploiting all opportunities of information exchange. They are therefore called *lifelong learners*, an essential twenty-first-century requirement that prepares them, according to Professor B.V.R. Chawdari of National University of Singapore, for a "life of careers instead of a career for life" (Bhatia, 2009).

Other advantages of developing autonomy have been listed by many: it enhances motivation, which in turn leads to more effective learning (Dickinson, 1995); it promotes rapid accomplishment and longer retention of learning since it facilitates learning in ways preferred by the individual (Claxton, 1996); and autonomous learners will have little difficulty in transferring their capacity for autonomous behaviour to other areas of social behaviour which in turn makes them better and more efficient members of society (Little, 1991).

Promoting learner autonomy does not mean sudden and total transfer of control over the learning process, tasks, pace and materials to learners. It is a gradual process that involves building "human potential through a continuously supportive process…to acquire knowledge, values, skills and understanding…and apply them with confidence…in all circumstances" (Longworth & Davies, 1996: 22). Within the parameters of teaching reading to ESL learners, this means teachers should endeavour to create readers who are capable of accessing any textual input and constructing meaning without external agent assistance.

As paradoxical as it may sound, throughout the process, learners need to be given direct and explicit expert guidance in learning. They need to be made aware of the need for autonomy, taught about and see demonstrated ways that can facilitate autonomous learning, in ways that respect and accommodate the learners' own current ways of thinking and learning, and eventually lead them to see the purpose of what they are learning (Benson, 2011).

The Process of Reading

The skill of reading has been described as a simple process that involves three competencies which help extraction of information from the text and construction of meaning by the reader:

- visual operations that lead to the recognition of letters and words, and decoding them in order to comprehend the meaning;

- sensitivity to grammatical relationships that adds meaning to the message and leads to construction of conceptual understanding; and
- construction of personal meaning that depends on one's background knowledge, purpose and techniques of reading (Kolers, 1970).

Through an active process of transactions between reader and text (Spiro et al., 1997; Swaffar, Arens, & Byrnes, 1991), meaning is constructed in a four-stage process of selection, acquisition, construction and integration (Weinstein & Mayer, 1986). Selection helps a reader focus on specific information relevant to the purpose at hand, which is then transferred to long-term memory. This acquisition of information through transfer is assisted by construction of connections between the new incoming information and the old information that is already stored within the reader. And finally in the integration stage, the newly gained information is accommodated, fitted into and blended with the old.

During each stage, reader interaction with information is shaped by knowledge that the reader already has. This knowledge is collected, formed and fashioned from his experiences in society, interaction with others, education, familiarity with text type, level of reading, language ability, cultural background, personal beliefs, etc. These different types of knowledge are represented as mental structures, also called schemata.

An autonomous reader would then be one who is able to identify and make use of relevant schemata to facilitate integration of textual information with existing schema using appropriate mental processes. Cognitive theories best explain knowledge representations in the form of schemata and the mental processes that make use of these.

Cognitivist View of Language Acquisition

During the 1950s, theories of language teaching and learning witnessed a paradigm shift from behaviourism to cognitivism. Cognitivism proposed the notion that humans do not receive input passively but are highly active while interacting with incoming sources of information. Cognitive psychologists use the concept of schema (plural: schemata) to explain the interaction of various sources of information during the comprehension process. According to the schema theory, knowledge already gained through prior experience is organized and stored as knowledge structures or units called schemata. Schemata can represent information gained about ideas, events, concepts, situations, actions and objects, and can also store information that connects these various units. Thus this mental framework helps the learner make sense of incoming information by choosing information that is familiar, recognizing what is unfamiliar, organizing knowledge based on patterns and structures, associating new information with previous knowledge and adding new elements to existing knowledge, selecting attention. It also enables storing and recall of information.

The theory has as its basis what Immanuel Kant claimed in 1781—that new information can acquire meaning only when it can be related to something the individual already knows. Our attempts to learn involve interaction between knowledge (or information structures) available within us (prior knowledge/ schema), and the incoming new information; assimilation and integration of information gained with existing mental structures/schemata; and construction of new schema to accommodate information that cannot be integrated with the old structures. This view adds a constructive element to the cognitive paradigm.

Different types of prior knowledge/schemata are summoned by a reader to facilitate reading comprehension and knowledge construction: linguistic (knowledge of language), content (knowledge of the topic) and formal (knowledge of text types and structures) schemata (Carrell, 1983). These schemata are products in flux fashioned through prior experience with and exposure to agents like family, community, school, socio-cultural environment, age, gender and affective factors like anxiety, self-esteem etc. (Abersold & Field, 1997) and consequently differ from one individual to another (Anderson, 1982; Omaggio, 1993).

A fourth type of schema is the process schema, a knowledge of mental or cognitive activities, or techniques, called strategies that a reader can employ to summon relevant schemata and implement appropriate comprehension activities to process incoming data. Process schema also helps a reader monitor comprehension and launch compensatory actions. Process schema is therefore made up of procedures that help a reader make use of content, language and formal schemata available and deploy them in a manner that best suits the reading purpose at hand.

Lee and Van Patten (2003) explain that the interplay of schemata that operate simultaneously and interactively help "disambiguate, elaborate, filter, and compensate" (p. 219) textual information. Comprehension activities that help meaning making like explanation, interpretation, inference, evaluation and compensation are all fashioned out of the schemata that a reader brings to the text, and a comprehension deficit arises when one or more of these schemata are missing. However, Bernhardt (2005) argues that inadequacies in one schema can be compensated by activating another schema.

The role of schema while reading in a second language is compounded by the fact that reader variables are also effected additionally by what the reader has gained from L1. A beginning L2 reader brings to the reading process content, process, formal and linguistic knowledge gained from his experience with L1. As expertise in L2 grows, so do the various schemata. Bernhardt's (2005) model of L2 reading comprehension ascribes considerable significance to roles played by L1 literacy, L2 proficiency and unidentifiable factors like personality, motivation, intelligence and attitude in facilitating reading comprehension. Faerch and Kasper (1983) list two resources that help a second-language reader make meaning of incoming information: declarative knowledge that consists of internalized L2 rules and memorized chunks of language, and procedural knowledge made up of mental activities and procedures, or strategies, employed by the learner to process L2 data for acquisition and use.

Birch (2007) concurs. The model of reading proposed by Birch lays down that the L2 reading process is made up of two main components: knowledge areas and strategies used to process the text. World knowledge and language knowledge belong to the former, and cognitive processing and language processing strategies make up the latter. Cognitive processing strategies are general actions like inferring, predicting, etc., while language processing strategies like chunking, word recognition, etc. are language-specific strategies without which reading will suffer.

A second-language learner is then someone who has an already developed and unique set of schemata to support his L2 reading comprehension process. Content, linguistic, formal and process schemata of an L2 reader are already developed due to exposure to L1. In addition, a threshold of linguistic and formal schemata in L2 is required for comprehension to be successful. What is required in our classrooms is therefore: first, an awareness that the reading process is not invariant, that it is reader dependent; and second that the L2 reader is not a total novice, that they come equipped with a lot of reading resources at their disposal.

Teaching Reading in the ESL Classroom

Most ESL classrooms adopt a product-based approach where the teacher teaches the reader how to read, how to comprehend and what to comprehend with scant attention paid to what the reader already knows. The focus is on what and how much content has been comprehended, and how to comprehend a text. In an L2 classroom where learners are already familiar with reading in L1, have a repertoire of content, structure and process knowledge to rely on, direct instruction in ESL reading where teacher decides the meaning of the text and explains how to understand it can be disconcerting. It might demotivate, decelerate or even impede learner progress.

From the point of view of the schema theorists, what might work better is a process-based approach which provides scope to activate each learner's prior experience with language learning, brings to the fore reading strategies (procedural knowledge/process schema) currently used, and leverages them to facilitate L2 comprehension. Such an approach would include enhancing awareness of strategies one employs; locating and correcting deficits in strategy use; demonstrating ways to increase their efficacy; giving opportunities to master their use; and providing exposure to a wider repertoire of strategies that could result in a richer process schema. The teacher does not assist with content, language or structure, but facilitates with techniques that can be employed to ensure adequate comprehension of textual information. This would help build readers who develop insights into their learning styles and strategies; take an active and conscious choice regarding how to address the task of reading in hand; and recognize and utilize the right strategies to exploit available schemata so that comprehension becomes more reader-controlled and autonomous.

This chapter believes that a rich process schema might help rectify inadequacies in topical, structural or language knowledge available to the reader.

What also works in favour of providing training in strategies/developing process schema is that procedural knowledge is finite in nature, unlike topic and language knowledge, and does not fluctuate much based on variables like culture, social background, age, intelligence, etc.

In the following sections we detail various procedural resources, also termed strategies, utilized by a reader.

Learner Strategies in Language Acquisition

Learners use a variety of mental or behavioural activities called strategies to assimilate new information to their mental structures/schema (Anderson, 1982). For Weinstein and Mayer (1986: 315), strategies control both mental and behavioural aspects of an individual. They are "behaviours and thoughts that a learner engages in during learning that are intended to influence the learner's encoding process". Oxford (1994: 1) defines them as "actions, behaviours, steps, or techniques students use, often unconsciously, to improve their progress in apprehending, internalizing, and using the L2".

Learners' procedural knowledge stores information about three major types of strategies used while learning a language: cognitive, socio-affective, and metacognitive (O'Malley & Chamot, 1990). Cognitive strategies are techniques or procedures that facilitate a learning task or the steps or operations used in learning or problem solving. They involve techniques used to select, acquire, construct and integrate information. Social strategies decide learners' interaction with peers, teachers and other individuals, and affective strategies affect learners' motivational or affective state, and help them control their emotions. Metacognitive strategies are controlling, monitoring and evaluating strategies; they are problem and outcome oriented and are deployed by learners when a particular learning problem is encountered. They help learners think about their thinking.

Oxford (1990) classified strategies for language learning into direct strategies that are knowledge based and meaning based, and are used for memorizing, cognitive processing and compensation, and indirect strategies that consist of metacognitive, social and affective strategies. A few examples of cognitive strategies are reviewing lessons, guessing word meaning from context, writing notes, skimming and using a dictionary; while metacognitive strategies include planning a schedule, setting goals, looking for opportunities to learn the language, etc. Strategies that we use to interact with others for language learning are social strategies like asking the speaker to slow down when the message is not clear, practising with others and asking for help with learning. Examples of affective strategies are trying to relax when nervous, giving encouragement to oneself and rewarding oneself for a lesson well learned.

There are no direct cause-and-effect relations between strategies and their purpose. In other words, there are no exclusive strategies directed to achieve specific results. Sometimes more than one strategy can be used to perform the same result.

For instance, once the reader identifies the presence of an unfamiliar word (inadequate linguistic schema), many strategies can be employed to repair the deficit, viz., guessing from context, translating the context to mother tongue, referring to a dictionary, ignoring the word, breaking up the word into familiar components, asking a more knowledgeable person, etc. The choice of strategies depends on the reader's level of expertise or preferred style of learning.

So also there are no good or bad strategies; efficiency of strategies depends on the number of strategies available for use and how they are used. A successful learner is one who has access to a wide number of strategies. The third aspect of successful strategy use is if the strategy was employed metacognitively (Carrell, 1989; Jimenez, Garcia, & Pearson, 1996; García et al., 1998). Unsuccessful learners lack strategic awareness and hence are unable to monitor their comprehension processes (Mokhtari & Reichard, 2002). Past researches in L1 and L2 indicate that ESL learners struggle primarily because of lack of knowledge of their own cognitive process, also known as metacognition, to monitor control and their learning abilities (Niemi, 2002). In the 1970s Flavell introduced the term metacognition to refer to the knowledge and awareness of one's cognitive learning processes. Metacognitive strategies are those that help learners plan learning activities, monitor achievements and repair unsuccessful activities by adjusting strategies to ensure successful performance (Jacob & Paris, 1987; Pressley, 2000).

Several reasons why metacognitive strategies contribute to effective language learning have been pointed out: metacognitive knowledge develops lifelong learners who can cope and adapt to new contexts and problems (Eggen & Kaucbak, 1995); awareness of metacognitive processing results in use of strategies which are purposeful, effortful, focused, essential and facilitative in promoting language acquisition (Alexander & Jetton, 2000); integrating metacognitive knowledge instruction into language instruction programmes helps develop learners who can take charge of their own learning (Garb, 2000).

Strategies in Reading

Fluent readers construct meaning using a combination of text-based information and their own prior knowledge (Rumelhart, 1977; Stanovich, 1980). Reading strategies are techniques that help facilitate this construction of meaning by

- retrieving information from prior knowledge
- storing new information
- recognizing obstacles/deficits
- deciding upon ways to overcome these
- launching correction measures to ensure comprehension

A successful language learner, according to Devine (1993) is one who has a good awareness of skills and strategies available at their disposal; has metacognitive knowledge about themselves as a learner and how they learn best; has clear understanding of the nature, purpose and demands of the task at hand; and knows the strategies that are appropriate to achieve goals of the task. Skilled readers are therefore those who are conscious of the reading strategies they use; have clear understanding of the purposes of the current reading task; are aware of their strategy needs to meet these purposes; are in control of their comprehension process by constant monitoring of the effect of strategies employed; and know what repair strategies to use should there be a comprehension deficit (Pressley & Afflerbach, 1995). As mentioned before, higher levels of metacognitive awareness enables efficient use of reading strategies (Carrell, 1983; Zhang, 2001); and successful reading comprehension depends on whether a strategy was employed metacognitively (Carrell, 1989). So in comparison, poor readers are not those who lack cognitive strategies (in fact, it is rare to find L2 readers who lack cognitive strategies) but those who fail to access them metacognitively. Many strategy research studies (Barnett, 1988; Auerbach & Paxton, 1997; Jimenez et al., 1996) support the finding that there is a positive relation between L2 reading comprehension and reader awareness of strategy use/metacognitive awareness.

Rosenblatt (1978) describes two kinds of reading: efferent reading and aesthetic reading. The former helps acquire information from the text that is being read, while reading aesthetically helps the reader focus on the mental activities that occur while reading, paying attention to processes, associations, feelings and attitudes. In other words, reading aesthetically and paying attention to how one's reading process works, helps develop metacognitive strategies. To ensure retention and application of information acquired, students need to be taught to develop both efferent and aesthetic ways of reading. This has the potential to develop autonomy in reading skills.

Expert learners are aesthetic readers who are continually active—constantly taking decisions regarding task requirements, accuracy and sufficiency of information acquired, sources of comprehension obstacles, deploying of appropriate correction strategies and making the language-learning environment conducive and favourable. The interactive model of the expert language learner 'learner self-management' (LSM) proposed by Rubin (in Johnson, 2005: 37) states that the learner's metacognition involves five procedures of planning, monitoring, evaluating, problem identification/solving and implementing corrective measures. According to this model, there is continual interaction between an expert reader's metacognition and procedural knowledge resources. Less successful language learners, then, are those who do not have the metacognitive knowledge that helps one become aware of cognitive and/or socio-affective strategies that are context/need appropriate (Chamot, 2005).

There is evidence to suggest that metacognitive strategies used by successful learners to make the right decisions are what distinguish good language learners. Reviewing Good Language Learner models proposed by researchers in strategy studies, Rubin (in Johnson, 2005) points out that there may be some variation in the cognitive and socio-affective strategies used by various learners but there is seemingly little or no variation in the use of metacognitive strategies. While both expert and novice learners may use the same cognitive and socio-affective strategies, research consistently shows that the difference in success depends on the use of effective metacognitive strategies. Learners who have a wider repertoire of metacognitive strategies and are in control of their metacognition in terms of choosing the right strategy that the context demands are therefore potential autonomous language learners (Hauck, 2005).

Metacognitive strategies help learners evaluate whether they have the schemata needed to accomplish a task, viz., topic knowledge, language knowledge, structure knowledge and even process/strategies required for successful completion of the task, and if they lack any of these, how to remedy it. According to Ertmer and Newby (1996: 3), expert learners are "strategic, self-regulated, and reflective"; they are more aware than novices of the need to check for errors in comprehension, how to address these, how to compensate for deficits in their ability and achieve success in their efforts. This upholds the view that expertise in reading is not a demonstration of automaticity of reading processes but that good readers are acutely conscious of their reading processes and are constantly monitoring them.

The cognitive-constructivist view upheld the view that comprehension instruction can be best strengthened through development of various strategies. This stems from the view that expert learners are those who have strategies that help assess the requirements of the task, know which procedures to deploy to serve the task purpose at hand, have a large repertoire of procedures to choose from, and are constantly monitoring and evaluating the efficacy of these procedures. As mentioned earlier, in a second-language context, reading strategies are developed primarily through reading in L1. Acquired through repeated encounters with language, while trying to solve problems encountered during acquisition or transmission of knowledge, strategies can also be learned through direct instruction.

Language Strategy Training Programmes

The sustained popularity of language strategy training lies in the potential it holds for shaping learning in and outside the classroom, and offering information that can accelerate the processes of language learning (Grenfell & Macaro, 2007). A large body of research documents the positive effects of strategy training on language learning. Strategy training can build effective and independent learning habits (Wenden & Rubin, 1987; O'Malley & Chamot, 1990) and learners who are confident and motivated to take charge of their learning process (Chamot & O'Malley, 1994). Research indicates that more proficient L2 learners tend to have a wider range of strategies, have a heightened sense of metacognitive awareness and employ strategies more often than less proficient learners (O'Malley & Chamot, 1990; Oxford, 1990). Factoring in these indicates that for a strategy training programme to be effective, activation of metacognition and instruction in the use of a large number of strategies should be enabled. However, in an L2 context, strategy training should allow learners to discuss and describe strategies already being used before familiarizing them with other strategies that are available. Strategy selection to be informed, "presupposes knowledge of strategies and knowledge of strategies presupposes instruction" (Nunan, 1991).

Nature of Strategy Instruction

O'Malley and Chamot (1990) list two approaches to instruction in teaching use of learning strategies: direct and embedded. In direct training students are taught the name, purpose, value and use of various learning strategies considered useful by the instructor, whereas in embedded strategy training guidance in the use of learning strategies is embedded or built into the materials used.

The research from which this chapter draws evidence is designed on the assumption that one effective way of developing independent reading skills is helping readers recognize the role of process schema, and promote use of and facilitate development of process schema through strategy training. In L2 contexts, however, both direct and embedded instruction could prove detrimental since strategies taught are pre-determined by the instructor/teacher/materials producer. This paper therefore recommends the use of a strategy training programme that first helps readers identify strategies that are currently used and determine their efficacy, and then provides exposure to a wider repertoire of strategies from which students can select, adopt, adapt or create new ones for use. This would not only support the fact that strategies have to be aligned with learning styles, but would also provide an essential opportunity to develop metacognition. It was hypothesized that process schema once developed would help bridge gaps in context and linguistic knowledge.

In the research reported here, individual think alouds and collaborative reading activities were used to help readers access their cognitive processes. The strategy training programme designed for the research works on the assumption that a cognitive-constructive learning environment that aims to achieve learning through dialogue with self, followed by dialogue with others through social participation, could be an ideal environment for a learner to understand and gain control over their reading processes and design a better process of their own by learning from others. Socio-constructivism, the second theoretical framework that forms the crux of the study—beside cognitivism—is explored below to explain how autonomy in L2 reading can be promoted in a collaborative learning environment that scaffolds strategy development with peer support and is preceded by activities that promote learner's self-awareness. Working first within the cognitive-constructive paradigm, the programme attempted to heighten learners' self-awareness before they collaborated to learn from peers in a socio-constructive setting. This was expected to make learning from others more purposeful and focused. Once learners are made aware of the processes they use and identify deficits in them, working with others, it was hoped this would help them choose and use strategies they found most needed, useful and suitable for their learning styles and contexts.

Social Constructive Learning

The cognitive paradigm viewed knowledge acquisition from texts as a process of selecting, interpreting and constructing meaning, based on the interaction between new knowledge in the text and knowledge structures already in the reader. Comprehension is the result of an active process of creating hypotheses, testing them and building new forms of understanding through trial and error. Constructing knowledge based on trial-and-error processes derived from an individual's observation and reasoning capabilities might have limited effects; for the trial-and-error process to be successful, learners need to be supported—either in terms of materials (proposed by cognitive theorists) or others/experts (proposed by constructive theorists) that can make the learning processes adopted richer. Accommodating this view, the cognitive paradigm explaining the skill of reading has witnessed a shift from focus on interaction of reader and text to a socio-constructive paradigm that upheld the role played by the interaction of reader and context/others in successful reading comprehension.

The addition of the social constructive view was directly in keeping with the contrasting views proposed by development psychologists Piaget and Vygotsky. While for Piaget (1957) it was the child's experiences that determined, regulated and constructed learning, Vygotsky (1978) argued that the role of others was primary in the cognitive development of the child. The theory of social constructivism believes that one's learning, ability and intelligence are not static constructs but dynamic, arising out of collaborated responses to specific social/interaction situations. Social interactions determine cognitive abilities.

The concept of distributed cognition proposed by Hutchins in the 1990s based on Vygotsky's views on the social aspect of cognition explains that, in a social environment, facts, knowledge and information of any sort are distributed among all the members of a group. Distributed cognition thus means a set of cognitive systems that interact not only within each other but also with each other. Collective performance, resulting from members socially coordinating to perform complex tasks, contributes to individual cognitive development. In other words, cognition embedded in all the individuals in a collective setting contributes to each member's individual learning. Salomon (1993), introducing the term 'shared cognition' to explain a type of distributed cognition, explains that social activities like conversations produce constant changes in individual's cognition based on the responses of other participants in the system (distributed cognition). Socially distributed individually embedded capacities, skills or knowledge can therefore be made to result in individual growth through scaffolding social activities.

Vygotsky (1978) and later researchers like Warschauer (1997) and Warschauer and Kern (2000) point out that in an environment where learning is facilitated through social interaction and is mediated by tools like teamwork, conversations and dialogue, each participant internalizes the new, co-constructed knowledge first on the social level, and later on the individual or personal level. From social interactions participants move towards independent thinking (Woolfolk, 2004).

Collaborative learning events can thus encourage learner independence and promote critical thinking.

Vygotsky (1978) introduced two terms to signify how social interaction promotes co-construction of knowledge and learning: scaffolding and zone of proximal development. At the social level, the acquisition of new knowledge is facilitated by the More Knowledgeable Other (MKO), any person who has a better skill, a higher level of knowledge, or an advanced ability or understanding than the learner. The MKO supports collaborative learning by scaffolding, i.e., by providing prompts, hints, clues, explanations, questions and suggestions to assist problem solving (Bonk & Cunningham, 1998). With scaffolding provided by the MKO, students can reach higher-level understanding of tasks or solve problems they would have been unable to solve alone. Vygotsky captures this enhanced learning through the concept of the zone of proximal development (ZPD). The ZPD is the difference between the ability of a learner to perform a specific task independently and to perform the same task under the guidance of an MKO. It is the distance between actual developmental level as determined by independent problem solving and the level of potential development as determined through problem solving in collaboration with more able peers or the MKO.

Socio-constructive theory explains that higher and effective learning occurs in ZPD; that given appropriate help a learner can perform a challenging task beyond his independent abilities (Woolfolk, 2004).

Constructivism in Practice

Two strategy teaching methods that implement socio-constructivism and cognitive constructivism in reading comprehension skills which are of significance to this chapter are reciprocal teaching and differentiated instruction respectively.

Reciprocal teaching, first developed by Palincsar and Brown (1986), is a small-group reading instruction activity in which students play the roles of the teacher. The teacher first demonstrates and then helps students to use the four reading strategies of summarizing, question generating, clarifying and predicting. Once the students master the use of these strategies, each one assumes the role of teacher and leads a dialogue with group members applying a specific strategy to the text segment that has been read.

While reciprocal teaching delivers a pre-determined set of strategies to students via direct instruction followed by group learning, differentiated instruction as a pedagogic framework believes that effective teaching ought to provide each student with personalized learning instruction opportunities in terms of materials for acquiring content; means/strategies for processing, constructing and comprehending information; type of learner output expected; context of learning; and materials for assessment (Anderson, 2007). This outlook is based on the assumption that learners vary based on their socioeconomic and cultural background, language used, gender, motivation, cognitive abilities, interest levels, etc.

Reciprocal teaching and differentiated instruction are of significance to the study reported here since the former makes use of peer teaching while the latter accommodates the view that learning processes are unique and vary depending on learners.

However, strategy training as implemented in these programmes is in danger of devaluing the individual L2 learner since both implement a set of strategies prescribed by an 'other'/expert and not by the individual, and hence may not match learner deficit or address learner need. While reciprocal teaching completely discounts the learner's available process schema, differentiated instruction does *attempt* to take into account the deficits in the process schema of learners but does not allow a choice of strategies. Like most collaborative learning activities, it might then get reduced to weaker members adopting strategies from those who are the most vociferous or assertive.

Keeping this in mind, one guiding influence for the strategy training programme designed for this programme was the extended view of reading as a social process that regards group interaction as capable of making up for individual deficits in topic/language/structure/strategies with the facility of distributed cognition. The second guiding principle was what Collins, Brown, and Newman (1989) pointed out in favour of making thinking visible for cognitive development: that concepts, like strategies, should be regarded as tools that need to be understood through use, rather than as notions or ideas that need to be taught through instruction.

The research from which the chapter draws its notions hypothesizes that learning together and co-construction of knowledge should be preceded by awareness raising of the processes involved in personal construction of knowledge, or metacognition. Social interaction can yield individual benefits, only if one first allows opportunities for individual construction of knowledge. Unless personal-level awareness precedes the social, the individual will not be ready to learn, adopt and adapt from peers; and social learning activities will not be purposeful. In the context of strategy training, working in the cognitivist-constructive paradigm enables in individuals awareness of strategies and their purposes. Thus strategies are not restricted to being mere ideas but are recognized as tools readers use. More than a strategy list, development of metacognition through individual think alouds facilitates readers with the language to discuss and share strategies used, and search for strategies needed.

Strategy Training to Develop Autonomy in Reading: An Experiment

Drawing on cognitive and socio-constructive theoretical frameworks, a strategy training experiment was conducted to exhort the need for fostering the pedagogy of collaboration in the ESL classroom in order to promote independent reading habits. The chapter argues that encouraging individual cognitive awareness before collaborative construction (the personal before the social) can lead to enhanced, focused and more purposeful individual cognitive development and consequently autonomy in learners.

Researchers like Wenden and Rubin (1987) and O'Malley and Chamot (1990) have claimed that an awareness of one's strategies will lead to independent and therefore effective learning. In the case of reading, this would mean that an awareness of one's reading strategies leads to effective reading without external assistance. However, awareness raising, this researcher felt, is an essential but not sufficient requirement for developing independent reading habits. Awareness of strategies one uses does not equip one with alternative strategies to solve one's comprehension blocks. A lack of awareness of alternative strategies limits an individual's ability to perform a learning task which requires new learning strategies (Dansereau, 1985). However, if the reader is made aware of a wide variety of strategies they might choose an alternative strategy or adapt, modify, adopt or even create a new one to fit their learning requirements and learning process, and thus use it confidently to satisfy their purpose of reading.

Second, it has been hypothesized (Vygotsky, 1978) that interpersonal development through a socio-constructive learning paradigm can promote intrapersonal development facilitated by a cognitive-constructive learning paradigm. Whereas this research argues that for collaboration/learning from others to have any learning effect, an individual should first be aware of themselves and the processes they use, and be able to detect the deficiencies in the processes. A cycle of stages of personal —social—personal development is recommended.

A strategy training programme was envisaged to test the efficacy of the hypothesis that providing exposure to alternative strategies through a programme that precedes collaborative learning activities with personal cognitive development activities might encourage learners to achieve independence in reading by giving them opportunities to develop a larger repertoire of individually chosen strategies. Three features formed the pivotal factors that determined the design of the strategy training programme.

It was felt that, in order to facilitate lifelong learning habits through a strategy training programme, we must first attempt to generate an awareness of one's cognitive process, i.e., metacognitive awareness (Flavell, 1978).

Second, it is over-simplistic to assume an individual termed a *student* will always respond within a system in ways consistent with this label (Elliott, 1999). Any individual is primarily a social being and hence lifelong learning should create opportunities for learners to engage and re-engage in learning with fellow members of their society (Elliott, 1999: 26). Hence, the researcher felt that social learning or learning in groups might be the most appropriate activities for developing lifelong learning habits in our learners.

Third, since it has been argued that we can facilitate a rapid accomplishment of learning, which will be retained longer if learning is provided in ways preferred by the individual (Claxton, 1996), it is advisable to allow the learner to choose those strategies that suit their preferences. In this context, what a strategy instructor can do is provide the learner with a number of strategies within the strategy instructional framework so that they are free to adopt what they feel will fit their learning style and purpose.

A strategy training programme was conducted:

(i) to identify the reading strategies used by the subjects and to determine if an awareness of their reading strategies would lead them to better comprehension on the one hand and independent reading on the other, and
(ii) to decide whether through group activities like collaborative reading and social think alouds, learners could be exposed to strategies used by peers, and if they could be encouraged to make use of these.

Methodology

The study was conducted in five phases with ten adult ESL learners (R1 to R10) at various levels of proficiency of reading (TOEFL reading scores ranging from 08 to 24). All the participants were students enrolled in short-term English proficiency development courses offered by the English and Foreign Languages University, Hyderabad. For convenience in managing students, the selected ten were divided randomly into two mixed-ability groups (groups A and B) with five members each. Group A had readers identified as R1, R2, R3, R4 and R6, and group B had members R5, R7, R8, R9 and R10.

Tools used for strategy awareness and strategy training included Oxford's (1990) Strategy Inventory for Language Learning (SILL), think alouds, a metacognitive response sheet designed by the researcher to facilitate think alouds, retrospective and introspective interviews, teacher discussions and consultations, and ten reading texts at various levels of difficulty (determined through Flesch-Kincaid reading difficulty measure) followed by comprehension questions. A simple calculation of average of reading comprehension scores was solely depended on as descriptive measure to determine growth, if any, in reading comprehension. The mean score was considered sufficient primarily because the focus of this research was on qualitative understanding of data obtained: delineating ways to raise awareness of strategies; understanding types of strategies used by readers; increasing efficacy of strategy training; investigating kinds of readers who benefitted from strategy training; and investigating retention of effects of strategy training. Statistical measures were not considered since the sample was too small, being chosen keeping in mind the exhaustive nature of parsing, coding and analysis of think aloud and interview data required for identifying strategies used.

The initial study extended over a period of seventeen days, and a delayed-effects study (phase 5) was conducted after a gap of 30 days.

In phase 0, before the commencement of the actual study, readers' entry-level comprehension was assessed using an academic reading text (Txt1) at reading difficulty of Flesch-Kincaid grade level 10. Based on levels of language proficiency demonstrated by responses to reading comprehension questions, readers were rank ordered and grouped as belonging to high, middle and low levels of language proficiency. This was purely for research purposes and not revealed to subjects. R4, R5 and R10 showed high levels of language proficiency, scoring an average of 9 out of 10; R6 and R8 scored 6 out of 10 and so were grouped as middle-level language proficiency; and R1, R2, R3, R7 and R9 were readers who demonstrated low language proficiency, having scored an average of 2.5 out of 10 in comprehension questions.

The goal of phase 1 was to identify strategies used by the subjects before group interaction activities and to raise self-awareness of strategies used. All the texts used here were read individually accompanied by think alouds. Think alouds were facilitated with the help of a metacognitive response sheet designed by the researcher. Two practice texts at reading difficulty of Flesch-Kincaid grade levels 6 and 7 were used for the cognitively demanding task of practising thinking aloud and identifying reading strategies used. Once they gained expertise in articulating their thought processes, readers were given texts at levels 8 and 9 (Txt2 and Txt3) and comprehension exercises.

Strategy profiles of each reader were drawn working with the reader, using inputs received from think alouds, retrospective and introspective interviews, and performance of comprehension tasks in addition to responses to Oxford's (1990) Strategy Inventory for Language Learning (SILL). These were then given back to the learners to make them aware of strategies they used. Equipped with individual strategy profiles, readers were then asked to read Txt4 at difficulty level 10 and respond to comprehension questions. Performance on these questions was compared with that at phase 0 to determine if an awareness of strategies alone would help improve comprehension.

In phase 2 readers were made aware of alternative strategies available by exposing them to strategies used by peers through group reading activities. Subjects read the texts (Txt5 and Txt6 at levels 10 and 11) individually first, and then discussed with peers parts they did not understand. Comprehension questions were discussed and answered as a group. Social think alouds were encouraged and soon became a tool that facilitated collaborative reading: less successful members clarified what they could not comprehend, while those who were successful discussed and demonstrated various strategies they used to understand the text. Group members questioned each other about the various strategies and learned how to use them.

Phase 3 was conducted to determine if exposure to alternative strategies resulted in learners adopting new strategies and demonstrating improvement in reading comprehension. So in this phase collaborative reading activities were conducted using texts (Txt7, Txt8) at levels 11 and 12, but comprehension tasks that followed the texts were attempted individually. This was followed by group discussion of responses to tasks, though readers were asked not to make any changes to their written responses.

In phase 4 a text (Txt9) at level 11 was used for individual reading assessment. Readers read the text individually and answered comprehension questions. This was followed by drawing up of reader strategy profiles, as in phase 1, to determine increase in strategy repertoire, if any. Reader responses to comprehension items were assessed to determine if exposure to other strategies and/or increase in individual learners' strategy repertoire resulted in enhanced levels of comprehension. All readers showed an increase in their strategy repertoire, and in keeping with findings derived in phase 3, a consequent growth in comprehension scores as well.

In phase 5 a text (Txt10) at level 11 was used to assess delayed effects of strategy instruction, i.e., to determine if learners were able to retain use of new strategies they had learned from peers. As in the previous stages, readers were asked to read a text and respond to comprehension questions. Later they were asked to recall strategies they employ currently, not only while reading the text but also elsewhere in other reading contexts.

Analysis and Interpretation of Data

Tables 5.1, 5.2 and 5.3 give the marks that the all readers scored in the tasks which accompanied the ten texts used for comprehension. Maximum marks for task items for each text are given in brackets. Group scores are given for texts 5 and 6 since tasks here were attempted as a group.

I. To answer the first research question (does awareness of strategies result in improvement of reading comprehension?), we take a look at the average of scores marked for texts 1 and 4. It is clear that readers do not show much growth from phase 0 to phase 1.
II. In phase 2, group A scored 4.5 out of a total of 5, and 4 out of 4 for texts 5 and 6 respectively, while group B scored 5 out of 5 and 4 out of 4 for both texts indicating the success of collaborative reading and group think aloud activities.

Table 5.1 Marks scored by subjects in reading comprehension tasks in phases 0 and 1

Level of proficiency	Phase 0 Txt1 (5)	Phase 1 Txt2 (4)	Phase 1 Txt3 (3)	Phase 1 Txt4 (5)
Low				
R1	1.5	1	0	1
R2	0.5	0	0.5	1.5
R3	0.5	1	1	1
R7	0	1.5	1	1
R9	1	1.5	1	1.5
Average	0.8			1.2
Middle				
R6	2.5	2.5	2	2.5
R8	2	2.5	2	2
Average	2.25			2.25
High				
R4	3.5	3	2	3
R5	4	3.5	3	3.5
R10	4	4	2.5	4
Average	3.6			3.5

5 Blending Cognitive and Socio-constructive Pedagogies ... 75

Table 5.2 Marks scored by subjects in reading comprehension tasks in phases 0–4

Level of proficiency	Phase 0 Txt1 (5)	Phase 1 Txt4 (5)	Phase 3 Txt7 (4)	Phase 4 Txt8 (4)	Phase 4 Txt9 (4)
Low					
R1	1.5	1	2.5	3	3
R2	0.5	1.5	3	3	3.5
R3	0.5	1	2	3	4
R7	0	1	2.5	3.5	4
R9	1	1.5	3	3	4
Average	0.8	1.2	2.6	3	3.7
Middle					
R6	2.5	2.5	3	3.5	4
R8	2	2	3.5	3	4
Average	2.25	2.25	3.25	3.25	4
High					
R4	3.5	3	3.5	4	3.5
R5	4	3.5	4	3.5	4
R10	4	4	4	4	3.5
Average	3.6	3.5	3.8	3.8	3.6

Table 5.3 Marks scored by subjects in reading comprehension tasks in phases 0–5

Level of proficiency	Phase 0 Txt1 (5)	Phase 1 Txt4 (5)	Phase 3 Txt7 (4)	Phase 4 Txt8 (4)	Phase 4 Txt9(4)	Phase 5 Txt10 (5)
Low						
R1	1.5	1	2.5	3	3	4
R2	0.5	1.5	3	3	3.5	3.5
R3	0.5	1	2	3	4	4
R7	0	1	2.5	3.5	4	3
R9	1	1.5	3	3	4	4.5
Average	0.8	1.2	2.6	3	3.7	3.8
Middle						
R6	2.5	2.5	3	3.5	4	4
R8	2	2	3.5	3	4	4.5
Average	2.25	2.25	3.25	3.25	4	4.25
High						
R4	3.5	3	3.5	4	3.5	4.5
R5	4	3.5	4	3.5	4	5
R10	4	4	4	4	3.5	5
Average	3.6	3.5	3.8	3.8	3.6	4.8

III. To answer the second question (does an awareness of alternate strategies result in improvement of reading comprehension?), we compare marks scored in phases 0 and 1 with marks scored in phases 3 and 4. It was observed that every reader showed some degree of growth in levels of comprehension when compared to their previous performances.
IV. To investigate the delayed effects of strategy training, i.e., the long-term benefits of strategy training for reading comprehension, in phase 5 which was conducted after a gap of 30 days, readers were given text 10 for comprehension. This was followed by a brief retrospection of the strategies used by each reader. Given below is a comparison of scores at all five phases.
V. Profiles of strategies used by readers at three differing levels of language proficiency are shown in Table 5.4. Strategies used before the training intervention are listed in the left column, and those demonstrated after the training in the right. The ones marked in bold in this column are those that were newly acquired.

Table 5.4 Reading strategies profiles of low-, mid- and high-proficiency learners

R1: low-level proficiency	
1. Using background knowledge 2. Reading aloud 3. Memorizing 4. Translating 5. Re-reading 6. Builds mental pictures 7. Underlining (almost the whole text)	1. **Division of words** 2. **Building mental images** 3. **Self-evaluating** (*summarizing and questions to self*) 4. **Translation and substitution** 5. **Translation and elimination** 6. **Summarizing (ongoing)** 7. **Paying attention to discourse markers** 8. **Skimming** 9. **Using context for word meaning** 10. **Underlining key words** 11. Using background knowledge 12. Re-reading 13. Reading aloud
R2: low-level proficiency	
1. Translating 2. Re-reading 3. Using background knowledge to relate to text information 4. Division of long sentences into shorter segments 5. Re-writing key words/sentences on a paper 6. Referring to dictionary	1. **Summarizing (ongoing)** 2. **Division of words into familiar components** 3. **Partial translation** 4. **Relates different sentences** 5. **Contextual guessing** 6. **Underlining** 7. **Self-monitoring** (*using mental summaries*) 8. **Note making** 9. **Builds mental pictures** 10. **Translation and substitution** 11. **Writing a language-learning diary of vocabulary and strategies learned; progress made** 12. Re-reading 13. Using background knowledge 14. Using dictionary

(continued)

5 Blending Cognitive and Socio-constructive Pedagogies ...

Table 5.4 (continued)

R6: mid-level proficiency	
1. Underlining 2. Relates text to background knowledge 3. Uses images of familiar words 4. Scanning 5. Builds mental pictures 6. Memorizing 7. Translation and substitution (paragraph level) 8. Writing a language-learning diary 9. Rhyming for memorizing word meanings 10. Using dictionary 11. Skimming 12. Clarifying with peers/teachers/experts	1. **Division of words** 2. **Guessing word meanings through linguistic clues** 3. **Making predictions by relating to background knowledge** 4. **Summarizing (write down main points)** 5. **Self-evaluating using summaries** 6. **Skipping (words or paragraphs)** 7. **Making notes on margin** 8. **Comparing new information with background knowledge** 9. Translation and substitution (sentence level) 10. Relates text to background knowledge 11. Uses images of familiar words 12. Scanning 13. Skimming 14. Builds mental pictures 15. Writing a language-learning diary
R8: mid-level proficiency	
1. Translation (partial) 2. Division of words and sentences 3. Uses background knowledge to compare 4. Uses background knowledge to predict 5. Guessing of word meaning using linguistic clues 6. Guesses with sound similarity 7. Uses images of words which are familiar 8. Self-monitoring (by asking questions to self) 9. Re-writing important points in notebook 10. Re-reading	1. **Skipping (of paragraphs)** 2. **Summarizing** 3. **Relates different sentences/paragraphs** 4. **Underlining** 5. **Writing a language-learning diary (on effective strategies, strategies used)** 6. **Skimming** 7. Contextual guessing (linguistic clues) 8. Relates to background knowledge (to compare) 9. Uses background knowledge to predict 10. Translating 11. Division of long sentences (for word meanings) 12. Scanning 13. Translation and elimination (sentence level) 14. Re-read 15. Translation and substitution (sentence level) 16. Self-evaluating *(ongoing questions to self)*
R5: high-level proficiency	
1. Re-reading (when there is a block in comprehension) 2. Skipping (of words) 3. Relates different paragraphs/sentences 4. Uses background knowledge to translate 5. Scanning 6. Guessing using linguistic clues 7. Summarizing (ongoing) 8. Self-evaluating (by asking questions) 9. Skipping words or paragraphs 10. Making summary notes of each paragraph 11. Reasoning 12. Inferring 13. Using dictionary 14. Making predictions by relating to background knowledge	1. **Division of words** 2. **Division of long sentences into shorter segments** 3. **Skimming** 4. **Predicting based on title followed by skimming** 5. **Translation and substitution (for word meanings)** 6. Contextual guessing (linguistic clues) 7. Self-evaluating *(set a goal; ask questions to see if comprehension is sufficient; identify problems and employ multiple strategies)* 8. Skipping (words or paragraphs) 9. Making notes marking relation between paragraphs 10. Relating different paragraphs/sentences 11. Re-reading (when there is a block in comprehension) 12. Summarizing (oral or written) 13. Reasoning 14. Inferring

(continued)

Table 5.4 (continued)

R10: high-level proficiency	
1. Frames mental pictures by remembering location of words on page 2. Relates sentences and words to larger text context to better comprehension 3. Translation and elimination (sentence level) 4. Translation and substitution (sentence level) 5. Reads aloud (only when there is a block in comprehension) 6. Self-evaluating using questions to self 7. Contextual guessing (linguistic clues) 8. Uses background knowledge to relate different parts of text 9. Skimming 10. Reasoning 11. Scanning	1. **Division of words and sentences** 2. **Reasoning deductively** 3. **Asking questions of peers and teacher for clarification** 4. **Making notes** 5. **Summarizing (main points for evaluation of comprehension)** 6. **Uses background knowledge to compare** 7. **Uses background knowledge to predict and skim** 8. Contextual guessing using linguistic clues 9. Self-evaluating asking questions 10. Forms mental pictures of textbook pages 11. Uses background knowledge to relate different parts of the text 12. Reasoning 13. Translation and elimination (partial) 14. Translation and substitution (partial) 15. Reading aloud 16. Scanning

Observation of strategy use before the training programme reveals that the number and types of strategies used by mid-level and high-proficiency readers almost match. As explained in strategy research (Oxford, 1994; O'Malley and Chamot, 1990) reading comprehension efficiency depends not on the type of strategies used but how effectively you use them. However, low-level readers in this study had fewer strategies, predominantly basic, word comprehension-level strategies, at their disposal. This could indicate the need to cultivate a larger strategy repertoire in our readers.

A most heartening observation regarding the effect of the strategy training programme is that all readers' strategy repertoire expanded towards the end of the training programme. The two most prominent strategy categories adopted/adapted by all are word meaning decoding strategies and metacognitive strategies.

For decoding meanings of unfamiliar words, three strategies used effectively and adopted extensively were *translation, division of words* and *using larger text context/linguistic clues*. The subjects of the study used the strategy of translation in four ways: *partial translation of text portions not understood; complete translation; translation and substitution* (translate and substitute with a more familiar word without changes in meaning); and *translation and elimination* (translate and eliminate the word if unnecessary for comprehension). The last two translation strategies are not listed in traditionally used strategy inventories.

The other word-based strategies most used are guessing word meaning by *dividing into familiar components* and *guessing word meaning through linguistic clues like words, sentences and other parts of the text* were also adopted by most readers.

While less proficient readers showed a marked increase in the number of cognitive strategies used, more proficient readers gained from the intervention programme by becoming more self-regulated and reflective of their processes, i.e., the strategy training programme helped good readers increase the number and quality of metacognitive strategies they used. Among metacognitive strategies, *self-evaluating* was adopted effectively by readers with low-level proficiency and adapted with a wider scope by good readers. While the more proficient readers included planning, monitoring, problem identification and problem solving by trying out multiple corrective measures as part of their process of self-evaluation, less proficient readers relied mainly on summarizing parts of text and asking themselves questions. The self-monitoring strategy of *writing language diaries* was also found useful by a few.

Another significant observation was that high-proficiency readers were able to extend the *use of background knowledge* to gain better bottom-up and/or top-down comprehension of text. *Relating the theme or topic to available background knowledge* (content schemata) as a strategy was used by most readers before the training intervention. However, training helped them also use background knowledge related to text layout, format, grammar and word structure to further both top-down and bottom-up comprehension by using information extensively to compare, contrast, predict and justify text content.

The beneficial effects of collaborative reading activities were evidenced by the fact that strategies were shared and used across levels; while mid- and low-proficiency readers adopted strategies used by high-proficiency readers, what is surprising is that there are instances of high-level readers adopting and adapting strategies used by low-and mid-level readers. Translating strategies and division of long sentences into shorter segments for easy comprehension are strategies that were learned from low-level readers, while asking others questions for clarification was acquired from mid-level readers.

Readers with high levels of language proficiency demonstrated their competency in strategy use by gradually widening the scope of strategies adapted; for example, prediction was followed by skimming; underlining progressed to making notes; and self-monitoring by asking questions was preceded by making mental summaries in order to help ask questions.

Delayed assessment revealed that translation strategies for *understanding word meaning* and metacognitive strategies of *self-evaluation* were the most effectively retained strategies. All translation strategies (for elimination and substitution) were used in the delayed-effects phase, and so were summaries and questions used for self-monitoring. Consequently, strategies for understanding word meaning increased, and use of the dictionary and dependence on others reduced.

All readers grew conscious of the fact that different sentences in a text are connected and that different parts of a text are related. This helped relate text input to the various schemata the reader has. Comprehension gains were also exhibited by the fact that low-proficiency readers started responding accurately to inferential questions.

In terms of contribution to the body of knowledge in strategy training, it was observed that awareness of strategies one uses does not result in improvement in comprehension. However, it helped give readers insights into their reading process, comprehension obstacles encountered and insufficiencies in their strategy repertoire. Due to individual cognitive and metacognitive development prior to training intervention, strategies did not remain mere concepts, they became tools to be used. This gave the readers the language to exhibit, discuss and demonstrate use of strategies by self and learn those used by others.

Collaborative learning became effective because of this individual cognitive and metacognitive growth since readers had the language to discuss strategies and their purposes. Peer collaboration, social think aloud, and strategy discussion-demonstration-sharing activities helped learners learn about alternative strategies which resulted in conscious adoption and use of repair strategies once a comprehension deficit was identified. Consequently improvement in reading performance was demonstrated by all.

Finally, learner interviews showed that participating in collaborative reading and group think aloud activities with more able peers gave readers insight into the reading process of good readers; they were able to observe a reader in action. It not only taught them good use of some effective strategies, but also the assurance that everyone encounters problems while reading as well as the confidence that one can successfully control and manage one's reading process.

Conclusion

The brief strategy training resulted in the following changes:

1. Learners grew more aware of their own reading process which resulted in conscious use of repair strategies.
2. All learners started to use new reading strategies gained from peers consciously and effectively.
3. All learners demonstrated improvement in task performance.
4. Readers gained confidence to read independently.

The peer-led collaborative strategy training programme gave explicit evidence for internalization of interactions between learners and their more capable peers. This research points out that dialogues with self should precede dialogue with and observation of others if collaborative learning is to achieve its full potential. All readers were found to model high-level metacognitive skills that guided them to regulate their thinking while reading a text, monitor actions and deploy contextually appropriate strategies choosing from a rich repertoire.

Socio-constructivism believes that lifelong learning should create opportunities for learners to engage and re-engage in learning with fellow members of their society (Elliott, 1999). Autonomy can best be promoted by creating opportunities for social learning. The underlying assumption of this research is that interaction with others can lead to individual cognitive development only if the individual has achieved a certain threshold level of cognitive growth. Discussions with self to understand one's cognitive processes can pave the way to better deployment of discussion with others. This strategy training programme provides evidence that comprehension obstacles caused by topic unfamiliarity or language deficits can be overcome when learners are allowed to interact with a heterogeneous peer group which helps gain exposure to a variety of strategies and enhanced metacognition. This holds immense promise for exploiting individual and group language resources to facilitate reading performance in academic contexts.

A significant contribution made by this research is the inclusion of social interaction and collaboration, two essential twenty-first-century life skills, in the design of the strategy training programme. The core of the opportunity posed by the strategy training as envisaged in this chapter is that the central purpose of learning with peers is to "learn how to do something better" (Novak, 2010), and that collaborative learning should lead to individual gains.

References

Abersold, J. A., & Field, M. L. (1997). *From reader to reading teacher. Issues and strategies for second language classrooms*. Cambridge, UK: Cambridge University Press.
Alexander, P. A., & Jetton, T. L. (2000). Learning from text: A multidimensional and developmental perspective. In M. L. Kamil, P. B. Mosenthal, P. D. Pearson & R. Barr (Eds.), *Handbook of reading research* (Vol. III, pp. 285–310). Mahwah, NJ: Erlbaum.
Anderson, J. R. (1982). Acquisition of cognitive skill. *Psychological Review, 89,* 369–406.
Anderson, N. J. (2002). *The role of metacognition in second language teaching and learning. ERIC clearinghouse on language and linguistics*. Retrieved April 2016 from http://files.eric.ed.gov/fulltext/ED463659.pdf.
Anderson, K. M. (2007). Tips for teaching: Differentiating instruction to include all students. *Preventing School Failure, 51*(3), 49–53. https://doi.org/10.3200/PSFL.51.3.49-54.
Auerbach, E., & Paxton, D. (1997). 'It's not the English thing': Bringing reading research into the ESL classroom. *TESOL Quarterly, 31,* 237–261.
Benson, P. (2011). *Teaching and researching autonomy*. London, UK: Longman.
Bernhardt, E. B. (2005). Progress and procrastination in second language reading. *Annual Review of Applied Linguistics, 24,* 133–150.
Bhatia, S. (2009). Vision 2010. *The Times of India*. December 28.
Birch, B. M. (2007). *English L2 reading: Getting to the bottom* (2nd ed.). Mahwah, NJ: Erlbaum.
Bonk, C. J., & Cunningham, D. J. (1998). Searching for learner-centered, constructivist, and sociocultural components of collaborative educational learning tools. In C. J. Bonk & K. S. King (Eds.), *Electronic collaborators: Learner-centered technologies for literacy, apprenticeship, and discourse* (pp. 25–50). Mahwah, NJ: Erlbaum.
Bonnett, M., & Cuypers, S. (2003). Autonomy and authenticity in education. In N. Blake, P. Smeyers, R. Smith, & P. Standish (Eds.), *The Blackwell guide to the philosophy of education* (pp. 326–340). London: Blackwell.
Boud, D. (1981). *Developing student autonomy in learning*. London: Kogan Page.
Bown, J. (2009). Self-regulatory strategies and agency in self-instructed language learning: A situated view. *The Modern Language Journal, 93*(4), 571–583.

Carrell, P. L. (1983). Some issues in studying the role of schemata or background knowledge in second language comprehension. *Reading in a Foreign Language, 1,* 81–92.

Carrell, P. L. (1989). Metacognitive awareness and second language reading. *The Modern Language Journal, 73*(2), 121–134.

Chamot, A. U. (2005). Language learning strategy instruction: current issues and research. *Annual Review of Applied Linguistics, 25*: 112–130.

Chamot, A. U., & O`Malley, J. M. (1994). *The CALLA handbook: Implementing the cognitive academic language learning approach.* White Plains, NY: Addison Wesley Longman.

Claxton, G. (1996). Implicit theories of learning. In G. Claxton, T. Atkinson, M. Osborn, & M. Wallace (Eds.), *Liberating the learner: Lessons for professional development in education* (pp. 45–56). London: Routledge.

Cohen, A. D., & Macaro, E. (Eds.). (2007). *Language learner strategies. Thirty years of research and practice.* Oxford: Oxford University Press.

Cohen, Andrew. (2003*). Strategy training for second language learners. ERIC clearinghouse on language and linguistics.* Retrieved April 2016 from http://www.cal.org/resources/digest/0302cohen.html.

Coiro, J. (2003). Reading comprehension on the Internet: Expanding our understanding of reading comprehension to encompass new literacies. *The Reading Teacher, 56*(5), 458–464.

Coiro, J., & Dobler, E. (2007). Exploring the online reading comprehension strategies used by sixth grade skilled readers to search for and locate information on the Internet. *Reading Research Quarterly, 42,* 214–257.

Collins, A., Brown, J. S., & Newman, S. E. (1989). Cognitive apprenticeship: Teaching the crafts of reading, writing, and mathematics. In L. B. Resnick (Ed.), *Knowing, learning, and instruction: Essays in honor of Robert Glaser* (pp. 453–494). Hillsdale, NJ: Lawrence Erlbaum Associates.

Dansereau, D. F. (1985). Learning strategy research. In J. W. Segal, S. F. Chipman, & R. Glaser (Eds), *Thinking and learning skills: Vol 1. Relating instruction to research.* Hillsdale, NJ: Erlbaum, 209–239.

Devine, J. (1993). The role of metacognition in second language reading and writing. In J. G. Carson & I. Leki (Eds.), *Reading in the composition classroom: Second language perspectives* (pp. 105–127). Boston: Heinle and Heinle.

Dickinson, L. (1995). Autonomy and motivation. A literature review. *System, 23*(2), 165–174.

Dörnyei, Z., & Ryan, Stephen. (2015). *The psychology of the language learner revisited.* New York: Routledge.

Eggen, P., & Kaucbak, D. (1995). *Strategies for teachers: Teaching content and thinking skills.* Boston: Allyn and Bacon.

Elliott, Geoffrey. (1999). *Lifelong learning. The politics of new learning environment.* London: Jessica Kingsley Publishers.

Ertmer, P., & Newby, T. (1996). The expert learner: Strategic, self-regulated, and reflective. *Instructional Science, 24,* 1–24.

Faerch, C., & Kasper, Gabriele (Eds.). (1983). *Strategies in interlanguage communication.* New York: Longman.

Flavell, J. H. (1978). Metacognitive development. In J. M. Scandura & C. Brainerd, (Eds.), *Structural/Process theories of complex human behaviour* (pp. 21–245). Alphenan der Rijn, Netherlands: Sijtoff and Noordhoff.

Garb, E. (2000). Maximizing the potential of young adults with visual impairments: The metacognitive element. *Journal of Visual Impairment and Blindness, 94*(9), 574–583.

García, G. E., Jiménez, R. T., & Pearson, P. D. (1998). Metacognition, childhood bilingualism, and reading. In D. Hacker, J. Dunlowsky, & A. Graesser, *Metacognition in educational theory and practice* (pp. 200–248). Mahwah, NJ: Lawrence Erlbaum.

Grenfell, M., & Macaro, E. (2007). Claims and critiques. In A. D. Cohen & E. Macaro (Eds.), *Language learner strategies. Thirty years of research and practice* (pp. 9–28). Oxford: Oxford University Press.

Hauck, M. (2005). Metacognitive knowledge, metacognitive strategies, and CALL. In J. L. Egbert, & G. Petrie (Eds.), *CALL research perspectives. ESL and applied linguistics professional series* (pp. 65–86). New Jersey: Lawrence Erlbaum.

Holec, H. (1981). *Autonomy and foreign language learning*. Oxford: Pergamon Press.

Hurd, S., & Lewis, T. (Eds). (2008). *Language learning strategies in independent settings*. Clevedon: Multilingual Matters.

Hutchins, E. (1995). *Cognition in the wild*. Cambridge, MA: MIT Press.

Jacobs, J. E., & Paris, S. G. (1987). Children's metacognition about reading: Issues in definition, measurement and instruction. *Educational Psychologist, 22*, 255–278.

Jimenez, R., Garcia, G., & Pearson, P. (1996). The reading strategies of bilingual Latina/o students who are successful English readers: opportunities and obstacles. *Reading Research Quarterly, 31*, 90–112.

Johnson, Keith (Ed.). (2005). *Expertise in second language learning and teaching*. New York: Palgrave Macmillan.

Kolers, P. A. (1970). Three stages of reading. In H. Levin & J. P. Williams (Eds.), *Basic studies on reading*. New York: Basic Books.

Lee, J. F., & VanPatten, B. (2003). *Making communicative language teaching happen* (2nd ed.). New York: McGraw.

Leu, D. J., O'Byrne, W. I., Zawilinski, L., McVerry, J. G., & Everett-Cacopardo, H. (2009). Expanding the new literacies conversation. *Educational Researcher, 38*, 264–269.

Little, D. (1991). *Learner autonomy. Definitions, issues, and problems*. Dublin: Authentik Language Learning Resources Ltd.

Longworth, N., & Davies, W. K. (1996). *Lifelong learning: New vision, new implications, new roles for people, organizations, nations and communities in the 21st century*. London: Kogan Page.

Macaro, E. (2001). *Learning strategies in foreign and second language classrooms*. New York: Continuum.

Mokhtari, K., & Reichard, C. (2002). Assessing students' metacognitive awareness of reading skills. *Journal of Educational Psychology, 94*(2), 249–259. http://citeseerx.ist.psu.edu/viewdoc/download?doi=10.1.1.456.5716&rep=rep1&type=pdf.

Niemi, H. (2002). Active learning. A cultural change needed in teacher education and schools. *Teaching and Teacher Education, 18*, 763–780.

Novak, J. D. (2010). *Learning, creating and using knowledge. Concept maps as facilitative tools in schools and corporations*. New York: Routledge.

Nunan, David. (1991). *Language teaching methodology*. London: Prentice Hall International.

Omaggio, A. (1993). *Teaching language in context*. Boston: Heinle & Heinle.

O'Malley, J. M., & Chamot, A. U. (1990). *Learning strategies in second language acquisition*. Cambridge: Cambridge University Press.

Oxford, Rebecca L. (1990). *Language learning strategies. What every teacher should know*. Boston: Heinle and Heinle Publishers.

Oxford, Rebecca L. (1994). *Language learning strategies: An update*. ERIC clearinghouse on languages and linguistics.

Palincsar, A. M., & Brown, A. L. (1986). Reciprocal teaching of comprehension monitoring activities. *Cognition and Instruction I*: 117–175.

Piaget, J. (1957). *Construction of reality in the child*. London: Routledge and Kegan Paul.

Pressley, M. (2000). What should comprehension instruction be the instruction of? In M. L. Kamil, P. B. Mosenthal, P. D. Pearson, & R. Barr (Eds.), *Handbook of reading research* (Vol. 3, pp. 545–561). Mahwah, NJ: Lawrence Erlbaum.

Pressley, M., & Afflerbach, P. (1995). *Verbal protocols of reading: The nature of constructively responsive reading*. Hillsdale, NJ: Erlbaum.

Rosenblatt, L. M. (1978). *The reader, the text, the poem: The transactional theory of the literary work*. Carbondale, IL: Southern Illinois University.

Rubin, J. (2005). The expert language learner: A review of good language learner studies and learner strategies. In K. Johnson (Ed.), *Expertise in second language learning and teaching* (pp. 37–63). New York: Palgrave Macmillan.

Rumelhart, D. E. (1977). Toward an interactive model of reading. In S. Dornic (Ed.), *Attention and performance* (Vol. VI, pp. 573–603). New York: Academic Press.

Salomon, G. (1993). *Distributed cognitions: Psychological and educational considerations*. New York: Cambridge University Press.

Spiro, R. J., et al. (1997). *Schemata as scaffolding for the representation of information in connected discourse*. Bolt Beranek and Newman Inc. Report no. 24. Cambridge, Massachusetts.

Stanovich, K. (1980). Toward an interactive-compensatory model of individual differences in the development of reading fluency. *Reading Research Quarterly, 16,* 32–71.

Swaffar, J. K., Arens, K., & Byrnes, H. (1991). *Reading for meaning*. New Jersey: Prentice Hall.

To read or not to read. (2007). Research Report no. 47. Washington, DC: The National Endowment for the Arts. Retrieved June 30, 2017 from https://www.arts.gov/sites/default/files/ToRead.pdf.

The Rose Review. (2008). *An independent review of the primary school curriculum*. DCSF Publications, Nottingham. Retrieved June 30, 2017 from http://www.educationengland.org.uk/documents/pdfs/2009-IRPC-final-report.pdf.

Vygotsky, L. S. (1978). *Mind in society: The development of higher psychological processes*. Cambridge, MA: Harvard University Press.

Wadsworth, B. J. (2004). *Piaget's theory of cognitive and affective development: foundations of constructivism*. NJ: Allyn and Bacon.

Warschauer, M. (1997). Computer-mediated collaborative learning: Theory and practice. *The Modern Language Journal, 81,* 470–481.

Warschauer, M., & Kern, R. (2000). *Network-based language teaching: Theory and practice*. Cambridge: Cambridge University Press.

Weinstein, C., & Mayer, R. (1986). The teaching of learning strategies. In M. C. Wittrock (Ed.), *Handbook of research on teaching* (pp. 315–327). New York: Macmillan.

Wenden, A., & Rubin, J. (Eds.). (1987). *Learner strategies in language learning*. Cambridge: Prentice-Hall.

Wenden, A. L. (1991). *Learner strategies in language learning*. Englewood Cliffs, NJ: Prentice Hall.

Wild, M., & Heck, J. (2011). *Expert learners*. http://www.expertlearners.com/el.php.

Woolfolk, Anita. (2004). *Educational psychology*. Boston, MA: Allyn and Bacon.

Zhang, L. J. (2001). Awareness in reading: EFL students' metacognitive knowledge of reading strategies in an acquisition-poor environment. *Language Awareness, 10,* 268–288.

Chapter 6
Using L1 Reading Strategies to Develop L2 Reading

Mahananda Pathak

Abstract This chapter reports an exploration of whether reading capabilities and strategies can be transferred from one language to another with the help of carefully developed instruction. This exploration is grounded in Indian multilingual reality and focuses on children studying in an Assamese (the official state language of Assam, one of the north-eastern states of India) regional-medium, under-resourced government primary school. The underlying premise is that the reading capabilities and strategies that exist in their more enabled language or 'own language' (Cook in Translation in language teaching: an argument for reassessment. Oxford University Press, Oxford, 2010), Assamese, can be transferred and exploited to develop reading capabilities in their second language, English. Children who are learning to read in a second language, by default, possess knowledge of the first language, literacy, reading capability and some strategies. However, these previous reading experiences are not recognized and even more rarely explored in the context of teaching reading in ESL classrooms. Such an exploration becomes essential in the context of Indian bi/multilingualism where children live with, and more importantly, very often function in at least two languages with considerable ease. Adopting a variant of the strategy-based instruction model (SBI model), Class VI children with minimum levels of both Assamese proficiency and English literacy were taught for about three weeks using Assamese–English parallel texts and tasks. The teaching intervention showed that children could infer the meaning of words and sentences in context, use background knowledge, word and world knowledge to comprehend text and use text-referring words. This enabling in English was made possible through an awareness and exploitation of existing reading strategies in Assamese, namely, word analysis, text and reader-initiated strategies and those using knowledge about language(s).

Keywords Reading capabilities · Reading strategies · Indian bi/multilingualism Strategy-based instruction model · Using knowledge about language(s)

M. Pathak (✉)
Department of Materials Development, Testing and Evaluation,
The English and Foreign Languages University, Tarnaka, Hyderabad 500007, India
e-mail: mahanandap@gmail.com

© Springer Nature Singapore Pte Ltd. 2018
R. Joseph Ponniah and S. Venkatesan (eds.), *The Idea and Practice of Reading*,
https://doi.org/10.1007/978-981-10-8572-7_6

Introduction

Children who are learning to read in an L2, by default, possess knowledge of the first language, literacy, reading capability and some strategies. In other words, L2 reading has access to various other resources including the L1. As Upton and Lee-Thompson rightly state, "Reading in a second language (L2) is not a monolingual event; L2 readers have access to their first language (L1) as they read, and many use it as a strategy to help comprehend an L2 text" (2001: 469). Such children's attempts at learning to read in a second language need to be perceived as providing opportunities to help them build on existing skills and also enable them to transfer skills from one language to another. Furthermore, for second-language learners, literacy knowledge from the first language must be perceived as something that can assist them to acquire high levels of reading comprehension in the second language (Bialystok, 2001). Reading capability in the first language has to be valued as a rich repertoire of resources that can be used to enable reading comprehension in a second language. If these resources are not exploited, it is like asking the children to keep their languages in two parts of the brain, thus creating 'semi-linguals'. In a grassroots multilingual country like India, where individuals switch between languages with ease as and when required, this would be like placing the two languages in two separate compartments. This, unfortunately, is the reality in most language classrooms in the country.

Teachers in English-language classrooms in India do not seem to be making use of their children's capability in L1. The ESL reading class, if it can be called that, is confined to some common, routinized classroom practices such as rote recitation of the alphabet, choral sounding out of a story word by word, repeating a sound and word a dozen times, copying the letters of the alphabet correctly over and over again, breaking down words into letters and sentences into words, 'explaining' a reading text followed by the dictation of answers to comprehension questions given in the text. Hence this attempt to use or rather build on the foundation of children's L1 (Assamese) reading strategies to enable reading comprehension in an L2 (English). The argument made in this chapter is that with assistance and training, teachers can be encouraged and enabled to use children's existing L1 reading strategies to develop L2 reading capabilities. It is hoped that eventually children will become confident, successful and proficient L2 readers.

Research on Reading Strategies Instruction

In L1 context, current research on strategy instruction is confined to the use of and training in various strategies such as summarizing, predicting, imaging, monitoring, using prior knowledge and forming questions for comprehension. However, there is a relative dearth of research focusing on L2 reading strategies instruction (Grabe, 2009: 239). There are some studies, however, that have been done; these span students from three continents, ranging in age from 15 to 40. The proficiency levels range from high to intermediate. The nature of the research has been both descriptive and interventional with some quantitative studies. Most of the studies, however, have used think-aloud protocols to capture strategy use in instructional contexts.

Carrell, Pharis, and Liberto (1989) reported a study on metacognitive strategy training for ESL reading. The research questions were: (a) Does metacognitive strategy training enhance L2 reading? (b) If so, does one type of strategy training facilitate L2 reading better than another? and (c) How is the effectiveness of metacognitive strategy training related to the learning styles of the students? The participants were 26 ESL students, with a wide range of first languages, in Level 4 of the intensive programme of the Center for English as a Second Language (CESL) at Southern Illinois University, USA. After a four-day training period, results showed that metacognitive strategy training (in semantic mapping and the experience-text relationship) was effective in developing second-language reading, and that the effectiveness of one type of training versus another may depend upon the way reading is measured. Also, the effectiveness of the training was related to differences in the learning styles of the students.

Kern (1989) also worked with university students with low to high levels of proficiency. He focused on two cognate languages, English and French, and investigated the effect of direct instruction of word, sentence and discourse analysis strategies on reading comprehension. He divided his subjects (53) into experimental and control groups. Pre- and post-tests for comprehension revealed that only the lower-ability students achieved a statistically significant gain in comprehension.

Raymond (1993) again worked with the English–French combination of languages and investigated the effects of structure strategy training on the comprehension of expository prose. The participants were 43 native English-speaking students learning French as a second language. He compared two groups of participants: a group that was taught five top-level structure strategies and a group that received no training. The selected strategies were: (1) description; (2) collection; (3) causation; (4) problem solution; and (5) comparison. The reason behind this selection was the frequency of their occurrence in the reading of prose. The participants were asked to read a text, complete a questionnaire and then do a written recall (in English). The study showed that after the treatment, the experimental group outperformed the control group by recalling more idea units from one text. This implies that training in structure strategy helped increase the amount of idea units recalled. It also showed that structure strategy use is a characteristic of skilled second-language readers. However, Raymond reiterates the need for more research that will explore the interaction of many different variables such as text content, reader interest, text difficulty and background knowledge with L2 reading comprehension.

Kitajima (1997) used a combination of word-level and metacognitive strategies for his strategy-based instruction programme with two non-cognate language.

It was located in the USA and examined whether or not strategy training that orients American college students' attention toward referential processes would help them comprehend a Japanese narrative. At the end of fifteen weeks of intervention, the experimental group of students comprehended the story at the macro level significantly better than the control group.

Bimmel, van den Bergh, and Oostdam (2001) reported on the effects of a strategies intervention study. Strategies for reading comprehension were taught both in L1 (Dutch) and English (L2), in the hope that strategies would be successfully transferred from L1 to L2. The four reading strategies were: looking for key fragments, paying attention to structure marking elements (hinge words), making up questions (questioning) and mapping the most important information from a text (semantic mapping). Students had to work in pairs on the execution of reading tasks following a consciousness-raising method, consisting of an orientation phase in which they explored the reading tasks and selected a reading strategy, a practice/application phase in which actual performance took place and a verbalization phase, in which the steps that lead to a correct solution had to be formulated explicitly. On the basis of this programme, 15-year-old Dutch students from the third year of regular secondary education ($N = 12$) were trained in applying these reading strategies while reading in their first language (Dutch). The results were compared with those of a control group ($N = 119$). The results showed that the training programme had an effect on the mastery of the four strategic reading activities and led to a substantial improvement of the reading comprehension in the first language (Dutch). The transfer effects for L2 reading, however, could not be determined.

Dreyer and Nel (2003) outlined the format and structure of a strategic reading instruction component of an English for Professional Purposes course offered within a technology-enhanced environment. Their study addressed the following research questions: (a) What does the reading comprehension and reading strategy use profile of first-year students at Potchefstroom University, South Africa look like? (b) Did the students in the experimental group attain statistically and practically significantly higher mean scores on their end-of-semester English, Communication and TOEFL reading comprehension tests than the control group, and did they differ significantly in terms of their reading strategy use? After participating in a thirteen-week strategic reading instruction module offered in the university, it was found that the experimental group differed statistically and practically significantly from the control group on all the reading comprehension measures. This was true for both successful and at-risk students.

The above studies were carried out in non-Indian contexts: America, Canada, the Netherlands and South Africa. There is very little research on this area from India. Three such studies rooted in the Indian context are presented below.

Indian Research Studies on Strategy Instruction

The first study, by Jose (2000), aims to make learners more independent in reading by generating awareness of reading strategies. She argues for a learner-chosen strategy training programme. Twenty adult ESL learners (graduates and postgraduates) who joined an English proficiency course in the Central Institute of English and Foreign Languages, Hyderabad participated in this study. Results showed that an awareness of and exposure to alternative strategies such as active reading strategies (chiefly strategies to get the meaning of unfamiliar vocabulary), comprehension monitoring strategies and metacognitive strategies (summarizing and self-evaluation) led to enhanced reading comprehension, manifested in improved task performance. As a result of learners' increased strategy repertoire, the readers also gained confidence and attempted independent reading.

Kaw (2006) attempted to find the role played by questioning in the teaching of reading comprehension in ESL classrooms. Her study provided an empirical justification for the use of questions in teaching second-language reading. Question-rich teaching sessions were conducted for a stipulated period of time to find out whether persistent questioning helps in making learners autonomous. The teaching sessions were based on question–answer exchanges with questions that were cognitively varied. In the feedback sessions, instead of giving away the correct answers to questions, the teacher posed further questions with the aim of simplifying the questions, helping the learners to understand the focus of the question and directing their attention to the textual clues that hold the correct answer.

The subjects for this study were 29 Class VIII students studying English as a second language in a Kendriya Vidyalaya, Hyderabad, Telangana. The findings of the study showed that the children copied answers (from the textbook) much less in the post-intervention test. It also showed that allowing learners to discover answers for themselves was beneficial as it helped them to grow autonomous and self-reliant in getting the meaning out of a text which meant that their cognitive problems in processing textual information had decreased.

Rajasekhar (2006) chose to work with three specific strategies—imagination, elaboration, prediction and confirmation (IEPC), semantic impression and mind modelling—to teach a group of Class 7, 8 and 9 students studying in a Navodaya Vidyalaya, Peddapuram, East Godavari district, Andhra Pradesh. As a result of the teaching, his students participated actively in class, became more articulate and responded to questions more confidently. The study does not document a pre- and post-intervention test but does claim that their comprehension abilities had increased. This claim is based only on teacher plausibility and in-class ongoing evaluation.

A critical look at both Indian and non-Indian studies reveals that the nature of the two languages that feature in them plays an important part. Two of the six studies dealt specifically with non-cognate languages, English and Japanese, and Afrikaans/Setswana and English. One study had a range of first languages but focused on English as a second or foreign language. The others all dealt with cognate languages. Cognitive strategies may transfer across non-cognate languages with ease, but it is possible that comprehension strategies need deliberate and focused instruction, when the distance across the two languages is vast and the script is also different.

The age group covered in these studies is another difference. The range is from eleven to 40; this implies that the focus has not been on younger children, with lower levels of proficiency. The nine research studies have either used inferential statistical measures or think-aloud protocols to capture strategy use. Also, although interventional, very few have attempted to capture developmental growth in reading comprehension. Therefore, there is a need to carry out research on strategy instruction with younger learners. Hence this attempt to work with children who are between the ages of ten and eleven, who are first-generation learners coming from homes with poor reading environments.

Proposing Hypothesis

Very few studies have attempted to explore the using of reading comprehension ability in a first language (that is not similar in structure to the language under focus) as a base to enable capability in the second. Moreover, there are hardly any studies that have attempted this with young first-generation learners. As such, the research questions posited were tentative and exploratory in nature, rather than attempting confirmation of existing work. The study has attempted to answer the following research questions:

- What are the aspects of reading capabilities of primary level Class VI bilingual children in Assam which are transferable from L1 (Assamese) to L2 (English)?
- How can these aspects of reading be tapped to enable this transfer to happen from Assamese to English?
- What are the reading strategies that exist in Assamese that can be tapped to enable this transfer to happen?
- Which of these strategies will be successful and will therefore enable reading comprehension in English?

In order to determine success in reading comprehension, the following hypotheses were postulated. By the end of the intervention, the Class VI regional-medium children will be able to:

- identify words, and infer meaning in context and sentence-level discourse;
- use text and background knowledge, word and world knowledge to answer comprehension questions;
- use knowledge of text structure to locate information and restate it;
- use knowledge of text-referring words (pronominals, adjectives) and be able to indicate their referents.

It needs to be remembered, however, that this intervention is not one that is governed by strategy-based instruction (SBI) (Rubin, Chamot, Harris, & Anderson, 2007: 141). This widely used SBI model is based on the demonstration and explanation of strategies and their conscious application by learners in new settings. Although there is some instruction of 'strategy', it is always done in an indirect or rather inconspicuous manner, through the use of texts and tasks. Texts which were age, proficiency-level, and background and cultural knowledge appropriate were selected. Suitable tasks that were in the zone of proximal development (Vygotsky, 1978) were created. Through the 'doing' of these tasks it was assumed that many strategies would be tapped and transferred. In other words, this can be a variant of SBI model, which seeks to activate certain strategies for the reading of L1 texts, and then facilitate/encourage their application in dealing with L2 texts with scaffolding provided by parallel tasks rather than direct instructions.

Design of the Study

Subjects

The intervention study was two weeks long and had eight Class VI Assamese-English children as subjects. They were aged ten to eleven and had a minimum of three years of exposure to English. For purposes of confidentiality and ethics the children have all been given pseudonyms such as Karabi and Kaberi (twins), Barsha, Anjali, Manisha (5 girls), and Manash, Rahul and Rohan (3 boys). Nearly fifteen lessons had to be held over 20 days to 'teach' the tasks. The timings were outside school hours (7–8 a.m. and 5–6 p.m.) as the schools did not allow such teaching to happen.

Locality

Participating children were from a remote village named Garemari, Barpeta district, Assam, one of the north-eastern states of India. Barpeta district is located in the western part of Assam, nearly 150 km from the capital city, Guwahati. Garemari is situated in the eastern part of the Barpeta district, sharing borders with Nalbari and Baksha districts. The Tihu-Doomni road (also popularly known as Saahebor Aali), one of the oldest roads in the district, passes through Garemari. The Bodoland Territorial Council (BTC) has elevated the portions which pass through their area to *pukka/pucca* road. However, the remaining portion is still lying as *kutcha* road, adding woe to the remoteness of the village.

The linguistic map of Garemari is quite complex with many languages: standard varieties of Assamese, Hindi for some specific purposes, and Bodo (or Boro), a language of the Tibeto-Burmese family, whenever the need arises. However, the people of Garemari and a few other neighbouring villages use a particular dialect called 'Bajaali dialect', part of the Kamrupi group of dialects, in their day-to-day life, which influences school instruction as well. Officially, standard Assamese is the medium of instruction but the teacher and the students use a lot of their dialect both inside and outside the classroom.

Reading Capabilities and Strategies of Class VI Children Across Two Languages

The children in Class VI could:

- locate print on a page very easily and had sufficient knowledge of left-to-right direction of print while reading,
- identify the front and back side of a book and identify the starting point of reading on a page,
- figure out the top and bottom of a page as well as a picture,
- point out the first and last word of a particular page in both languages,
- point out the end of the story in English after the instruction for the tasks was translated into Assamese,
- handle *juktakkhor* or cluster *akshara* that retain most of the original symbol details,
- read words given in the Bajaali dialect.

Furthermore, they had

- the knowledge of print to enable them to distinguish a word from a letter or the space between words in both languages,
- a fairly good amount of word reading ability.

However, it seemed that they did not exhibit, in an overt manner, strategies of reading comprehension. At this level, using their reading capabilities as a base, it was felt that strategies like word analysis, rephrasing a text in a simpler manner, using text structure or background knowledge to understand meaning, and being able to locate key information in the text (by underlining) are probably already being exploited by the children in Assamese. However, it is likely that these are done automatically and are therefore not being transferred to another language. The argument made in this chapter is that children's knowledge and capabilities of using reading strategies in their L1 (Assamese) can be used to develop reading capabilities in an L2 (English).

It was hypothesized that if a 'make them aware by giving a parallel task' trigger was provided, the children would be able to use word analysis and other simple reading strategies like using background knowledge, locating specific information in a text, and using time and place indicators. Tasks in the language with more enabled capability, Assamese, would be used as a scaffold to spark off its use in the language with less enabled capability, English.

Procedure

Tasks to Enable Reading Capability in L2 Through L1

The intervention study was conceptualized as consisting of five tasks (Appendix 1), which focused primarily on areas such as words in context, the ability to locate key information (and then use that information to either restate it, use it where needed, or order it in a different manner), using knowledge about language(s). These tasks were graded from easy to difficult, keeping the processing demand and linguistic requirements in mind.

The tasks were conceptualized as similar across the two languages and were to be administered in that manner. As such a coding scheme has been used where the task in L1, Assamese, is mentioned as 1A, 2A etc., where 'A' refers to the Assamese task. This is to be followed by the task in L2, English, and is coded as 1E, 2E etc., where 'E' refers to the English task. It was found prudent to write and deliver all L2 task instructions also in L1 to ensure comprehension and eradicate 'construct irrelevant variance' (Bachman, 1990).

Task Modality

The tasks were bilingual in two ways: first in the format of the task, i.e., first the children were given the task in L1, followed by the parallel L2 task. Second, in the administration of the L2 tasks, all the instructions to these tasks (oral and written) were in the children's L1. The deliberate attempt to use parallel tasks was to filter the declarative knowledge of the children in the best possible way to ensure that the knowledge can be put into use immediately to perform the task in L2 (Macaro, 2001). Thus, it was hoped that the children would very easily be able to perceive the strategy and that transfer would happen with ease.

Scoring Criteria

The two sets of tasks are parallel and make similar demands, except for one task (No. 5) where the amount of information required is different. The marks, however, remain the same. This alone is indicated separately (see Appendix 2).

Plausible L1 Strategies to Enable L2 Reading Comprehension

As mentioned earlier, the transfer of strategies has been rarely attempted with students who are first-generation learners. As such, the choice of strategy selection was governed by the researcher's sense of plausibility (Prabhu, 1987) and has been grounded in an understanding of the actual contexts in which the teaching and learning part of the study would take place. As a teacher-researcher, I had to trust my own 'grounded' self-conceptualization of the strategies that would most effectively improve the reading comprehension of my Class VI, year three of English, Assamese-medium, first-generation learners. From the long list of strategies available, the ones selected included the exploitation of word analysis along with text- and reader-initiated strategies. Since these students are all bilingual learners who can use their knowledge about language(s) to learn another language much earlier and very easily (Mohanty, 1994), strategies that would invoke such knowledge were also added. It is observed that knowledge about own language/known language/L1 and basic cognitive skills are *likely* to transfer to L2 reading and are *unlikely* to be a source of potential interference (Grabe, 2009).

Selected Reading Strategies

From the long list of strategies deemed as teachable, the first one was **word analysis**, part of a strategy broadly called words in context. This strategy involves breaking bigger words into smaller meaningful chunks for an easy decode.

The second set of strategies that I felt could be exploited were **text-initiated strategies** (Jimenez, Garcia, & Pearson, 1996). The first of them is **restating the text**, which requires the student to simply re-write the information given in the text to customize the questions in hand (see tasks 2A and 2E).

The second is **using text structure** which could be viewed as simply using the visual representation of information in the text to comprehend it better (see tasks 3A and 3E). The third is **referring to the context**. Instead of just using text structure to get information, the reader is expected to determine the meaning of an unknown or hitherto unencountered word or a difficult portion of the text by referring to its L1 counterpart (provided of course that the reader has access to the parallel texts/tasks).

Although the learners are only at the primary level of education, I felt that four **reader-initiated strategies** (Jimenez et al. 1996) could also be exploited. The first of these is **using background knowledge**. It involves asking the learner/reader to consciously draw on general knowledge of the world (schema), culture-specific knowledge, formal knowledge, domain knowledge (a threshold level of knowledge about the topic under discussion) while decoding a text. In this context, it was assumed that this was 'tapped' in tasks 1A and 1E where their knowledge of the meaning of the terms 'poor' and 'rich' and its connotations were invoked. **World/word knowledge**, which is the second, is a part of the previous strategy.

World/word knowledge has to be considered an essential component of reading comprehension, since every text takes for granted the readers' familiarity with a lot of facts about the cultural and natural world and knowledge of words. Therefore, readers should be encouraged to apply such facts while reading and comprehending a text during the reading event.

Another reader-initiated strategy which is very important for beginners is the ability to **underline key information**. It includes locating key information in texts and showing it by underlining. In order to do this, it is important to teach learners how to **locate key information** in the text. Children can be taught to detect these by identifying the topic and main ideas, supporting details, by paying attention to connecting words during reading.

At early levels of reading (year 3 of English), it would be assumed that such learners, unless adults, would not possess any knowledge about language(s). While this may be true of monolingual learners, research has shown that bilinguals are able to use such knowledge much earlier (Mohanty, 1994). Accordingly, a few strategies that invoke the use of knowledge about language(s) were also selected as teachable. They are not very complex ones, but I saw them as essential and more importantly, plausible. The first is the use of **text-referring words** in tasks 5A and 5E. This strategy refers to asking learners/readers to pay attention to text-referring words such as pronominals and adjectives and figure out the function of these words in texts to aid comprehension. The second is teaching learners to **form adjectival phrases** such as 'dark clouds' and **adverbial phrases**, using the available knowledge in their first language, Assamese. The third was **awareness of the most basic of punctuation marks, the full stop**. I felt that this, along with an awareness of capital and small letters (a distinction that is not there in Assamese script) could be exploited.

Results and Discussion

Using the scoring criteria (Appendix 2), the responses were analysed in two ways. First the marks were computed and performances compared to find out whether the children were actually able to comprehend reading texts in English. It was observed that the scores of the students as a whole were similar. This may be attributed to their socio-economic background and the print-starved environment that they live in. However, their actual responses were then examined in detail to check whether any of the strategies 'taught' through the Assamese tasks were used to comprehend the English texts and answer the corresponding questions.

Capturing Reading Capability in English

The tasks had five broad areas as their focus: understanding the meaning of words in context, locating and restating information, using text structure, and using knowledge about language(s). Each of these aspects is discussed separately. All tasks were attempted by eight children.

Words in Context

These tasks required the children to activate background knowledge to understand the meaning of words. While observing the performance of the children in the L1, Assamese task and the parallel L2, English task (Appendix 3, Table 6.1), it was noticed that all the children had got the correct answers. This shows that the children were able to activate background knowledge while reading, to infer the meaning of words. This task has implications for the second-language reading class and also in designing classroom activities to facilitate the activation of background knowledge. Culturally familiar content could be incorporated to activate background knowledge. The explicit teaching of appropriate background information will facilitate second-language reading.

Locating Key Information

Information in a text can be stated both explicitly and implicitly. To identify and process text-explicit information, one needs to locate a key word or a phrase in a text, whereas to decipher text-implicit information one needs to go beyond mere location (Koda, 2005: 230–38). Such deciphering demands inferencing.

Locating and restating: This was the focus of tasks 2A and 2E. It required the student to locate the key information and state it as an answer to a comprehension question. The performance in the L1 Assamese task (Appendix 3, Table 6.2) shows that the children can locate specific information in texts. However, the L2 English task, 2E, created problems for all the children except one. This task required the reader to define a polyglot. But the children provided an example of a polyglot, which is stated explicitly in the statement. This does not mean that they cannot locate the specific information in the text. A post-task discussion with the children revealed that the wording of the question misled them. Once the task was clarified by the teacher-researcher, Kaberi and Rahul got it perfectly correct, which included the definition of a polyglot with an example.

It was interesting to note that those who performed poorly in the L1 Assamese task also performed poorly in the L2 English task. They randomly copied words from the given text as an answer to the question. Hence, Kaberi, Manisha, Rahul and Rohan scored 0 in the L2 task. One of the children (Manash) got the first item of the English task correct, but the second item was wrong. Although both the items focused on the same sub-skills of reading, the performance in both the tasks varied. This may be because in the first item the text matched the cultural background of the reader. However, in the second item, there was a mismatch between the text and the reader because of the unfamiliar text. Hence, the comprehension was higher in the first item than in the second one. In other words, the child made incorrect inferences and distortion such as "The Flamenco is Spain" (Grabe, 2009) appeared in the second item as an answer.

Locating and using appropriately: This task expected the children to identify information available in a text and write it in the appropriate box in a chart. The marks obtained by all eight students in task 3A (Appendix 3, Table 6.3) show that the children can locate specific information in a text, and use it appropriately in correct places. This suggests that they can separate and identify content words (noun, e.g., all kinship terms such as father, mother and grandfather) from function words (determiners, pronouns) in sentences. They can also represent/reproduce information, which is a combination of content and function words, as broken into two content words. Only Manash could not distinguish between the content word and the function word, and therefore, copied both the words (*bhani dujani* means two sisters, where *bhani* (sister) is a content word and *dujani* (two) is a function word) as an answer.

While reviewing the marks obtained by the students in the third English task, 3E, it was noticed that those children who scored low in the Assamese task also performed badly in the English task. They could not separate the content words from the function words and therefore copied the entire portion (e.g., "mother does work at home", "mother does") and included unnecessary words like 'two', 'little' from the text.

Locating and ordering: This reading comprehension task is based on the chronology of events in an individual's life. Children have to read the passage and answer questions with the help of time-referring words to express chronology of events such as *aagot* (before), *paasot* (after), *taar paasot* (after that), *xei xomoyot* (during that time). The results (Appendix 3, Table 6.4) show that all the children got two of the five statements given in item 1 in the Assamese task 4A, wrong. These two statements (i) and (v) were not directly taken from the reading passage, unlike the other three statements. These two statements were based on a sentence in the reading passage. One was presented as a general statement about Bishnu Rabha's higher education in Calcutta and the other stated the names of the institutions he attended in Calcutta. This probably misled the children, and led them to answer incorrectly. However, all the children scored full marks in the *wh*-question and the true-false one.

While reviewing the children's performance in this reading comprehension task in English, 4E, it was noticed that all the children could rearrange the facts of

Kalpana Chawla's life correctly. The children later informed the researcher in one of the informal post-task discussions, that the knowledge of time indicators in the L1 task and numerals helped them to complete the task correctly. The children also performed well in the three other 'literal questions' in the text. The first question provided the scope to copy directly from the text, whereas the other two needed slight modifications. In the second question children had to use the noun *Kalpana* rather than its pronominal counterpart 'she'. However, half of the children used 'she' or rather copied the third sentence of the passage "She liked flying and aerobatics most" instead of "Kalpana liked flying and aerobatics most" as an answer. In the third question, where there was less scope for copying from the text, two of the children wrote only the expansion of NASA 'National Aeronautics and Space Administration', and not the whole answer: "The full form of NASA is 'National Aeronautics and Space Administration'."

Using Knowledge About Language(S)

This task required the children to identify text-referring words such as pronominal antecedents (e.g., they) and adjectival phrases (e.g., blue sky) and show the link between these words and the head words by drawing a line in the text. Performance in the Assamese task (Appendix 3, Table 6.5) shows that the children have a fair knowledge of text-referring words in a text. They can identify and show the relationship between words by drawing lines connecting both the head word and the referring words. However, Rohan identified some unnecessary words like *e-taa* (one-classifier) and missed relevant words such as *thopaa-bor* (bunch of grapes), *xei-bor* (those). As far as the performance in the English task 5E is concerned (Appendix 3, Table 6.6), the children performed reasonably well. None of them could identify 'two boys' which refers to both Manash and Abhijit in the task. However, they identified both the pronominal antecedents 'they' and 'them'. This indicated that the children can identify text-referring words such as pronominal antecedents, but have problem with adjectival phrases like 'two boys'. In line with this Brunerian observation, these children were able to use a pencil to draw linking lines between pronominals and their antecedents. As with other task performances, here too it was noticed that those children who performed badly in the Assamese task also performed badly in the English task. They identified some extra words like 'a', and 'the' as text-referring words which actually do not refer to the nouns in the text.

The purpose of this chapter was to report whether strategy instruction would help the Class VI children to transfer their reading capability from Assamese to English. So, a detailed analysis of the strategies used by them, as revealed in their response sheets, had to be undertaken to capture strategy use.

Capturing Evidence of Strategy Use

Because of the small number of subjects, as the teacher-researcher, I was able to discreetly make a note of the strategies used by the children. Whenever an opportunity presented itself, or was found necessary, strategy use was explored during the intervention. The children were able to employ quite a few strategies while reading texts and comprehending them.

Underlining Key Information While Reading

This reading behaviour was noticed by the researcher during the administration of the Assamese tasks 1A and 2A. While reading the supporting sentences of the tasks, the children underlined the key words and information which gave them a clue and helped them to choose the most appropriate word. This is an early sign of the strategic behaviour of a good reader. It also indicates the children's awareness of one of the important reading comprehension strategies in the beginning stages of reading: **underlining the important parts of texts while reading**. This particular behaviour was deliberately used by the researcher as a teaching aid while the children were engaged in reading the English tasks, 1E and 2E. This behaviour was again observed by the researcher while the children were engaged in tasks 4A and 4E. They underlined the key words of small paragraphs to infer the most appropriate words.

Word Analysis

This strategy involves breaking big words into smaller meaningful parts, also related to task 1E. Children had a problem with reading and understanding the meaning of the word 'businessman' (task 1E, item 1). They were encouraged to break it into smaller parts, i.e., business and man, citing examples such as *xobdokox* (dictionary) *xobdo* (word) and *kox* (a treasury) from their L1. Thus, a simple word analysis strategy can be used efficiently in the classroom to understand meaning and also encourage fluency in oral reading.

Refer to Context/Description in L1 While Reading Its L2 Equivalent

In task 1E, item 2, the children had problems with words like 'thunder and lightning', and 'clouds'. The meanings of those words were unknown to them. Realizing this, I asked the children to look at the description of the Assamese item, since item 2 in the English task is a pragmatic translation of the item used in the L1 task. After a while, they themselves 'identified' the Assamese equivalents of the difficult words and were therefore able to work out the meaning. This suggests that a simple prompt such as 'look at the Assamese item' could help the children to understand the meaning of difficult words in context. In cases where a parallel task does not exist, the teacher could draw their attention to the equivalent word in their respective first/more enabled language.

Form an Adjectival Phrase

A language awareness task, by using children's existing knowledge about L1, was deliberately tried out by the teacher-researcher. The task focused on the phrase 'dark clouds' (used in task 1E, item 2) where dark and cloud were used as an adjective and a noun respectively. The children provided the Assamese equivalent as *kolaa megh*. They were then encouraged to develop a similar combination in L1 focusing on the meaning of the expression, which resulted in phrases like *nilaa megh* (blue clouds), *nilaa aakaax* (blue sky), *kolaa aakaax* (dark sky), *phorokaal aakaax* (clear sky). Once these were available, with a little bit of help, the students were able to come up with 'blue sky', 'dark sky', etc. Children coming from an English-poor environment with low levels of proficiency in English would be intimidated by the idea of forming their own compound adjectives. Tapping such ability in the first language is a good second-language teaching and learning strategy.

Apply Word/World Knowledge to Aid Comprehension

The results of the Assamese task (4A) item I, where the children had to order events related to Bishnu Rabha's education, showed that all the children got the sequence of the statements (i) and (v) wrong. This was therefore taken up for further discussion. The teacher-researcher explained in Assamese the chronology of events in Bishnu Rabha's education, relating it to the children's own life. This explanation included a discussion on the various stages of education—primary, secondary and higher education—which can be perceived as a part of shared world knowledge or 'text-to-self/world connection' (Nag & Sircar, 2008: 16). After the explanation, the children were able to arrange the events related to Bishnu Rabha's education in the correct order, starting with the primary education in Dhaka, followed by the Matric examination, then the incident where he left for Kolkata and Koch Bihar for higher studies, according to the reading passage given. This kind of demonstration of connecting ideas presented in a text to one's experience/life/world can be a starting point to teach children how to make connections in reading which will eventually help them to read between the lines.

Knowledge of Full Stop Use

This instance is associated with task 2A, item 1, which required children to locate specific information in a sentence and write answers for definitional *wh*-factual questions. In response to this, Karabi underlined the necessary information in the prompt sentence and copied it as an answer. She even used a comma at the end of the answer rather than a full stop (*daari* in Assamese). This suggests that she could copy information successfully, but was yet to develop the basic knowledge of punctuation. The non-use of *daari* was found in the responses of Kaberi and Manash as well. Interestingly, the non-use of full stops featured in the same set of children in the English task 2E. Therefore, the use of full stops as a punctuation mark (or, in Assamese *daari*) was taken up for discussion.

In a whole-class discussion session, as a response to the teacher-researcher's question, some of the children told me that '|' (*daari*) is used to mark the end of a sentence in Assamese. They also provided some examples to show its use in Assamese. This indicates that the children have the knowledge of the recognition as well as the use of *daari* in their L1. After that, they were informed that in English '.' (full stop) is used to mark the end of an English sentence like the Assamese *daari*. The children understood that there is no difference between Assamese and English as far as the usage of 'full stop' is concerned, but that only the symbol which is used to mark it was different. As a result all the children used the '*daari*/full stop' appropriately in a writing task.

Strategy Instruction Enabled L2 Comprehension

At the beginning of this chapter, research questions were posited regarding the aspects of reading capabilities of Class VI regional-medium children that may transfer from Assamese to English, and the manner in which this transfer would happen. It was also posited that these children are proficient readers in Assamese because they do use some reading strategies, and that some of these, with the help of parallel tasks and necessary instruction/awareness raising, will enable them to read and comprehend texts in English.

The hypotheses postulated are rephrased below as 'can do' descriptors with a qualitative judgement of partial or full success or failure, as the case may be. This is because although scoring criteria were created and marks allotted for every correct answer indicated/written for a reading comprehension question, a mark cannot be equated with the existence or absence of a sub-skill/strategy. Such 'measurement' is not tenable, for in a sense all testing is indirect and the validity of an inference is a matter of degree. As such, the 'can do' descriptors are based on the performance of the children and the marks given and the teacher-researcher's 'sense of plausibility' (Prabhu, 1987). The task numbers that the 'can do' descriptors are based on are given in brackets.

The eight children of Class VI can

- identify words and infer meaning in context (task 1E)
- use text and background knowledge to answer comprehension questions (task 1E, 4E)

- use knowledge of text structure to locate information and restate it (task 2E, 3E)
- use knowledge of text-referring words (pronominals, adjectives) indicate their referents (task 5E).

From the above descriptors, it is apparent that the children were extremely successful with the tasks that required reading comprehension of texts and demanded only an indication of answers through selection or partial one-word/one-sentence responses.

Limitations of the Study

This study cannot be described as a case study, as individual performances and growth and variations between them was not its focus. At the same time, the 'experiment', if it could be called that, was not conducted inside the institution called 'school'. For genuine academic reasons, it had to be conducted in the verandah of the teacher-researcher's house and this meant that an external observer could not be brought in. Thus in a sense, the nature of the study itself, and the nature of data collected, are the two crucial limitations.

Nature of the Study

First, the study was located in a remote part of Assam, and the social and geographical location of this district (Barpeta) imposed certain limitations on it. The study was carried out with school students who study in a village which is situated in the rural area of Barpeta, a district in Lower Assam. This implies that it cannot be replicated within Assam itself without modifications, even, for instance, in the districts of Upper Assam. This is because in Lower Assam certain distinctive dialects are used as the initial mediums of instruction, while in Upper Assam standard Assamese is used. Thus the study may show different results if it is carried out in Upper Assam. On the other hand, it could be argued that the modifications are inherent to such a study and that absolute replication is not an essential condition.

Second, this kind of study is possible only in schools and contexts where both teachers and students share the same 'vernacular language' or dialect. In this sense, this study is narrow, but rooted or grounded in its context.

Another argument that could be made is that the period of the intervention was too short to observe any substantial growth of the children. But unless institutional support is provided, an extended (over a school term) experiment is not possible. If this were feasible then the teacher-researcher would also be the class teacher who could document their own work. Such an 'insider intervention' or rather 'teaching cum observation' would also enable a larger number of tasks for each focused sub-skill/strategy. This would possibly provide a richer picture of growth in the children.

Another problem is that the researcher was the only 'teacher' who tried out the intervention. If one or two more teachers could have been persuaded to also try out the experiment, the study would have benefited from it.

Nature of Data Collection

In terms of the nature of data collection and tools, information about the kind of teaching that was taking place in classes within schools was recorded only in the form of classroom observations and researcher's notes. For practical reasons it was not possible to tape these classes. Video recordings of classroom interactions would have provided richer data. Also, the 'documentation' was done only by the researcher, primarily because no like-minded teacher/researcher who believed in using capability in one language to augment it in another was available. It is possible that because of this, some minute details, which may have contributed to the reliability of the study, were not taken into account.

One argument that is posited in the literature is that classroom observations do not really constitute data. In the words of Byram, "it is an open question as to whether it is at all possible to obtain data through observation that have not been influenced in some way, either by the presence of the observer, or by the data collection procedures themselves" (2004: 517). While this stance has to be accepted, one also has to remember that in the context of this study, no other documentation was possible.

The study also did not have a pre-and a post-test. Performance on the intervention tasks themselves was used as an indicator of 'growth' or rather, 'small gains' (Tharu, 1981). It was felt that in the span of twenty classes, nothing more tangible would have been possible. If institutional support had been available, a lot more could have been accomplished.

Pedagogical Implications

For Instruction

The study has serious implications for instruction, specifically for reading comprehension instruction in the ESL classroom. Strategy instruction could be a central component of reading comprehension instruction to promote strategic reading among learners (in line with Grabe, 2009: 227).

With the beginning-level learner one could think of reading instructions that focus on 'scaffolding' through parallel tasks (both in L1 and L2) and reading texts where children are expected to use certain strategies. With the slightly proficient learner, consistent modelling of strategy use by teachers could be useful. With the advanced learner who can articulate the transfer of strategies, consistent modelling of strategy use by students and retrospective/reflective practice of strategy use by them could promote strategic reading. This way it is hoped that strategy instruction can be embedded in everyday reading instruction rather than being taught as a separate topic/lesson in the classroom.

For Instructional Materials

To represent the societal and individual bi/multilingual nature of Indian society, one could envisage a language curriculum initiated by bilingual word cards followed by theme-based bilingual word cards (e.g., words related to *family*, *festivals*). Bilingual reading passages can then be developed around these words and themes. To create such bilingual reading passages/texts, teachers can use texts that children are reading for other subjects like science and social studies. These 'texts' will enable them to activate background and word/world knowledge very easily for better comprehension. Teachers who teach at the primary level in India can be of great help in the creation of such materials because one teacher handles all the subjects including the languages.

For Teachers' Continuing Professional Development

One valuable by-product of negotiating bilingual tasks/texts with children in the classroom is the discovery of teachers' own knowledge systems, whether in their first language or in English, resulting in a fundamental attitudinal change in teachers who then continue on the path of professional development. Thus, bilingual instructional materials and teaching procedures in language classrooms will indirectly help the teacher to reflect on the usefulness of using the first language as a resource in the English classroom.

Appendix 1

Description of Intervention Tasks in Assamese

Tasks S. No.	Task type	Skills focused	Description
1A	Selected-response item: multiple choice task (McKay, 2006: 99)	*The ability to identify words (noun and adjective) from a context* (Using background knowledge to understand meaning of words) (Grabe, 2009: 74–75)	Children have to read two sets of short texts and fill in the given sentences by choosing the right words given in brackets • The first text is about a person called Anil and his properties. The two options are **rich** and **poor**. Both these options are adjectives and opposite words • The second text is about **rain**. The word **earthquake** is given as a distracter. These two are nouns
2A	Limited production task: very short-answer task (McKay, 2006: 106)	*The ability to locate specific information in a text and restate it as an answer* (Using simple reading strategies such as identifying key information in a sentence stated in-between commas)	This task has two items. The first is a short text (12 words) about Jeng Bihu, a dance form from Assam, followed by one definitional *wh*-factual question and one true/false question. The second has a slightly longer text (21 words) dealing with one of the cultural stalwarts of Assam, Kolaaguru Bishnuprasad Rabha, with two inferential questions, one definitional and one informational. Both questions require the reader to go beyond information explicitly stated in the text
3A	Read-and-do tasks: information transfer (McKay, 2006: 242)	*The ability to locate specific information in a text and use appropriately in correct places* (Processing, selecting and classifying information for diagrammatic representation) (Adapted from Mathew & Kunnan, 2006)	There is a small text about family followed by a visual representation of it, with ten gaps. Children have to read the text and fill the gaps with words and information from the text

(continued)

(continued)

Tasks S. No.	Task type	Skills focused	Description
4A	Read-and-do tasks: ordering of events and short-answer tasks (McKay, 2006: 238)	*The ability to locate and order information in a text by using time indicators/ connectors, numerals* (Adapted from Mathew & Kunnan, 2006)	This is a passage of 121 words describing Kolaaguru Bishnuprasad Rabha's life and education (Natun Path, 2002: 18). It gives details in chronological order and does not have too many inter-sentential connections. The first item asks children to arrange the 'happenings' during his education in the right order. There are five statements about his education. They have to read and arrange them in order by writing 1, 2, 3, etc. in the space provided. These simple statements are not directly taken from the passage. There are subtle changes here and there in terms of language. For example, in statement IV, 'High School Leaving Certificate Examination' is used instead of 'matric' (as used in the text). The second item is a *wh-*question asking the name of Rabha's grandfather. The third is a true/false question related to his education. The first item is a 'literal question' (Gunderson, 2009: 66), whereas the next two are 'inferential questions' (Gunderson, ibid.), which require low-level inference
5A	Read-and-do task: (Objective-type matching task)	*The ability to identify text-referring words such as pronominal antecedents and also understand the function of these words in the text by drawing line/ arrow to indicate the relation to the head words (both nouns)* (Adapted from Grabe, 2009: 246)	The story 'The Fox and the Sour Grapes' is given. Students have to identify and draw lines to words referring to 'fox' and 'grapes'. One example is provided to them

Description of Intervention Tasks in English

Tasks S. No.	Task type	Skill focused	Description
1E	Selected-response item: multiple choice task (McKay, 2006: 99)	*The ability to identify words (noun and adjective) from a context* (Using background knowledge to understand meaning of words) (Grabe, 2009: 74–75)	Children were asked to read two short texts and choose the right words given in brackets. This task is a direct translation of task 1A, only the name of the person involved is different. It has **rich** and **poor**, both adjectives, as two options. The contextual clues are related to the word **rich**. The second sentence is about **rain**. The word **earthquake** is given as a distracter. Both are nouns
2E	Limited production task: short-answer task (McKay, 2006: 106)	*The ability to locate specific information in a text and restate it as an answer* (Using simple reading strategies such as identifying key information in a sentence stated in-between commas)	It has two items, each containing one statement, followed by one definitional literal question. First item is the direct translation of the Assamese task 2A. Second statement is about the flamenco, a Spanish dance
3E	Read-and-do tasks: information transfer (McKay, 2006: 242)	*The ability to locate specific information in a text and use appropriately in correct places* (Processing, selecting and classifying information for diagrammatic representation), (Adapted from Mathew & Kunnan, 2006).	There is a small text about family, followed by a visual representation of it, with ten gaps. Children have to read the text and fill the gaps with words and information from the text
4E	Read-and-do tasks: ordering of events and short-answer tasks (McKay, 2006: 238)	*The ability to locate and order information in a text by using time indicators/ connectors, numerals* (Adapted from Mathew & Kunnan, 2006)	This reading passage contains 88 words describing Kalpana Chawla, who lost her life when she went on a space mission. It gives details about her birth, early life and education in chronological order. The first item asks children to put five statements about Kalpana Chawla's education in the right order. These statements are taken directly from the text with

(continued)

(continued)

Tasks S. No.	Task type	Skill focused	Description
			some minor changes in terms of language. For example, 'passed' is used in statement (i) instead of 'finished', which is used in the text. Similarly, 'started' is used in statement (ii) instead of 'began'. There are two 'literal questions' (Gunderson, 2009: 66) that ask for details about her birth and about NASA, and one 'inferential question', which requires low-level inference (Gunderson, ibid.) about what she likes most
5E	Read-and-do task: spot the text-referring words	*The ability to identify text-referring words such as pronominal antecedents, adjectival phrases and also understanding the function of these words in the text by drawing line/arrow to indicate the relation to the head words (both nouns)* (Adapted from Grabe, 2009: 246)	A small reading passage is given. Students have to identify and draw lines to those words referring to Manash and Abhijit (names of two boys)

Appendix 2

Scoring Criteria Used for Assamese and English Intervention Tasks

Tasks A + E	Score breakdown	Total score
Task 1	1 mark for each correct response	2
Task 2	Answers are usually one word, one or two sentences in length. 1 mark is given for each correct answer regardless of the length	4
Task 3	Answers are one or two words in length. Each correct response carries 1 mark	10

(continued)

(continued)

Tasks A + E	Score breakdown	Total score
Task 4	The first item does not require much writing. The second and the third item can be answered in one or two words or in one sentence. Irrespective of the length of the answers, each correct answer carries 1 mark	7
Task 5A	Score 0.5 marks for each correct response	5
Task 5E	Score 1 mark for each correct response for a total score of 3. Also, 2 marks for the reading of the passage in English. So the total marks for this task are 5	5

Appendix 3

Distribution of Marks for Intervention Tasks

Table 6.1 Tasks 1A and 1E

Marks obtained by children in 1A				Marks obtained by children in 1E			
Subjects	Item 1	Item 2	Total (2)	Subjects	Item 1	Item 2	Total (2)
Karabi	01	01	02	Karabi	01	01	02
Kaberi	01	01	02	Kaberi	01	01	02
Barsha	01	01	02	Barsha	01	01	02
Anjali	01	01	02	Anjali	01	01	02
Manisha	01	01	02	Manisha	01	01	02
Manash	01	01	02	Manash	01	01	02
Rahul	01	01	02	Rahul	01	01	02
Rohan	01	01	02	Rohan	01	01	02

Table 6.2 Tasks 2A and 2E

Marks obtained by children in 2A				Marks obtained by children in 2 E			
Subjects	Item 1	Item 2	Total (4)	Subjects	Item 1	Item 2	Total (4)
Anjali	1 + 1	1 + 1	04	Karabi	1.5	1.5	03
Karabi	1 + 1	0 + 1	03	Anjali	1.5	1.5	03
Barsha	1 + 1	0 + 1	03	Barsha	1	1	02
Manisha	1 + 1	0 + 1	03	Manash	1.5	0	1.5
Manash	1 + 1	0 + 1	03	Kaberi	0	0	0
Rahul	0 + 1	1 + 1	03	Manisha	0	0	0
Kaberi	0 + 1	0 + 1	02	Rahul	0	0	0
Rohan	0 + 1	0 + 1	02	Rohan	0	0	0

Table 6.3 Tasks 3A and 3E

Marks in 3A		Marks in 3E	
Subjects	Marks obtained (10)	Subjects	Marks obtained (10)
Karabi	10	Karabi	10
Kaberi	10	Barsha	10
Barsha	10	Kaberi	09
Anjali	10	Anjali	09
Manisha	10	Manisha	09
Rahul	10	Rahul	09
Rohan	10	Manash	06
Manash	09	Rohan	06

Table 6.4 Tasks 4A and 4E

Marks obtained by children in 4A					Marks obtained by children 4E					
Subjects	Item 1 (5)	Item 2 (1)	Item 3 (1)	Total (7)	Subjects	Item 1 (4)	Item 2 (1)	Item 3 (1)	Item 4 (1)	Total (7)
Karabi	03	01	01	05	Karabi	04	01	01	01	07
Kaberi	03	01	01	05	Kaberi	04	01	01	01	07
Barsha	03	01	01	05	Barsha	04	01	01	01	07
Anjali	03	01	01	05	Anjali	04	01	01	01	07
Manisha	03	01	01	05	Manash	04	01	01	01	07
Manash	03	01	01	05	Rahul	04	01	01	01	07
Rahul	03	01	01	05	Manisha	04	01	01	0.5	6.5
Rohan	03	01	01	05	Rohan	04	01	01	0.5	6.5

Table 6.5 Task 5A

Subjects	Xi (he)	Taar (his)	Thopaa-bor (bunch of)	Xei-bor (those)	Xi (he)	Taar (his)	Xi (he)	Taar (his)	Xi (he)	Taar (his)	Marks obtained (5)
Karabi	0.5	0.5	0.5	0.5	0.5	0.5	0.5	0.5	0.5	0.5	05
Kaberi	0.5	0.5	0.5	0.5	0.5	0.5	0.5	0.5	0.5	0.5	05
Manash	0.5	0.5	0.5	0.5	0.5	0.5	0.5	0.5	0.5	0.5	05
Barsha	0.5	0.5	0	0	0.5	0.5	0.5	0.5	0.5	0.5	04
Anjali	0.5	0.5	0	0	0.5	0.5	0.5	0.5	0.5	0.5	04
Manisha	0.5	0.5	0	0	0.5	0.5	0.5	0.5	0.5	0.5	04
Rahul	0.5	0.5	0	0	0.5	0.5	0.5	0.5	0.5	0.5	04
Rohan	0.5	0.5	0	0	0.5	0.5	0.5	0.5	0	0	03

Table 6.6 Task 5E

Subjects	They	Them	Two boys	Reading in English	Marks obtained (5)
Karabi	01	01	0	02	04
Kaberi	01	01	0	02	04
Barsha	01	01	0	02	04
Anjali	01	01	0	02	04
Manisha	01	01	0	02	04
Manash	01	01	0	02	04
Rahul	01	0	0	02	03
Rohan	01	0	0	02	03

References

Bachman, L. F. (1990). *Fundamental considerations in language testing.* Oxford: Oxford University Press.
Bialystok, E. (2001). *Bilingualism in development: Language, literacy, and cognition.* Cambridge: Cambridge University Press.
Bimmel, P. E., van den Bergh, H., & Oostdam, R. J. (2001). Effects of strategy training on reading comprehension in first and foreign language. *European Journal of Psychology of Education, 16*(4), 509–529.
Byram, M. (Ed.). (2004). *Routledge encyclopedia of language teaching and learning.* London and New York: Routledge.
Carrell, P. L., Pharis, B. G., & Liberto, J. C. (1989). Metacognitive strategy training for ESL reading. *TESOL Quarterly, 23,* 647–678.
Cook, G. (2010). *Translation in language teaching: An argument for reassessment.* Oxford: Oxford University Press.
Dreyer, C., & Nel, C. (2003). Teaching reading strategies and reading comprehension within a technology-enhanced learning environment. *System, 31,* 349–365.
Grabe, W. (2009). *Reading in a second language: Moving from theory to practice.* New York: Cambridge University Press.
Gunderson, L. (2009). *ESL (ELL) literacy instruction: A guidebook to theory and practice* (2nd ed.). New York: Routledge.
Jimenez, R. T., Garcia, G. E., & Pearson, D. P. (1996). The reading strategies of bilingual Latin/o students who are successful English readers: Opportunities and obstacles. *Reading Research Quarterly, 31*(1), 90–112.
Jose, K. (2000). *Reading strategies used by adult ESL learners: Implications for strategy training* (M. Phil. Thesis). Central Institute of English and Foreign Languages, Hyderabad.
Kaw, M. (2006). *Questioning and cognitive processing: A study of question-answering in the L2 reading classroom* (M. Phil. Thesis). Central Institute of English and Foreign Languages, Hyderabad.
Kern, R. G. (1989). Second language reading strategy instruction: Its effects on comprehension and word inference ability. *The Modern Language Journal, 73*(2), 135–149.
Kitajima, R. (1997). Referential strategy training for second language reading comprehension of Japanese texts. *Foreign Language Annals, 30*(1), 84–97.
Koda, K. (2005). *Insights into second language reading: A cross-linguistic approach.* New York: Cambridge University Press.
Macaro, E. (2001). *Learning strategies in foreign and second language classrooms.* London: Continuum.

Mathew, R., & Kunnan, A. J. (2006). Achievement testing to proficiency testing: Myth or reality? *FORTELL Newsletter, 9,* 6–11.

McKay, P. (2006). *Assessing young language learners.* Cambridge: Cambridge University Press.

Mohanty, A. K. (1994). *Bilingualism in a multilingual society: Psycho-social and pedagogical implications.* Mysore: Central Institute of Indian Languages.

Nag, S., & Sircar, S. (2008). *Learning to read in Bengali: Report of a survey in five Kolkata primary schools.* Bangalore: The Promise Foundation.

Path, N., & Bhaag, C. (2002). *An integrated text cum work-book for Class IV.* Guwahati: The Assam State Textbook Production and Publication Corporation Limited.

Prabhu, N. S. (1987). *Second language pedagogy.* Oxford: Oxford University Press.

Rajasekhar, G. (2006). *The effect of strategy instruction on teaching ESL reading* (M.Phil. Thesis). Central Institute of English and Foreign Languages, Hyderabad.

Raymond, T. M. (1993). The effects of structure strategy training on the recall of expository prose for university students reading French as a second Language. *The Modern Language Journal, 77,* 445–458.

Rubin, J., Chamot, A. U., Harris, V., & Anderson, N. J. (2007). Intervening in the use of strategies. In A. D. Cohen & E. Macaro (Eds.), *Language learner strategies: Thirty years of research and practice* (pp. 141–160). Oxford: Oxford University Press.

SCERT (2002). Natun Path (Chaturtha Bhaag) [*An integrated text cum work-book for Class IV*] Guwahati: The Assam State Textbook Production and Publication Corporation Limited.

Tharu, J. (1981). *Measuring small gains in the context of language instruction.* Paper presented at National Seminar on Aspects of Evaluation and Testing in Language Education. Mysore: Central Institute of Indian Languages.

Upton, T. A., & Lee-Thompson, L. C. (2001). The role of the first language in second language reading. *Studies in Second Language Acquisition, 23*(4), 469–495.

Vygotsky, L. S. (1978). *Mind in society.* Cambridge, MA: Harvard University Press.

Chapter 7
First-Language Reading Promotes Second-Language Reading and Acquisition: Towards a Biolinguistic Approach

R. Joseph Ponniah

Abstract The chapter explores the possible transfer of L1 pleasure-reading habits to L2 and the acquisition of a second language by reading L2 texts with a biolinguistic perspective. Human beings in general have an inherent propensity to learn and grow, and this innate tendency is facilitated by supportive conditions in the environment. In this study, the subject evinces keen interest in learning business English, as her working environment requires her to speak and write for a specific purpose. In order to acquire both written and spoken language, she was instructed to read a few historical novels provided by the experimenter but she expressed difficulty in reading the novels, as the themes did not interest her despite the innate propensity to acquire the specific language. This is because the inaccessible part of the brain does not allow a person to become involved and immersed in an activity if it is not interesting. But when she was provided with English novels with themes like those of L1 novels which were read for pleasure, she could continue reading for enjoyment and pleasure by using the reading strategies picked up subconsciously while reading L1 texts. The pleasure extracted from L2 reading provides compelling input that facilitates acquisition.

Keywords L1 and L2 reading · Innate tendency · Language problem Pleasure reading · Language acquisition

Studies analysing the correlation between L1 and L2 reading have hypothesized that proficiency in one language contributes to the development of reading ability in another language (Mezek, 2013; Mickiewicz, 2016; Spies, Lara-Alecio, Tong, Irby, Garza, & Huerta, 2017). The complex brain networks required for L2 reading are shaped by L1 (Kim, Liu, & Cao, 2017; Yamashita, 2002), which facilitates the transfer of reading skills to a second language. The L1 knowledge transferred is the

R. J. Ponniah (✉)
Department of Humanities and Social Sciences, National Institute of Technology Tiruchirappalli, Tiruchirappalli, Tamil Nadu, India
e-mail: joseph@nitt.edu

© Springer Nature Singapore Pte Ltd. 2018
R. Joseph Ponniah and S. Venkatesan (eds.), *The Idea and Practice of Reading*, https://doi.org/10.1007/978-981-10-8572-7_7

"conceptual knowledge rather than specific linguistic elements" (Cummins, 1991: 77) and the conceptual knowledge combined with L2 linguistic knowledge enhances comprehension. Moreover, the cognitive ability developed by reading L1 text can be used for reading L2 text and the use of L1 reading strategy in L2 reading positively affects comprehension and a wide range of cognitive skills. But "limited control over the language 'short circuits' the good reader's system, causing him/her to revert to poor reader strategies when confronted with a difficult or confusing task in the second language" (Clarke, 1980: 206) as there are common underlying principles that govern both L1 and L2.

The effective use and transfer of L1 skills require a reader to have a certain amount of linguistic competence in L2, which is referred to as the "threshold level of linguistic competence" (Cummins, 1991). This claim prompts researchers to examine the L2 linguistic knowledge of readers; studies confirm that L2 linguistic knowledge helps enhance comprehension and facilitate reading in L2 (Artieda, 2017; Lee & Schallert, 1997). Brisbois (1995) assessed the L2 vocabulary and grammar knowledge of 131 (88 beginners and 43 upper-level) native English-speaking students learning French as a second language to test how proficiency of one language contributed to the development of the other language. The findings of the study confirmed that the subjects who had breadth and depth of vocabulary and grammar knowledge could transfer the L1 reading skills more easily than the less proficient students; moreover, the L1 reading scores were consistent with the L2 reading scores. Tsai, Ernst and Talley (2010), in their experimental study with 222 Chinese students, revealed that L1 reading can be transferred to L2, but L2 grammar and vocabulary knowledge were crucial for the transfer. Further, the reading strategies to increase reading comprehension employed by the skilled readers differed from those of the less skilled learners. The skilled readers could easily transfer reading strategies used in L1 to L2. Studies have confirmed that readers who have the threshold level of language competence in L2 had increased comprehension and did more reading. This is consistent with the threshold hypothesis, which maintains that transfer of reading is possible only when the proficiency of a learner reaches the threshold level of competence.

While underlying competence can help a reader comprehend a text, it cannot motivate and create an innate desire for reading despite one's inherent propensity to explore and learn (Ryan & Deci, 2002). Human beings are biologically wired to seek out challenges of learning and achievement, and this can be observed in the behaviour of children. Children, in general, are inquisitive and curious; this implies they have the natural inclination towards assimilation, mastery and exploration that is essential for cognitive and social development (Harter, 1978; Ryan, 1995; Ryan & Deci, 2000). Similarly, adults have an innate propensity towards academic and professional growth, and to sustain and enhance this inherent desire, they need proper guidance and support from the environment. This implies that competence in the target language alone cannot promote reading; supportive conditions are required to fuel the intrinsic motivation to learn and achieve.

Alderson's (1984) thought-provoking question "Is reading, a reading problem or a language problem?" is relevant in this context. Studies have attempted to partially answer the most commented upon question of Alderson—whether reading is a 'language problem' but little has been done to answer the other half of the question: could reading be a 'reading problem'? A wealth of research (Dmitrenko, 2017; Hadadi, Abbasi, & Doodarzi, 2014; Lasagabaster, 1998) on language transfer claims that acquisition of threshold level of language competence makes reading easier but this does not guarantee more autonomous reading. If learners are uninterested and are intrinsically less motivated to read, the underlying threshold level of language that has developed cannot motivate reluctant readers to read as the brain is guided by the pleasure it extracts from an activity. If reading does not give pleasure, then the process of reading will become an unrewarding experience that creates anxiety, which in turn will not facilitate continued reading. The pleasure hypothesis (Krashen, 1994) claims that the reading experience must be pleasurable for the acquisition of language. The pleasure element is the crucial motivating ingredient that compels readers to immerse themselves in reading and to find time to read despite their regular day-to-day work.

The pleasure extracted from L1 reading will create a positive attitude towards L2 reading because for readers, reading itself is a rewarding experience. It is the attitude to reading that is crucial for the development of a reading habit in L2 and not the years of experience studying the language (Ro & Chen, 2014), because the attitude influences reading behaviour and the choice of texts is guided by feelings and beliefs about reading (Smith, 1990). Positive reading behaviour that is intrinsic in nature compels readers to immerse themselves in the content and they even forget that the text is in a second language. The L1 reading habit intrinsically motivates a reader to read in L2 if the reading is enjoyable and pleasurable. The quest to read in a second language is an innate desire (Dhanapala & Hirakawa, 2015) for growth that operates in an individual; supportive conditions in the environment should facilitate fulfilment of the desire to read. Therefore, before determining which strategies are appropriate to support a reader, it is important to find out, through discussion with the reader, which L1 reading strategies they have picked up incrementally and subconsciously.

If the L2 reading theme is not interesting to readers, scaffolding them with various reading strategies will not help continued reading, as the reader "automatically and routinely applies combinations of effective and appropriate strategies depending on reader goals, reading task, and strategic processing abilities" (Grabe, 2009: 220) to enhance comprehension and sustain interest.

Gaining insight into the reader's interests could help with the choice of appropriate texts for reading. If the reader is interested in reading romance and the instructor provides science fiction, it may not motivate them to read. Here the brain is guided by the pleasure it can extract from the reading experience and if the experience is not pleasurable, the brain does not allow the person to read and continued insistence on reading such texts ends up developing a hatred of reading. This is consistent with the food pleasure equation hypothesis (Witherly, 2007), which maintains that the brain has the ability to quantify the amount of pleasure that it can extract from an eating experience, leading to choice of type and amount of food. Similarly, the choice and the amount of reading are determined by the brain.

Research has also demonstrated that 'pleasure readers' do more bedtime reading which promotes peaceful sleep at night (Ponniah & Priya, 2014) and reduces stress and anxiety, as the pleasurable activity of reading helps secrete more serotonin. Serotonin is a neurotransmitter that works synergistically with melatonin, the sleep-inducing hormone, to give contentment and peaceful sleep (Buchanan, 2007). The instinctive desire to experience pleasure from reading is an involuntary one, guided by the inaccessible part of the brain. In fact, most of our decisions are taken by the subconscious mind. For instance, in an experiment, men who were given photographs of women's faces and asked to identify the beautiful ones, were attracted towards women with dilated eyes. The men obviously had no reason to choose those pictures but the inaccessible workings of the brain knew well that dilated eyes correlate with sexual excitement (Eagleman, 2011). This confirms that the notions of beauty, pleasure and attraction are hard-wired in the brain and in the hidden neural system.

It is because the brain seeks the path of pleasure to fulfil the innate desire for growth that language learners who read for pleasure devote more time to reading. Reading provides compelling input that results in the acquisition of all measures of language competence; any attempts to acquire language by learning explicit rules of grammar will distort learning, as this learning method is not the natural approach to language. Further, learning grammar is a tedious process devoid of pleasure (Ponniah, 2008). Learners who are trained to focus on the properties of language will continue to think about its grammatical aspects, preventing them from focusing on meaning and experiencing language with pleasure. Further, depending more on grammar for acquiring language is ineffective because grammar books merely scratch the surface of the basic properties of language (Chomsky, 2000) and not the meaning at a deeper level.

The process of language acquisition, which occurs easily with input through either listening or reading, is inaccessible to the conscious mind. Indeed, the acquisition of a second language is similar to the process of learning the first language. Inherited genetic codes pick up any language and this is evident in the babbling of babies. "Deaf children babble in the same way that hearing children do, and the children in different countries sound similar even though they are exposed to radically different languages. So the initial babbling is inherited as a preprogrammed trait in humans." (Eagleman, 2011). This genetic trait triggers the development of a language during exposure to it, and the course of language acquisition depends on the amount of input and the capacity of the language genes, resulting in the differences in the language of individuals. A child living in London will acquire English without explicit instruction and a child in Japan will acquire Japanese language subconsciously. Similarly, an adult living in the Tamil-speaking province of India who migrates to a Hindi-speaking state acquires Hindi as a second language without receiving any explicit instruction. However, in the input-impoverished environment, reading can be an effective tool for acquiring a second language. Further, spoken language is lexically impoverished compared to the written language; and reading volume, rather than oral input, is a prime contributor that expands the learners' vocabulary knowledge (Cunningham & Stanovich, 1998).

The acquisition of language happens when learners understand the text they read. The language of the text should provide ($i + 1$) input, where (i) is the current language level of the learner and (+1) is the next level. Indeed, the current language will help move to the next level (Krashen, 2003). More precisely, when a reader encounters unknown language properties such as words, syntax and structures while reading a text, they will use current language knowledge to fix the contextual meaning. This is consistent with the hypothesis that readers can make reading more comprehensible by acquiring the threshold level of language competence and the acquired language can help readers move beyond the threshold level of competence. The learners do not know how acquisition happens: it is a subconscious process more powerful than the conscious way of acquiring language. Moreover, the brain uses the subconscious mind to acquire any complex human language.

Material for effective reading must provide pleasurable input in addition to exposing readers to comprehensible input. Comprehension can make the text readable but cannot motivate a learner to read the text. Continuous reading is possible only when learners get pleasure from a reading experience. Pleasure reading is a powerful tool that contributes to the development of language because readers read the text with full attention, unaffected by affective filters such as anxiety and fear of understanding (Ponniah & Priya, 2014). The pleasure component in reading becomes the driving force for readers to read more and eventually they may spend more time on reading (Ujiie & Krashen, 2002). In fact, pleasure readers will somehow find time to read as the brain is guided by the pleasure it can extract from an activity.

Reading contributes to the development of the composition skills required for writing by affecting both language knowledge and cognitive abilities. Immersion in the content of the text while reading helps absorb the nuances used by the writer to construct meaning; these subconsciously acquired nuances can be used for writing. While writing, a writer may experience difficulty generating ideas and synthesizing them coherently, leading to writing apprehensions and block. In such a situation, the writing provides compelling input by prompting the person to read more for further insights and clarity, and the repeated reading enhances composing skill by affecting cognition. Thus reading and writing are reciprocal in nature, and the two skills go beyond mere lifting of meaning from texts. The decoded message from reading is synthesized in the brain to improve comprehension and the synthesized comprehended idea helps generate new ideas for writing.

Despite the clear benefits of pleasure reading, it has been a challenge for teachers and instructors to motivate students to read for pleasure. Readers who have a pleasure-reading habit continue to read and non-readers show reluctance to read. This compelled the researcher to design a study that explains how an L1 pleasure-reading habit promotes reading in a second language if the L2 reading text provides both comprehensible and pleasant input. The amount of pleasure extracted from the reading text is the crucial determining factor contributing to reading.

Hypotheses

The researcher proposes the following two hypotheses to examine the possible transfer of L1 reading skills to L2 and the impact of general L2 reading on discipline-specific spoken and written language.

- The first hypothesis postulates that the pleasure-reading habit of the first language transfers to second language, if the reading theme of L2 is similar to L1 and if the reading material is within the linguistic competence of the reader.
- The second hypothesis posits that the desire to read is a biological instinct guided by the pleasure experience of the brain, and that pleasure reading can result in the acquisition of general language which can be comfortably used in a professional environment.

Background

The subject approached the researcher asking for assistance and suggestions for improving her telephone conversation skills and language used in business contexts. The working environment requires the subject to speak by telephone with colleagues from different states in India. As the L1 of the subject and the interlocutors is different, they only communicate in English, the lingua franca of India.

The Subject

The subject, a well-educated grade I officer in a state-owned company, is interested in developing fluency in business English. She is familiar with technical terms and has general language proficiency but is interested in improving her language for a specific purpose. She is highly motivated to use the language effectively.

Procedure

The experimenter discussed with the subject the potential of comprehensible input, explaining how narrow reading promotes acquisition of discipline-specific language. The experimenter then explained that exposure to business English would help her improve business communication and she was instructed to watch the following videos: *BBC Business English*; *Business English (Can I help you?)*; *Business English (Negotiation)*; and *Business English (We might have a deal)*.

The subject watched the video for about ten minutes and expressed reluctance to continue watching, claiming that the content did not interest her despite her strong desire to acquire the specific language. She was then asked to read books such as *Bring the war home* (Barry Willdorf), *Caribbee* (Thomas Hoovers) and *Berserk revenge* (Mark Coakley).

She read a few pages, flipped through the rest and did not continue reading, stating that the book did provide comprehensible input but did not interest her despite her pleasure-reading experience in L1 (Tamil). As the subject is a voracious reader of Ramanichandran's novels, she was asked to choose novels in English that share themes with Ramanichandran. She collected more than 50 novels published by Mills and Boon and Harlequin and started reading them one after another without any assistance from the experimenter. In six months she completed 27 novels in L2 (English), including *Song of the wave* (Anne Hampson), *Scandalous* (Charlotte Lamb), *Temporary bride* (Patricia Wilson), *Kiss the moonlight* (Barbara Cartland) and *Married in a moment* (Jessica Steele). She read at bedtime as she had more work during the day, and now she continues to read novels in L2 for pleasure.

Discussion with the subject confirmed that reading such novels is a pleasurable experience and this kind of reading gave her not only the confidence to speak on the telephone but also helped her clearly communicate the intended meaning both in written and spoken language. When asked about her L2 reading experience, she said that she read for pleasure and did not feel that she was reading in a second language. She further explained that she strategically skipped uninteresting pages and would continue reading, the strategy used while reading L1 texts. In fact, she had not read any book for pleasure in L2 before the intervention of the experimenter.

She used to seek the experimenter's assistance to draft business letters, but once she had been reading English novels for pleasure for about a month she developed the ability to draft without the support of the experimenter. She explained that she never experienced writing apprehensions after reading the novels in L2. Further, her confidence level increased when telephoning in English as she had acquired the skills required for conversation. In the course of the discussion, the experimenter informally enquired about her L1 reading experience in order to understand about her passion for reading on a specific theme. While she was unable to give definitive answers, she replied from vague memory that she developed the habit of reading extracts of stories from bits of papers she had come across, and that she had read for pleasure. However, she could not recollect how she had incrementally developed the habit of reading a specific genre.

Results and Discussion

The results of the study proved that a first-language pleasure-reading habit transferred to second-language reading as the reading theme in L2 gave pleasure and provided compelling input. The pleasure extracted from the L2 reading experience made her forget that she was reading in a second language, as she had had the experience that she was reading in L1. This is consistent with Witherly's (2007) food pleasure equation hypothesis, which states that the brain is wired to quantify the pleasure it can extract from an eating experience, resulting in choice and amount of food. Similarly, the choice of reading material is determined by the brain; biological instinct avoids or chooses a reading text involuntarily, guided by the subconscious mind and with the conscious mind having little access to the reason behind the action. Attempting to read uninteresting texts demotivates the reader and inhibits reading as the decision comes from the subconscious mind.

Most decisions are taken by the brain involuntarily, so compelling the mind to read any uninteresting activity would end in failure, but this does not mean that language acquisition is impossible. The neural circuits in the brain have evolved by natural selection to solve problems (Eagleman, 2011) and therefore the subconscious mind will continue to find solutions to any problem. The brain assigns priority to unresolved problems according to need. In this study, the subject desperately sought ways of acquiring discipline-specific language, which of course is a problem-solving instinct, and when the researcher provided her with historical novels to read, she flipped through pages and showed reluctance to read, indicating that the reading theme was not the brain's natural choice. But this did not demotivate her from exploring other possible ways of acquiring language because she was subconsciously motivated by the compelling requirements of her working environment. Persuaded by the desire and passion to acquire business language, she read novels on family themes and romantic relationships, the themes she used to read in L1. She was intrinsically motivated to read such novels because the themes were the natural selection of her brain.

The subject did not know how her passion for reading a specific genre had developed, which confirms that the choice of reading material and the notion of pleasure are hard-wired in the inaccessible part of the brain. In her case, enjoyment of a specific reading content had been nurtured incrementally for years, hence she could not recollect the exact moment that triggered reading. Further, studies on developmental neuroscience confirm that early life experiences directly affect the underlying capacities of genes through the environment (Mc Ewen, 2015). Caspi et al. (2007) have demonstrated that genes can be nurtured by environment if they have the ability to process signals received from neurones and neurotransmitters. For example, such nature-and-nurture interaction explains how breastfed children attain higher IQ than children not fed breast milk, provided they have a specific variant of the FADS2 gene, which is involved in the metabolism of polyunsaturated fatty acids uniquely available in mother's milk. In the absence of the FADS2 gene (nature), the mother's milk (nurture or environment) cannot be processed for strengthening cognition. Similarly, creating a passion for reading is difficult in the absence of the inbuilt skills required for decoding ideas and the desire for exposure to a specific genre.

Reading experience differs from individual to individual depending on cognitive ability and attitude. The subject has a positive attitude towards reading and this prompted her to devise reading strategies to facilitate reading. The strategies were developed progressively to speed up reading, to avoid redundant ideas and to enhance comprehension. She skipped uninteresting pages to make the reading lively as she had prior knowledge and cognition to infer the meaning of the skipped passages because reading itself is a guessing game (Goodman, 1967). Where prediction of the meaning conveyed by uninteresting passages was difficult she speeded up reading to avoid anxiety. She was not aware of when and how her strategies evolved but it was subconscious and she did use them to read L2 novels. In the process of reading an L2 text, the brain uses the acquired L1 strategies and techniques for better comprehension. Acquisition of reading strategies depends on the capacity of genes affecting both language and cognition, and further research has implicated reduced expression of the ROBO1 gene in reading disability irrespective of normal intelligence, education and socio-economic background (Hannula-Jouppi et al., 2005; Tran et al., 2014). This indicates that if the genes that support both language and cognitive abilities have reduced expression or if the genes are mutated, devising and using reading strategies would be difficult for readers.

The genetic make-up of an individual facilitates acquisition of language if the environment provides input. The subconscious mind can take in and process the received language effortlessly, and the stored intake can easily be used for speaking and writing because the brain is hard-wired to naturally acquire and produce language. Similarly, as the subject received pleasurable comprehensible input, she never expressed difficulty in reading the identified novels in English; moreover, she had the threshold level of language competence for comprehending the text. Her reading experience was consistent with the comprehension hypothesis, which maintains that language acquisition happens when focusing on meaning and not when focusing on form, provided the text is comprehensible. While reading she never used a dictionary or grammar texts, and focused only on meaning for comprehension, which in turn made reading more pleasurable in addition to the benefit of acquiring language.

Fear of committing errors while speaking and writing is the result of incomplete language acquisition. Providing the required input will not only lower apprehensions but also promote acquisition. The subject's difficulty communicating with peers increased anxiety in the working environment, but reading positively affects language, and lowers writing apprehensions and fear of speaking with interlocutors. Since her reading contributed to the incremental development of language, she could use the acquired language to write business letters and conduct conversations. She did not read any business letters to improve acquisition of the specific language, but her brain used the acquired general language to generate a different kind of language, as human beings have an innate ability to generate language even when there is scarcity of a specific language. Before reading the English novels the subject sought the researcher's help with drafting business letters and after reading them she could draft letters with ease and never had any doubts about language use. Further, she could convey the intended meaning with ease, confirming that language acquired by reading can be put to use in real-life situations.

Pleasure reading in English helped her acquire general and business language in a short space of time as she immersed herself in the content because reading gave her pleasure. This is consistent with the pleasure hypothesis that learners acquire more language when they get more pleasure while reading. Since the reader gets pleasure in reading, the subconscious mind compels the reader to read with more concentration. Since pleasure was the only motivating factor for reading, she never felt that she was reading in a second language. Further, she did not use a dictionary as it could demotivate her, which confirms readers acquire vocabulary and grammar of words incidentally (Ponniah, 2011). Moreover, the brain is wired to acquire human language by focusing on the meaning of the text; this is consistent with the comprehension hypothesis, which states acquisition happens when learners focus on meaning and not form. The current language level of the learners will help fix the contextual meaning of unknown words and structures subconsciously if the reading text is comprehensible (Krashen, 2003).

Despite the commitments of a hectic working day, she prefers bedtime reading both in L1 and L2 as reading gives pleasure and comfortable sleep. Several studies of pleasure reading have confirmed that pleasure readers find time to read and they do more bedtime reading (Krashen, 2003; Nell, 1988), which has the propensity to reduce stress and anxiety and promote peaceful sleep. The brain compels people to immerse themselves in an activity that gives pleasure to prevent anxiety, and this compulsion has a therapeutic effect on readers who get pleasure from reading.

References

Alderson, J. C. (1984). Reading in a foreign language: A reading problem or a language problem? In J. C. Alderson & A. H. Urquhart (Eds.), *Reading in a foreign language* (pp. 1–24). New York: Longman.

Artieda, G. (2017). The role of L1 literacy and reading habits on the L2 achievement of adult learners of English as a foreign language. *System, 66,* 168–176. https://doi.org/10.1016/j.system.2017.03.020.

Brisbois, J. I. (1995). Connections between first- and second-language reading. *Journal of Reading Behavior, 27,* 565–584. https://doi.org/10.1080/10862969509547899.

Buchanan, B. (2007). Seasonal affective disorder: Treatment without a prescription. *The Avante Times, 3*(3). Retrieved from http://www.avantemedicalcenter.com/images/Avante_Times/pdf/atoct07.pdf.

Caspi, A., Williams, B., Kim-Cohen, J., Craig, I. W., Milne, B. J., Poulton, R., et al. (2007). Moderation of breastfeeding effects on the IQ by genetic variation in fatty acid metabolism. *Proceedings of the National Academy of Sciences, 104*(47), 18860–18865. https://doi.org/10.1073/pnas.0704292104.

Chomsky, N. (2000). *New horizon in the study of language and mind.* Cambridge: Cambridge University Press.

Clarke, M. A. (1980). The short circuit hypothesis of ESL reading—or when language competence interferes with reading performance. *Modern Language Journal, 64,* 203–209.

Cummins, J. (1991). Conversational and academic language proficiency in bilingual contexts. *AILA Review: Reading in Two Languages, 8,* 75–89.

Cunningham, A. E., & Stanovich, K. E. (1998). What reading does for the mind. *American Educator, 22*(1–2), 8–15.
Dhanapala, K. V., & Hirakawa, Y. (2015). L2 reading motivation among Sri Lankan university students. *Reading Psychology, 36*, 1–28.
Dmitrenko, V. (2017). Language learning strategies of multilingual adults learning additional languages. *International Journal of Multilingualism, 14*(1), 6–22.
Eagleman, D. (2011). *Incognito: The secret lives of the brain*. New York: Pantheon Books.
Goodman, K. S. (1967). Reading: A psycholinguistic guessing game. *Journal of Reading Specialist, 6*, 126–135.
Grabe, W. (2009). *Reading in a second language: Moving from theory to practice*. New York: Cambridge University Press.
Hadadi, A., Abbasi, H., & Goodarzi, A. (2014). How L1 influence changes with regard to L2 proficiency increase. *Procedia—Social and Behavioral Sciences, 98*, 614–617. https://doi.org/10.1016/j.sbspro.2014.03.458.
Hannula-Jouppi, K., Kaminen-Ahola, N., Taipale, M., Eklund, R., Nopola-Hemmi, J., Kääriäinen, H., et al. (2005). The axon guidance receptor gene ROBO1 is a candidate gene for developmental dyslexia. *PLoS Genetics, 1*(4), 0467–0474. https://doi.org/10.1371/journal.pgen.0010050.
Harter, S. (1978). Effectance motivation reconsidered: Toward a developmental model. *Human Development, 1*, 661–669.
Kim, S. Y., Liu, L., & Cao, F. (2017). How does first language (L1) influence second language (L2) reading in the brain? Evidence from Korean–English and Chinese–English bilinguals. *Brain and Language, 171*, 1–13. https://doi.org/10.1016/j.bandl.2017.04.003.
Krashen, S. D. (1994). The pleasure hypothesis. In J. Alatis (Ed.), *Georgetown University round table on languages and linguistics* (pp. 299–322). Washington, DC: Georgetown University Press.
Krashen, S. D. (2003). *Explorations in language acquisition and use*. Portsmouth, NH: Heinemann.
Lasagabaster, D. (1998). The threshold hypothesis applied to three languages in contact at school. *International Journal of Bilingual Education and Bilingualism, 1*(2), 119–133. https://doi.org/10.1080/13670059808667678.
Lee, J.-W., & Schallert, D. L. (1997). The relative contribution of L2 language proficiency and L1 reading ability to L2 reading performance: A test of the threshold hypothesis in an EFL context. *TESOL Quarterly, 31*, 713–739.
Mc Ewen, B. (2015). Epigenetics and learning. *Trends in Neuroscience and Education, 4*(4), 108–111. https://doi.org/10.1016/j.tine.2015.11.002.
Mezek, S. (2013). Multilingual reading proficiency in an emerging parallel-language environment. *Journal of English for Academic Purpose, 12*(1), 166–179. https://doi.org/10.1016/j.jeap.2013.02.001.
Mickiewicz, A. (2016). L1 based strategies in learning the grammar of L2 English and L3 Russian by Polish learners. 61, 65–74.
Nell, V. (1988). The psychology of reading for pleasure: Needs and gratifications. *Reading Research Quarterly, 23*(1), 6–50. https://doi.org/10.2307/747903.
Ponniah, R. J. (2008). Free voluntary reading and the acquisition of grammar by adult ESL students. *The International Journal of Foreign Language Teaching, 4*(1), 20–22.
Ponniah, R. J. (2011). Incidental acquisition of vocabulary by reading. *The Reading Matrix, 11*(2), 135–139.
Ponniah, R. J., & Priya, J. (2014). Pleasure reading and the acquisition of second language by adult ESL students. *The International Journal of Foreign Language Teaching, 4*(1), 16–22.
Ro, E., & Chen, C. A. (2014). Pleasure reading behavior of attitude of non-academic ESL students: A replication study. *Reading in a Foreign Language, 26*(1), 49–72. Retrieved from: https://eric.ed.gov/?id=EJ1031309.
Ryan, R. M. (1995). Psychological needs and the facilitation of integrative processes. *Journal of Personality, 63*, 397–427. https://doi.org/10.1111/j.1467-6494.1995.tb00501.x.

Ryan, R. M., & Deci, E. (2000). Self-determination theory and the facilitation of intrinsic motivation, social development and well being. *American Psychologist, 55*(1), 68–78.

Ryan, R. M., & Deci, E. L. (2002). Overview of self-determination theory: An organismic dialectical perspective. In R. M. Ryan & E. L. Deci (Eds.), *Handbook of self-determination research*. Rochester, NY: The University of Rochester Press.

Smith, M. C. (1990). A longitudinal investigation of reading attitude development from childhood to adulthood. *Journal of Educational Research, 83*(4), 215–219.

Spies, T. G., Lara-Alecio, R., Tong, F., Irby, B. J., Garza, T., & Huerta, M. (2017). The effects of developing English language and literacy on Spanish reading comprehension. *The Journal of Educational Research*. https://doi.org/10.1080/00220671.2017.1306686.

Tran, C., Wigg, K. G., Zhang, K., Cate-Carter, T. D., Kerr, E., Field, L. L., et al. (2014). Association of the ROBO1 gene with reading disabilities in a family-based analysis. *Genes, Brain and Behavior, 13*(4), 430–438. https://doi.org/10.1111/gbb.12126.

Tsai, Y. R., Ernst, C., & Talley, P. C. (2010). L1 and L2 strategy use in reading comprehension of Chinese EFL readers. *Reading Psychology, 31*(1), 1–29. https://doi.org/10.1080/02702710802412081.

Ujiie, J., & Krashen, S. (2002). Home run books and reading enjoyment. *Knowledge Quest, 31*(7), 36–37.

Witherly, S. A. (2007). *Why humans like junk food: The inside story on why you like your favourite foods, the cuisine secrets of top chefs, and how to improve your own cooking without a recipe*. Lincoln, NE: iUniverse Inc.

Yamashita, J. (2002). Mutual compensation between L1 reading ability and L2 language proficiency in L2 reading comprehension. *Journal of Research in Reading, 25*(1), 81–95. https://doi.org/10.1111/1467-9817.00160.

Chapter 8
Genetics of Reading Ability and Its Role in Solving Reading Difficulties

Radhakrishnan Sriganesh, D. R. Rahul and R. Joseph Ponniah

Abstract Reading is a heritable and biologically endowed ability that is enabled by the exaptation of genetic sub-skills that are readily available as language and object recognition abilities. The significant role of genes in biological processes such as the formation and plasticity of the specialized neural networks that accompany reading, the role of epigenetic modification of genes in reading, and the reciprocal effect of emotion and cognition in reading are discussed in this chapter. With due consideration of the genetic make-up of individuals, its effect on formation of the neural circuits corresponding to reading and the gene–environment interaction, the chapter proposes how knowledge of these aspects of a reader is pertinent to providing effective pedagogical solutions.

Keywords Reading genes · Neural plasticity · Epigenetics · Cognition
Affect · Personalized learning

Introduction

Recent research on biology of reading calls for an understanding of the interplay between genes and neurons that affect language, cognition and emotion. Reading is a cognitive-linguistic process enabled by an interface between the predisposed areas of the human brain responsible for visual, auditory and linguistic capacities. This interface is a result of the ability of the brain to modify neural connections in response to environmental reading input (Pascual-Leone, Amedi, Fregni, & Merabet, 2005). The ability of the brain to form new cortical structures (widely known as neuroplasticity) is found to be regulated by a hereditary mechanism known as epigenetics (Allen, 2008; Borrelli, Nestler, Allis, & Sassone-Corsi, 2008; Felling & Song, 2015; Kennedy et al., 2016). Additionally, language acquisition,

R. Sriganesh · D. R. Rahul · R. J. Ponniah (✉)
Department of Humanities and Social Sciences, National Institute of Technology Tiruchirappalli, Tiruchirappalli, India
e-mail: joseph@nitt.edu

© Springer Nature Singapore Pte Ltd. 2018
R. Joseph Ponniah and S. Venkatesan (eds.), *The Idea and Practice of Reading*, https://doi.org/10.1007/978-981-10-8572-7_8

cognition and affective factors, which are also remarkably innate, can act both as cause and effect of reading. The above propositions suggest that reading overall is an outcome of simultaneous expressions of multiple genes with multiple functionalities which result in inter-individual differences in reading. This wider understanding of reading is necessary for an all-round development of reading pedagogy, considering learners with and without reading difficulties.

Reading as a Gene-Enabled Ability

Reading must have a high genetic association since it is a union of several sub-skills that are instinctively available to human beings, including in particular orthographic coding, phonological decoding and a set of language sub-skills (Dehaene, 2010). Orthographic coding is an extension of innate object recognition ability that aids letter recognition. Phonological decoding, the ability to decode letters to sounds, is found to be genetically correlated to orthographic coding (Gayán & Olson, 2001). This shows that genes play a major role in both the reading sub-skills. Moreover, other reading sub-skills corresponding to morphological, syntactic and semantic processing are part of language, indicating reading requires language ability. Since language sub-skills are biological and gene-rendered abilities (Berwick & Chomsky, 2016; Brzustowicz, 2014), it can be deduced that reading also makes use of those genetic abilities.

The afore-mentioned reading sub-skills are biologically encoded into dedicated areas of the human brain. Neuroimaging studies prove that these areas are universal among humans (therefore, genetic), with individual languages only effecting local changes in brain activation (Chen, Fu, Iversen, Smith, & Matthews, 2002; Dehaene, 2010; Fu, Chen, Smith, Iversen, & Matthews, 2002). The universal reading areas among humans can perhaps be attributed to the fact that many of these areas share their functions with innate capacities (language, for instance). Some of these universal areas are slightly modified from their genetic function to aid in reading. For example, visual word form area (VWFA) is one such universal area that underwent slight modification from face recognition ability to result in visual word-forming ability, an ability unique to reading (Dehaene & Cohen, 2011). Understandably, a functional MRI study has proved that literacy results in reduced neural activation of VWFA for faces as opposed to increased activation for letters (Dehaene et al., 2010). Another study conducted among subjects across the world found that illiterate individuals were better at face recognition than literate counterparts (Dehaene, Cohen, Morais, & Kolinsky, 2015), indicating that the innate face recognition ability is partly taken over by reading. Therefore, for effective reading ability, genes corresponding to all reading brain areas including VWFA must have normal expressions.

Another important aspect of reading is that it is defined by the biological capabilities of human beings. This means that human beings have developed reading by innovatively making use of available human capabilities. Similarities in letter patterns across languages (Changizi, Zhang, Ye, & Shimojo, 2006) indicate that reading could have evolved within the boundaries of the visual coding abilities of human beings (Dehaene, 2010). A study finds that the neural reorganization of the visual pathway in the brain corresponding to reading acquisition is genetically constrained (Chang et al., 2015). This evidence, along with the fact that object recognition and language abilities are prerequisites for reading, suggest that reading developed within the constraints posed by our genetic capacities. Thus, one would expect normal expression of genes related to vision and language for reading.

Reading Disability and Genes

Reading disability or dyslexia is a complex neurobehavioural disorder mainly affecting reading skill which is known to affect approximately 5–10% of individuals across the globe. Dyslexia provides an indirect gateway to understanding what enables reading in human beings.

Neuroimaging studies have revealed that dyslexia corresponds to reduced activation in the left temporo-parietal cortex (Gabrieli, 2009). Hyperlexia, an ability to read well ahead of age-mates, is characterized by higher activation in the left superior temporal cortex and the same area was characterized by hypoactivation among dyslexic individuals (Turkeltaub et al., 2004), suggesting similarity in the functioning of the reading brain across all individuals and hence a genetic basis for reading. Research has also confirmed that dyslexia is heritable and therefore genetic (Eicher & Gruen, 2013; Fisher & DeFries, 2002; Gialluisi, Newbury, Willcutt, Consortium, & Luciano, 2014; Paracchini, Diaz, & Stein, 2016).

Genome-wide association studies (GWAS) provide insights into the genes responsible for the disorder. During the previous decade, several candidate genes for dyslexia, namely DYX1C1 (dyslexia susceptibility 1 candidate 1) on 15q21.3 (Taipale et al., 2003), ROBO1 (roundabout Drosophila homolog 1) on 3p12.3 (Hannula-Jouppi et al., 2005; Tran et al., 2014), DCDC2 (double cortin domain-containing protein 2) on 6p22.3 (Meng et al., 2005), KIAA0319 on 6p22.3 (Cope et al., 2005) and MRPL19/C2ORF3 on 2p12 (Scerri et al., 2012). More recently, another set of genes, namely CCDC136 (coiled-coil domain containing 136)/FLNC (filamin C) on 7q32.1 and RBFOX2 (RNA-binding protein, fox-1 homolog 2) were identified as candidate genes associated with both reading and language disabilities (Gialluisi et al., 2014). CMIP, a candidate gene for specific language impairment (SLI) is also found to be associated with reading (Scerri et al., 2011). So far, more than 20 dyslexia candidate genes have been identified by the Human Gene Nomenclature Committee (Raskind, Peter, Richards, Eckert, & Berninger, 2013).

Specific variants of these candidate genes are also identified to have associations with reading sub-skills such as phonological awareness, phonological decoding, orthographic coding and rapid serial naming. Substantially, the presence of genetic variants for dyslexia could indicate that each reading sub-skill involves specific genes. SNPs of KIAA0319, namely rs761100 and rs2038137 are found to be associated with rapid naming and rs6935076, which again is an SNP of KIAA0319, is associated with word reading fluency. Similarly, rs17236239, an SNP of CNTNAP2, is associated with non-word repetition. Population dyslexia studies show that the above abilities differ among individuals, resulting in inter-individual differences in brain circuitry (McGrath et al., 2011; Peterson & Pennington, 2012). These differences are also found to be genetic (Willcutt et al., 2010). Research in this direction could further highlight the genetic associations with the key reading sub-skills.

The candidate genes for reading, apart from DYX1C1, are responsible for brain development as well, implying multiple functions of the candidate genes (McGrath, Smith, & Pennington, 2006). As in the case of general language ability (Centanni, Green, Iuzzini-seigel, Bartlett, & Hogan, 2015), reading ability is manifested through multiple genes, with no specialist gene corresponding to reading disability identified. Also, the above-mentioned candidate genes are not yet known to have been mutated among dyslexic subjects (McGrath et al., 2006). However, involvement of multiple genes and their variants, and the absence of mutation in dyslexia does not undermine the heritability of the disorder, for even a simple genetic trait like eye colour may involve multiple genes and the absence of mutation (White & Rabago-Smith, 2011).

The discussion so far suggests that genes play an important role in making people dyslexic, but the role of genes and environment cannot be quantified unless twin or family studies are employed. Twin studies provide a natural setting for the genetic etiology estimations. Monozygotic (MZ) twins, who share all their genes, and dizygotic (DZ) twins, who share half the genes, are studied to show how a certain trait or disease is genetic or environmental. In such studies, people with a trait or disease (known as probands), their co-twins and co-siblings of the twins are studied for the corresponding variance from expected results which is: shared trait/ disease for all MZ twins and shared trait or disease in 50% of the DZ twin population. Then, based upon the comorbidity of a condition among MZ and DZ twins, further analysis is conducted to find the attribution (in percentage) to genetic and environmental causes (Olson, 2006). One such twin study of dyslexic children conducted by Gayán & Olson (2001) with a sample of 215 MZ and 159 DZ twins throws light on three reading sub-skills: word recognition, phonological decoding and orthographic coding. The genetic etiology estimation (with 95% confidence level) for word recognition attributed 54% to genetic influence, 40% to shared environment and 6% to non-shared environment. The percentages for phonological decoding were estimated to be 71, 18 and 11% for genetic influence, shared environment and non-shared environments respectively. For orthographic coding, it was 67% genetic, 17% shared environment effects and 16% non-shared environmental effects (Gayán & Olson, 2001; Olson, 2006). Several other twin and family studies point towards the dominant genetic determination of the disorder along with environmental causes (Bates et al., 2007; Gayán & Olson, 2003; Ho, Wong, Chow, Waye, & Bishop, 2017; Little & Hart, 2016; Olson, 2006; Swagerman et al., 2017).

Having fairly concluded that dyslexia has a major genetic etiology, a question arises as to how the disability is passed on to future generations in the absence of genetic mutations. As it is known that we inherit genetic diseases not only through mutation but also through epigenetic processes such as DNA methylation and histone modification, it could well be the case that genes responsible for reading are impaired through epigenetic processes. The fact that reading and writing could be restored to a limited extent to dyslexic children through interventions points to the possibility of an extremely conducive environment modifying the genetic disability. The role of environmental impact on gene expression in dyslexia could be understood by turning our focus towards the acquisition of reading.

Biology of Reading Acquisition and Fluent Reading

Genetic and neural mechanisms play a causal role in successful reading acquisition. As human biology is an enabler of the ability, it cannot be neglected in seeking an understanding of reading, both in health and disability. The biological process of acquiring reading involves simultaneous expression of genes that enable reading along with support from genes related to cognition and emotion. As these gene expressions trigger the formation of neural networks, reading is materialized in the human brain through the establishment of neuronal connections among various brain areas corresponding to the innate capacities involved in reading. This formation of neural networks of brain areas requires neuroplasticity, the ability to alter the interconnection of neurons located in different areas in response to environmental input. For example, as a child learns to read, letter–sound–meaning correspondences take place through intricate brain structures that connect visual-auditory areas and language areas in the brain (Dehaene, 2010; Norton, Beach, & Gabrieli, 2015; Wandell & Le, 2017).

A study suggests that the functional networking of the brain is found to be associated with polymorphisms of a set of genes promoting individual differences in functional connectivity of the brain (Richiardi, Altmann, & Jonas, 2015). Since reading is a result of a complex network of functional areas of the brain, the above finding can be extended to reading ability as well. It can thus be predicted that individual differences in reading ability result from the influence of genetic polymorphisms on functional brain circuits. Similarly, variants of genes also contribute significantly to inter-individual differences in reading achievement among non-dyslexic children. For example, the gene variants, i.e., SNPs, of CCDC136/FLNC and RBFOX2 were found to be associated with reading scores and restructuring of brain tissues (Gialluisi, Guadalupe, Francks, & Fisher, 2017; Gialluisi et al., 2014). Thus, functional networks corresponding to reading have molecular genetic associations and the gene variants correspond to individual differences in reading.

The discussion so far suggests that genetic make-up of individuals influences reading. However, reading can also influence gene–environment interactions, which leads to modification of the genes corresponding to the innate sub-skills of reading by epigenetic mechanisms. Recent breakthrough evidence suggests that an epigenetic process (DNA methylation) in reading-related gene KIAA0319 plays an important role in language lateralization (Schmitz, Kumsta, Moser, Güntürkün, & Ocklenburg, 2018). We can reasonably predict that environmental modification of KIAA0319, which helps language lateralization, comes to the aid of reading acquisition as well. This prediction is in line with a study that finds left hemisphere lateralization of object recognition is observed among children as they acquire reading skills (Caffarra et al., 2017). Additionally, since language sub-skills such as phonological decoding and meaning associations are shared between reading and spoken language (Olson, 2006), one could expect epigenetic effects of language genes passed on to reading skill as well.

Emotion and Cognition in Reading

Affective factors such as pleasure, motivation and self-determination in reading are important factors in reading achievement (McKenna & Kear, 1990; Ölmez, 2015). Self-determined learning is found to be fruitful for struggling learners of reading (Wehmeyer, Shogren, Toste, & Mahal, 2016). Reading for pleasure is linked to a positive attitude towards reading and greater self-confidence (Guthrie & Alvermann, 1999). When reading is pleasurable, it motivates people to read more and it also results in better cognition and language acquisition. The increased cognition, improved language and the pleasure derived drive them to read more, resulting in a cyclic relationship. Positive affective factors have a positive correlation to reading achievement in addition to various cognitive, psychological and physiological benefits. They also have genetic pathways which underlie inter-individual differences. Rs322931, an SNP of LINC01221 on chromosome 1, was found to be associated significantly with positive emotions (Wingo et al., 2017). The study also shows that the minor allele of rs322931 predicts the expression of microRNAs, namely miR-181a and miR-181b and it also postulates that the miRNA is associated with positive emotional stimuli and inhibition of fear. Thus, positive emotions are gene regulated and could positively affect reading acquisition, suggesting the possibility of reading achievement being heritable.

Conversely, if reading is forceful or stressful, it will have a detrimental effect on reading and language acquisition. Studies on reading have confirmed that anxiety is negatively correlated to reading comprehension (Blicher, Feingold, & Shany, 2017; Hewitt & Stephenson, 2012; Knickerbocker, Johnson, & Altarriba, 2015). To illustrate this mechanism in a typical classroom environment, imagine a second-language reading session where a teacher assigns a common text with the intention of enhancing comprehension and acquisition of vocabulary and grammar. The teacher may have chosen the text based on her preference or based on what she perceives as interesting to students. However, in reality, people have a wide variety of preferences such as novels and short stories of different genres, gadget reviews, cooking recipes, newspaper articles, magazines, investment tips, etc. The choice of such texts is dependent on the innate drive to seek knowledge and pleasure through reading. Therefore, when students read a text that is not of their choosing, it may not relate to their innate drive to read and they may not be motivated to continue reading. In effect, they will be demotivated to read. Krashen's second-language acquisition theories too point out that such anxiety in learning negatively affects language acquisition (Krashen, 1982). This could well be the case in first-language (L1) reading if the L1 reading session is dealt with in a similar manner.

The effects of stress in reading can be explained in terms of biology. As seen earlier, the reading process changes the structure of the brain and new cortical networks are established as a result of its acquisition. Stress acts in a detrimental way in establishing the change in brain connection since it restricts learning and physical growth by inhibiting the required neuronal plasticity (McEwen, Eiland, Hunter, & Miller, 2012). In addition, stress is also epigenetically heritable (McEwen, 2016; Nieto, Patriquin, Nielsen, & Kosten, 2016; Palmisano & Pandey, 2017), raising concerns over stressful methods of language learning.

In addition to the affective factors, human cognition is also influenced by reading. As discussed earlier, reading itself is a complex cognitive process that involves several sub-skills. As we learn to read, these reading sub-skills get better. Apart from this, reading is favourably correlated with several cognitive dimensions. For example, acquisition of grammar (Cox & Guthrie, 2001; Lee, Schallert, & Kim, 2015), and incidental vocabulary enhancement and retention (Ghanbari & Marzban, 2014; Wasik, Hindman, & Snell, 2016) are highly influenced by extensive reading. Moreover, reading enhances social cognitive abilities such as interpersonal sensitivity (Fong, Mullin, & Mar, 2013), and general knowledge and understanding of other cultures (Clark & Rumbold, 2006). Reading is also positively correlated with the theory of mind (Black & Barnes, 2015; Kidd & Castano, 2013), which is the ability to predict or infer our own and other people's beliefs, desires and intentions (Malle, 2005). Conversely, improvements in several constructs of cognition result in better reading ability (Cox & Guthrie, 2001).

Cognition developed while reading is influenced by human biology. A study suggests that the amygdala, a part of the brain implicated in cognitive mechanisms of learning and memory, releases higher dopamine during reading tasks (Fried et al., 2001). A variety of cognitive processes are linked to genes responsible for dopamine, a neurotransmitter that is a critical modulator of those cognitive processes (Elvevåg & Weinberger, 2009). Another study proposes that cognitive processes such as selective attention, working memory and decision making are genetically associated, leading to individual differences in cognition (Parasuraman, 2009). In addition, human intelligence has been found to have neurobiological and genetic associations (Deary, Penke, & Johnson, 2010). Moreover, cognition is found to be regulated by epigenetic mechanisms (Day & Sweatt, 2011). These findings point towards reading as a complex cognitive process that is genetically enabled and regulated.

Interaction Between Emotion and Cognition in Reading

Emotion and cognition work in tandem in almost all communication situations. For example, if a person wants to express happiness, cognition helps readily by fetching the necessary words to use in the context. Similarly, our emotional experiences help us learn, accentuate thinking processes and solve problems by making decisions (Zambo & Brem, 2004). It is also known that emotion affects cognitive processes such as perception, attention, long-term memory, working memory and decision making; and cognition also affects emotional factors (Dolcos, Iordan, & Dolcos, 2011).

Research in neuroscience reports that the dynamic interaction between cognition and emotion emerges from brain activation (Deary et al., 2010). Cognition- and emotion-based neural circuits are so intertwined that it is difficult to differentiate them (Gray, 1990). It has been argued that there are no different systems in the brain for cognition and emotion because both cognitive and emotional behaviour emerge from a complex, dynamic interaction between brain networks (Pessoa, 2008). In fact, both cognition and emotion are regulated by the amygdala (Dolcos et al., 2011; Fried et al., 2001; Gallagher & Chiba, 1996; Laeger et al., 2012).

Further, research on this topic has pointed to a genetic link in cognition–emotion interactions. It has been found that PCDH17 (Protocadherin 17) and its polymorphisms are associated with cognition, emotion (mood disorders) and the functioning of amygdala (Chang et al., 2017). Genetic association studies point to the fact that interaction between cognition and emotion is highly heritable (ranging from 30–80%) (Scult & Hariri, 2018). A branch named integrative neuroscience calls for the neuroscience of cognition and emotion, and their brain and genetic correlates, to be brought together (Williams, Tsang, Clarke, & Kohn, 2010).

Despite overwhelming evidence of the reciprocal relationship between cognition and emotion, most reading sessions in academic contexts discard the importance of emotion. In a typical reading-based classroom setting, learners experience a diverse set of emotions from the same reading passage. Some may be anxious because they cannot comprehend the text, some may find it uninteresting, some may find it informative, and so on. However, most learning environments tend to ignore emotion and focus on cognition. Emotion is more basic than cognition and can be expected to have a greater impact on learner outcomes.

The Need for Personalized Learning

Classroom reading/writing is one of the important ways people gain knowledge, enhance first-language skills and acquire a second language. However, formal classrooms that still follow one-size-fits-all policy of education are nightmares for many language learners (Hashemi, 2011). This policy goes against the genetic and epigenetic aspects of reading which perpetrate diversity among learners. A large-sample study postulates that 40% of variance in educational attainment is due to differences in the genetic make-up of individuals (Rietveld et al., 2013), suggesting reading-based training modules should be in tune with genetic variations in learning among individuals. Most importantly, people with learning difficulties such as reading disability and specific language impairment must have access to specialized teaching aids and personnel. Healthy learners also require personalized training since they differ greatly owing to inter-individual differences in learning methods and capacity. Moreover, the biological view of reading has shown the adverse effects of stress and positive effects of self-motivation in reading. This calls for a revisit of the formal classroom environment to make classrooms inclusive, with provision for stress-free, personalized and self-motivated learning.

A basic knowledge of neurological functions and epigenetics leading to inter-individual learning differences is as important to teachers as medical examination of a patient is important to doctors. However, the formal language teaching environment does not take into account the variety in brain functions that are due to genetic and epigenetic factors. An analogy from the field of medicine can provide a parallel insight into how personalized teaching makes the environment conducive to natural reading/language acquisition. The emerging field of pharmacogenomics studies the role of genes in inter-individual differences in drug response (Weinshilboum & Wang, 2006). Patients are tested for their neural, genetic and epigenetic markers and the physiological effect is predicted in advance. A suitable drug is then prescribed as a response to the genetic make-up of each patient. Similarly, in the pursuit of personalizing reading/language acquisition, a personalized teaching strategy that takes into account genetic make-up and an individual's response to learning methods, might be proposed.

A review of the topic (Wong, Vuong, & Liu, 2017) has suggested that the emerging personalized medicine can be extended to personalized learning as well. Personalized learning would aim to use genetic, neuronal and behavioural predictors to identify learning ability and needs of individuals, thereby arriving at an optimal teaching-learning solution. Neuroimaging studies (Bach, Richardson, Brandeis, Martin, & Brem, 2013; Hoeft et al., 2007, 2011; Molfese, 2000) have shown that neuromarkers (initial brain measures such as cortical volume and thickness) of reading have successfully predicted future reading gains in dyslexic patients. Since epigenetic mechanisms influence neuromarkers, their role in neurodevelopment of reading can also be understood. A study confirms this view and suggests that genetic variants can be linked to neuroimaging of the brain which in turn is connected to reading impairments (Eicher & Gruen, 2013). This could be the future of personalized learning in reading classrooms.

Conclusion

This chapter has demonstrated that several dimensions of reading such as reading sub-skills, reading brain areas, functional neuroplasticity (of reading), the dyslexic brain, positive affect and cognition are effected in the brain as neurobiological dispensations caused by genetic underpinnings of individuals. Therefore, reading must be viewed in its totality as a genetic ability that causes inter-individual difference in learning ability. Such a view is a prerequisite to understanding differing reading environment needs for dyslexics and healthy learners with differences in gene expression. A great deal of evidence pointing to neurobiology and genetics of reading ability suggests the direction of personalized learning that reading classrooms must take. Only a holistic approach to reading and switching to personalized learning methods will help us effectively tackle the inherent learning gaps between individuals.

References

Allen, N. D. (2008). Temporal and epigenetic regulation of neurodevelopmental plasticity. *Philosophical Transactions: Biological Sciences, 363*(1489), 23–38. https://doi.org/10.1098/rstb.2006.2010.

Bach, S., Richardson, U., Brandeis, D., Martin, E., & Brem, S. (2013). Print-specific multimodal brain activation in kindergarten improves prediction of reading skills in second grade. *Neuroimage, 82,* 605–615. https://doi.org/10.1016/j.neuroimage.2013.05.062.

Bates, T. C., Castles, A., Luciano, M., Wright, M. J., Coltheart, M., & Martin, N. G. (2007). Genetic and environmental bases of reading and spelling: A unified genetic dual route model. *Reading and Writing, 20*(1–2), 147–171. https://doi.org/10.1007/s11145-006-9022-1.

Berwick, R. C., & Chomsky, N. (2016). *Why only us: Language and evolution*. Cambridge, MA: MIT Press.

Black, J. E., & Barnes, J. L. (2015). The effects of reading material on social and non-social cognition. *Poetics, 52,* 32–43. https://doi.org/10.1016/j.poetic.2015.07.001.

Blicher, S., Feingold, L., & Shany, M. (2017). The role of trait anxiety and preoccupation with reading disabilities of children and their mothers in predicting children's reading comprehension. *Journal of Learning Disabilities, 50*(3), 309–321. https://doi.org/10.1177/0022219415624101.

Borrelli, E., Nestler, E. J., Allis, C. D., & Sassone-Corsi, P. (2008). Decoding the epigenetic language of neuronal plasticity. *Neuron, 60*(6), 961–974. https://doi.org/10.1016/j.neuron.2008.10.012.

Brzustowicz, L. M. (2014). Molecular genetic approaches to the study of language. *Human Biology, 70*(2): 199–213. Retrieved from http://www.jstor.org/stable/41465641.

Caffarra, S., Martin, C. D., Lizarazu, M., Lallier, M., Zarraga, A., Molinaro, N., et al. (2017). Word and object recognition during reading acquisition: MEG evidence. *Developmental Cognitive Neuroscience, 24*(16), 21–32. https://doi.org/10.1016/j.dcn.2017.01.002.

Centanni, T. M., Green, J. R., Iuzzini-seigel, J., Bartlett, C. W., & Hogan, T. P. (2015). Evidence for the multiple hits genetic theory for inherited language impairment: A case study. *Frontiers in Genetics, 6*(August), 6–11. https://doi.org/10.3389/fgene.2015.00272.

Chang, C. H. C., Pallier, C., Wu, D. H., Nakamura, K., Jobert, A., Kuo, W. J., et al. (2015). Adaptation of the human visual system to the statistics of letters and line configurations. *Neuroimage, 120,* 428–440. https://doi.org/10.1016/j.neuroimage.2015.07.028.

Chang, H., Hoshina, N., Zhang, C., Ma, Y., Cao, H., Wang, Y., et al. (2017). The protocadherin 17 gene affects cognition, personality, amygdala structure and function, synapse development and risk of major mood disorders. *Molecular Psychiatry, 23,* 1–13. https://doi.org/10.1038/mp.2016.231.

Changizi, M., Zhang, Q., Ye, H., & Shimojo, S. (2006). The structures of letters and symbols throughout human history are selected to match those found in objects in natural scenes. *The American Naturalist, 167*(5), E117–E139. https://doi.org/10.1086/502806.

Chen, Y., Fu, S., Iversen, S. D., Smith, S. M., & Matthews, P. M. (2002). Testing for dual brain processing routes in reading: A direct contrast of Chinese character and pinyin reading using fMRI. *Journal of Cognitive Neuroscience, 14*(7), 1088–1098. https://doi.org/10.1162/089892902320474535.

Clark, C., and Rumbold, K. (2006). *Reading for pleasure: A research overview.* National Literacy Trust. London. Retrieved from http://www.scholastic.com/teachers/article/collateral_resources/pdf/i/Reading_for_pleasure.pdf.

Cope, N., Harold, D., Hill, G., Moskvina, V., Stevenson, J., Holmans, P., et al. (2005). Strong evidence that KIAA0319 on chromosome 6p is a susceptibility gene for developmental dyslexia. *American Journal of Human Genetics, 76*(4), 581–591. https://doi.org/10.1086/429131.

Cox, K. E., & Guthrie, J. T. (2001). Motivational and cognitive contributions to students' amount of reading. *Contemporary Educational Psychology, 26,* 116–131. https://doi.org/10.1006/ceps.1999.1044.

Day, J. J., & Sweatt, J. D. (2011). Epigenetic mechanisms in cognition. *Neuron, 70*(5), 813–829. https://doi.org/10.1016/j.neuron.2011.05.019.

Deary, I. J., Penke, L., & Johnson, W. (2010). The neuroscience of human intelligence differences. *Nature Reviews Neuroscience, 11*(3), 201. https://doi.org/10.1038/nrn2793.

Dehaene, S. (2010). *Reading in the brain: The science and evolution of a human invention.* New York, NY: Viking.

Dehaene, S., & Cohen, L. (2011). The unique role of the visual word form area in reading. *Trends in Cognitive Sciences, 15*(6), 254–262. https://doi.org/10.1016/j.tics.2011.04.003.

Dehaene, S., Cohen, L., Morais, J., & Kolinsky, R. (2015). Illiterate to literate: Behavioural and cerebral changes induced by reading acquisition. *Nature Reviews Neuroscience, 16*(4), 234–244. https://doi.org/10.1038/nrn3924.

Dehaene, S., Pegado, F., Braga, L. W., Ventura, P., Filho, G. N., Jobert, A., et al. (2010). How learning to read changes the cortical networks for vision and language. *Science, 330*(6009), 1359–1364. https://doi.org/10.1126/science.1194140.

Dolcos, F., Iordan, A. D., & Dolcos, S. (2011). Neural correlates of emotion—cognition interactions: A review of evidence from brain imaging investigations. *Journal of Cognitive Psychology, 23*(6), 669–694. https://doi.org/10.1080/20445911.2011.594433.

Eicher, J. D., & Gruen, J. R. (2013). Imaging-genetics in dyslexia: Connecting risk genetic variants to brain neuroimaging and ultimately to reading impairments. *Molecular Genetics and Metabolism, 110*(3), 201–212. https://doi.org/10.1016/j.ymgme.2013.07.001.

Elvevåg, B., & Weinberger, D. R. (2009). Introduction: Genes, cognition and neuropsychiatry. *Cognitive Neuropsychiatry, 14*(4–5), 261–276. https://doi.org/10.1080/13546800903126016.

Felling, R. J., & Song, H. (2015). Epigenetic mechanisms of neuroplasticity and the implications for stroke recovery. *Experimental Neurology, 268,* 37–45. https://doi.org/10.1016/j.expneurol.2014.09.017.

Fisher, S. E., & DeFries, J. C. (2002). Developmental dyslexia: Genetic dissection of a complex cognitive trait. *Nature Reviews Neuroscience, 3*(10), 767–780. https://doi.org/10.1038/nrn936.

Fong, K., Mullin, J. B., & Mar, R. A. (2013). What you read matters: The role of fiction genre in predicting interpersonal sensitivity. *Psychology of Aesthetics, Creativity, and the Arts, 7*(4), 370–376. https://doi.org/10.1037/a0034084.

Fried, I., Wilson, C. L., Morrow, J. W., Cameron, K. A., Behnke, E. D., Ackerson, L. C., et al. (2001). Increased dopamine release in the human amygdala during performance of cognitive tasks. *Nature Neuroscience, 4*(2), 201–206. https://doi.org/10.1038/84041.

Fu, S., Chen, Y., Smith, S., Iversen, S., & Matthews, P. M. (2002). Effects of word form on brain processing of written Chinese. *Neuroimage, 17*(3), 1538–1548. https://doi.org/10.1006/nimg.2002.1155.

Gabrieli, J. D. E. (2009). Dyslexia: A new synergy between education and cognitive neuroscience. *Science, 325*(5938), 280–283. https://doi.org/10.1126/science.1171999.

Gallagher, M., & Chiba, A. A. (1996). The amygdala and emotion. *Current Opinion in Neurobiology, 6*(2), 221–227. https://doi.org/10.1016/S0959-4388(96)80076-6.

Gayán, J., & Olson, R. K. (2001). Genetic and environmental influences on orthographic and phonological skills in children with reading disabilities. *Developmental Neuropsychology. Developmental Neuropsychology, 20*(2), 483–507. https://doi.org/10.1207/S15326942DN2002_3.

Gayán, J., & Olson, R. K. (2003). Genetic and environmental influences on individual differences in printed word recognition. *Journal of Experimental Child Psychology, 84*(2), 97–123. https://doi.org/10.1016/S0022-0965(02)00181-9.

Ghanbari, M., & Marzban, A. (2014). Effect of extensive reading on incidental vocabulary retention. *Procedia—Social and Behavioral Sciences, 116*, 3854–3858. https://doi.org/10.1016/j.sbspro.2014.01.854.

Gialluisi, A., Guadalupe, T., Francks, C., & Fisher, S. E. (2017). Neuroimaging genetic analyses of novel candidate genes associated with reading and language. *Brain and Language, 172*, 9–15. https://doi.org/10.1016/j.bandl.2016.07.002.

Gialluisi, A., Newbury, D. F., Wilcutt, E. G., Consortium, T. S. L. I., & Luciano, M. (2014). Genome-wide screening for DNA variants associated with reading and language traits. *Genes, Brain and Behavior, 13*(7), 686–701. https://doi.org/10.1111/gbb.12158.

Gray, J. A. (1990). Brain systems that mediate both emotion and cognition. *Cognition and Emotion, 4*(3), 269–288. https://doi.org/10.1080/02699939008410799.

Guthrie, J. T., & Alvermann, D. E. (1999). *Engaged reading: Processes, practices and policy implications*. New York: Teachers College Press.

Hannula-Jouppi, K., Kaminen-Ahola, N., Taipale, M., Eklund, R., Nopola-Hemmi, J., Kääriäinen, H., et al. (2005). The axon guidance receptor gene ROBO1 is a candidate gene for developmental dyslexia. *PLoS Genetics, 1*(4), 0467–0474. https://doi.org/10.1371/journal.pgen.0010050.

Hashemi, M. (2011). Language stress and anxiety among the English language learners. *Procedia—Social and Behavioral Sciences, 30*, 1811–1816. https://doi.org/10.1016/j.sbspro.2011.10.349.

Hewitt, E., & Stephenson, J. (2012). Foreign language anxiety and oral exam performance: A replication of Phillips's MLJ study. *Modern Language Journal, 96*(2), 170–189. https://doi.org/10.1111/j.1540-4781.2011.01174.x.

Ho, C. S. H., Wong, S. W. L., Chow, B. W. Y., Waye, M. M. Y., & Bishop, D. V. M. (2017). Genetic and environmental etiology of speech and word reading in Chinese. *Learning and Individual Differences, 56*, 49–58. https://doi.org/10.1016/j.lindif.2017.04.001.

Hoeft, F., McCandliss, B. D., Black, J. M., Gantman, A., Zakerani, N., Hulme, C., et al. (2011). Neural systems predicting long-term outcome in dyslexia. *Proceedings of the National Academy of Sciences, 108*(1), 361–366. https://doi.org/10.1073/pnas.1008950108.

Hoeft, F., Meyler, A., Hernandez, A., Juel, C., Taylor-Hill, H., Martindale, J. L., et al. (2007). Functional and morphometric brain dissociation between dyslexia and reading ability. *Proceedings of the National Academy of Sciences of the United States of America, 104*(10), 4234–4239. https://doi.org/10.1073/pnas.0609399104.

Kennedy, A. J., Rahn, E. J., Paulukaitis, B. S., Michael, T. P., Day, J. J., David, J., et al. (2016). Tcf4 regulates synaptic plasticity, DNA methylation, and memory function. *Cell Reports, 16*, 2666–2685. https://doi.org/10.1016/j.celrep.2016.08.004.

Kidd, D. C., & Castano, E. (2013). Reading literary fiction improves theory of mind. *Science, 342*(6156), 377–380. https://doi.org/10.1126/science.1239918.

Knickerbocker, H., Johnson, R. L., & Altarriba, J. (2015). Emotion effects during reading: Influence of an emotion target word on eye movements and processing. *Cognition and Emotion, 29*(5), 784–806. https://doi.org/10.1080/02699931.2014.938023.

Krashen, S. D. (1982). *Priniciples and practice in second language acquisition* (1st ed.). London: Penguin Press Inc.

Laeger, I., Dobel, C., Dannlowski, U., Kugel, H., Grotegerd, D., Kissler, J., et al. (2012). Amygdala responsiveness to emotional words is modulated by subclinical anxiety and depression. *Behavioural Brain Research, 233*(2), 508–516. https://doi.org/10.1016/j.bbr.2012.05.036.

Lee, J., Schallert, D. L., & Kim, E. (2015). Effects of extensive reading and translation activities on grammar knowledge and attitudes for EFL adolescents. *System, 52,* 38–50. https://doi.org/10.1016/j.system.2015.04.016.

Little, C. W., & Hart, S. A. (2016). Examining the genetic and environmental associations among spelling, reading fluency, reading comprehension and a high stakes reading test in a combined sample of third and fourth grade students. *Learning and Individual Differences, 45,* 25–32. https://doi.org/10.1016/j.lindif.2015.11.008.

Malle, B. F. (2005). Folk theory of mind: Conceptual foundations of human social cognition. In R. Hassin, S. J. Uleman, & J. A. Bargh (Eds.), *The new unconscious* (pp. 225–255). New York: Oxford University Press. https://doi.org/10.1093/acprof:oso/9780195307696.003.0010

McEwen, B. S. (2016). In pursuit of resilience: Stress, epigenetics, and brain plasticity. *Annals of the New York Academy of Sciences, 1373*(1), 56–64. https://doi.org/10.1111/nyas.13020.

McEwen, B. S., Eiland, L., Hunter, R. G., & Miller, M. M. (2012). Stress and anxiety: Structural plasticity and epigenetic regulation as a consequence of stress. *Neuropharmacology, 62*(1), 3–12. https://doi.org/10.1016/j.neuropharm.2011.07.014.

McGrath, L. M., Pennington, B. F., Shanahan, M. A., Santerre-Lemmon, L. E., Barnard, H. D., Willcutt, E. G., et al. (2011). A multiple deficit model of reading disability and attention-deficit/ hyperactivity disorder: Searching for shared cognitive deficits. *Journal of Child Psychology and Psychiatry and Allied Disciplines, 52*(5), 547–557. https://doi.org/10.1111/j.1469-7610.2010.02346.x.

McGrath, L. M., Smith, S. D., & Pennington, B. F. (2006). Breakthroughs in the search for dyslexia candidate genes. *Trends in Molecular Medicine, 12*(7), 333–341. https://doi.org/10.1016/j.molmed.2006.05.007.

McKenna, M. C., & Kear, D. J. (1990). A new tool for teachers. *The Reading Teacher, 43*(8), 626–639. https://doi.org/10.1598/RT.43.8.3.

Meng, H., Smith, S. D., Hager, K., Held, M., Liu, J., Olson, R. K., et al. (2005). DCDC2 is associated with reading disability and modulates neuronal development in the brain. *Proceedings of the National Academy of Sciences, 102*(47), 17053–17058. https://doi.org/10.1073/pnas.0508591102.

Molfese, D. L. (2000). Predicting dyslexia at 8 years of age using neonatal brain responses. *Brain and Language, 72*(3), 238–245. https://doi.org/10.1006/brln.2000.2287.

Nieto, S. J., Patriquin, M. A., Nielsen, D. A., & Kosten, T. A. (2016). Don't worry: Be informed about the epigenetics of anxiety. *Pharmacology, Biochemistry and Behavior, 146–147,* 60–72. https://doi.org/10.1016/j.pbb.2016.05.006.

Norton, E. S., Beach, S. D., & Gabrieli, J. D. E. (2015). Neurobiology of dyslexia. *Current Opinion in Neurobiology, 30,* 73–78. https://doi.org/10.1016/j.conb.2014.09.007.

Ölmez, F. (2015). An investigation into the relationship between L2 reading motivation and reading achievement. *Procedia—Social and Behavioral Sciences, 199,* 597–603. https://doi.org/10.1016/j.sbspro.2015.07.561.

Olson, R. K. (2006). Genes, environment, and dyslexia the 2005 Norman Geschwind Memorial Lecture. *Annals of Dyslexia, 56*(2), 205–238. https://doi.org/10.1007/s11881-006-0010-6.

Palmisano, M., & Pandey, S. C. (2017). Epigenetic mechanisms of alcoholism and stress-related disorders. *Alcohol, 60,* 46. https://doi.org/10.1016/j.alcohol.2017.01.001.

Paracchini, S., Diaz, R., and Stein, J. (2016). Advances in dyslexia genetics—new insights into the role of brain asymmetries. In T. Friedmann, J. Dunlap, & G. S. F. (Eds.), *Advances in genetics* (1st ed., Vol. 96, pp. 53–97). Cambridge, MA: Elsevier Inc. https://doi.org/10.1016/bs.adgen.2016.08.003.

Parasuraman, R. (2009). Assaying individual differences in cognition with molecular genetics: Theory and application. *Theoretical Issues in Ergonomics Science, 10*(5), 399–416. https://doi.org/10.1080/14639220903106403.

Pascual-Leone, A., Amedi, A., Fregni, F., & Merabet, L. B. (2005). The plastic human brain cortex. *Annual Review of Neuroscience, 28*(1), 377–401. https://doi.org/10.1146/annurev.neuro.27.070203.144216.

Pessoa, L. (2008). On the relationship between emotion and cognition. *Nature Reviews Neuroscience, 9*(2), 148–158. https://doi.org/10.1038/nrn2317.

Peterson, R. L., & Pennington, B. F. (2012). Developmental dyslexia. *The Lancet, 379*(9830), 1997–2007. https://doi.org/10.1016/S0140-6736(12)60198-6.

Raskind, W. H., Peter, B., Richards, T., Eckert, M. M., & Berninger, V. W. (2013). The genetics of reading disabilities: From phenotypes to candidate genes. *Frontiers in Psychology, 3*(1), 1–20. https://doi.org/10.3389/fpsyg.2012.00601.

Richiardi, J., Altmann, A., & Jonas, R. (2015). Correlated gene expression supports synchronous activity in brain networks. *Science, 348*(6240), 11–14. https://doi.org/10.1126/science.1255905.

Rietveld, C. A., Medland, S. E., Derringer, J., Yang, J., Esko, T., Martin, N. W., ... Koellinger, P. D. (2013). GWAS of 126,559 Individuals identifies genetic variants associated with educational attainment. *Science, 340*(6139): 1467–1471. https://doi.org/10.1126/science.1235488.

Scerri, T. S., Darki, F., Newbury, D. F., Whitehouse, A. J. O., Peyrard-Janvid, M., Matsson, H., et al. (2012). The dyslexia candidate locus on 2p12 is associated with general cognitive ability and white matter structure. *PLoS ONE, 7*(11), 50321. https://doi.org/10.1371/journal.pone.0050321.

Scerri, T. S., Morris, A. P., Buckingham, L., Newbury, D. F., Miller, L. L., Bishop, D. V. M., et al. (2011). DCDC2, KIAA0319 and CMIP are associated with reading-related traits. *Biological Psychiatry, 70*(3), 237–245. https://doi.org/10.1016/j.biopsych.2011.02.005.

Schmitz, J., Kumsta, R., Moser, D., Güntürkün, O., & Ocklenburg, S. (2018). KIAA0319 promoter DNA methylation predicts dichotic listening performance in forced-attention conditions. *Behavioural Brain Research, in press.*. https://doi.org/10.1016/J.BBR.2017.09.035.

Scult, M. A., & Hariri, A. R. (2018). A brief introduction to the neurogenetics of cognition-emotion interactions. *Current Opinion in Behavioral Sciences, 19*, 50–54. https://doi.org/10.1016/j.cobeha.2017.09.014.

Swagerman, S. C., van Bergen, E., Dolan, C., de Geus, E. J. C. C., Koenis, M. M. G. G., Hulshoff Pol, H. E., et al. (2017). Genetic transmission of reading ability. *Brain and Language, 172*, 3–8. https://doi.org/10.1016/j.bandl.2015.07.008.

Taipale, M., Kaminen, N., Nopola-Hemmi, J., Haltia, T., Myllyluoma, B., Lyytinen, H., et al. (2003). A candidate gene for developmental dyslexia encodes a nuclear tetratricopeptide repeat domain protein dynamically regulated in brain. *Proceedings of the National Academy of Sciences of the United States of America, 100*(20), 11553–11558. https://doi.org/10.1073/pnas.1833911100.

Tran, C., Wigg, K. G., Zhang, K., Cate-Carter, T. D., Kerr, E., Field, L. L., et al. (2014). Association of the ROBO1 gene with reading disabilities in a family-based analysis. *Genes, Brain and Behavior, 13*(4), 430–438. https://doi.org/10.1111/gbb.12126.

Turkeltaub, P. E., Flowers, D. L., Verbalis, A., Miranda, M., Gareau, L., & Eden, G. F. (2004). The neural basis of hyperlexic reading: An fMRI case study. *Neuron, 41*(1), 11–25. https://doi.org/10.1016/S0896-6273(03)00803-1.

Wandell, B. A., & Le, R. K. (2017). Diagnosing the neural circuitry of reading. *Neuron, 96*(2), 298–311. https://doi.org/10.1016/j.neuron.2017.08.007.

Wasik, B. A., Hindman, A. H., & Snell, E. K. (2016). Book reading and vocabulary development: A systematic review. *Early Childhood Research Quarterly, 37*, 39–57. https://doi.org/10.1016/j.ecresq.2016.04.003.

Wehmeyer, M. L., Shogren, K. A., Toste, J., & Mahal, S. (2016). Self-determined learning to motivate struggling learners in reading and writing. *Intervention in School and Clinic*. https://doi.org/10.1177/1053451216676800.

Weinshilboum, R. M., & Wang, L. (2006). Pharmacogenetics and pharmacogenomics: Development, science, and translation. *Annual Review of Genomics and Human Genetics, 7,* 223–245. https://doi.org/10.1146/annurev.genom.6.080604.162315.

White, D., & Rabago-Smith, M. (2011). Genotype–phenotype associations and human eye color. *Journal of Human Genetics, 56*(1), 5–7. https://doi.org/10.1038/jhg.2010.126.

Willcutt, E. G., Betjemann, R. S., McGrath, L. M., Chhabildas, N. A., Olson, R. K., DeFries, J. C., et al. (2010). Etiology and neuropsychology of comorbidity between RD and ADHD: The case for multiple-deficit models. *Cortex, 46*(10), 1345–1361. https://doi.org/10.1016/j.cortex.2010.06.009.

Williams, L. M., Tsang, T. W., Clarke, S., & Kohn, M. (2010). An "integrative neuroscience" perspective on ADHD: Linking cognition, emotion, brain and genetic measures with implications for clinical support. *Expert Review of Neurotherapeutics, 10*(10), 1607–1621. https://doi.org/10.1586/ern.10.140.

Wingo, A. P., Almli, L. M., Stevens, J. S., Jovanovic, T., Wingo, T. S., Tharp, G., et al. (2017). Genome-wide association study of positive emotion identifies a genetic variant and a role for microRNAs. *Molecular Psychiatry, 22*(5), 774–783. https://doi.org/10.1038/mp.2016.143.

Wong, P. C. M., Vuong, L. C., & Liu, K. (2017). Personalized learning: From neurogenetics of behaviors to designing optimal language training. *Neuropsychologia, 98,* 192–200. https://doi.org/10.1016/j.neuropsychologia.2016.10.002.

Zambo, D., & Brem, S. K. (2004). Emotion and cognition in students who struggle to read: New insights and ideas. *Reading Psychology, 25*(3), 189–204. https://doi.org/10.1080/02702710490489881.

Chapter 9
Reading Comprehension in ESL Contexts: An Applied Cognitive Semantics Perspective

N. P. Sudharshana

Abstract 'Cognitive semantics' is an umbrella term applied to several streams of research sharing the common premise that language and general cognition are interrelated and interdependent. Stemming from this concept are the following principles which have been found to be relevant for language pedagogy: all linguistic elements have a conceptualization dimension and thus they are 'meaningful'; all linguistic elements are abstracted from their real-life usage contexts; discourse, just like individual linguistic elements, is highly structured and rooted in usage contexts; metaphoric and metonymic concepts prevail in our thought process; and linguistic elements represent categorization in human cognition based on perceived commonalities and motivated extensions. The first part of this chapter briefly sketches out these salient principles and the second part discusses implications of these principles for reading in ESL contexts. Extending on some current cognitive semantics-based practices in other areas of pedagogy, the paper argues that cognitive semantics (CS) can facilitate an in-depth reading comprehension in ESL contexts mainly by offering tools for detailed linguistic analyses and reconstruction of meaning. The application of CS principles is also illustrated with a sample text.

Keywords Reading in ESL contexts · Applied cognitive semantics
Conceptual metaphor · Cognitive grammar

Introduction

Reading is a crucial skill for success in ESL academic contexts. Learners are often required to employ different reading strategies to achieve different goals. They read for specific details and for an overall understanding (known as 'scanning' and 'skimming' respectively), for general comprehension and information, and also

---

N. P. Sudharshana (✉)
Department of Humanities and Social Sciences, IIT Kanpur, Kanpur, India
e-mail: sudh@iitk.ac.in

© Springer Nature Singapore Pte Ltd. 2018
R. Joseph Ponniah and S. Venkatesan (eds.), *The Idea and Practice of Reading*,
https://doi.org/10.1007/978-981-10-8572-7_9

sometimes for entertainment. Reading in academic contexts typically also involves two other important dimensions: reading for a critical understanding; and reading to acquire proficiency in second language (Grabe, 2009; Nation, 2009). When ESL learners read for a critical understanding, particularly at advanced levels, they are expected to carefully examine the choice of words/structures, understand the structure of the given text, delve deeply into the main thesis and examine evidence and arguments to form an opinion about the issue in question and integrate the given knowledge with the previous to form a global view of the topic. Reading has also been recognized as a tool to enhance proficiency. ESL learners are often directed towards use of specific structures and vocabulary items in actual discourse contexts, leading to consciousness raising and the acquisition of forms while making meaning (Ellis, 2003, 2010).[1]

This paper discusses how cognitive semantics (CS), a theory of language based on actual use of language in real-life contexts, can offer some insights for ESL reading. An attempt is made to explain how theories of the conceptual nature of language, the cognitive nature of cohesion and coherence in a discourse, prototypes and radial categories, and conceptual metaphor can enhance critical reading skills and facilitate acquisition of second-language proficiency.

The chapter is organized in the following way. First, the salient principles of CS and also some previous attempts at applying these principles into areas of pedagogy other than reading are summarized. Next possible ways that CS can enhance reading skills in ESL contexts are discussed, and the application of CS principles to a sample text is illustrated. The final section consists of concluding remarks.

Cognitive Semantics and Second-Language Pedagogy

The term 'cognitive semantics' is collectively applied to different streams of research such as Langacker's (1987, 1991, 2008) cognitive grammar; Lakoff's theories of metaphor (Lakoff & Johnson, 1980) and categorization (Lakoff, 1987); Talmy's (2000a, 2000b) theories on concept structuring and motion event typology; and Goldberg's (1995) construction grammar, among others. All these approaches to language differ from the formal approaches in their claim that "language is part of cognition and that linguistic investigation contributes to understanding the human mind" (Langacker, 2008: 7). CS presumes that linguistic knowledge is organized and retrieved in much the same way as other kinds of knowledge, and the processes and abilities employed in linguistic comprehension and production are similar to those applied to other cognitive tasks such as reasoning (Croft & Cruse, 2004). Linguistic structures, thus, cannot be segregated from *more basic systems and*

---

[1]Interpretation tasks and consciousness-raising tasks are examples which make use of authentic reading texts to direct learner attention to specific forms. Ellis (2003, 2010) argues that such form-focused meaningful activities help develop accuracy in communicative contexts.

utilities such as perception, categorization and memory (Langacker, 2008: 8, emphasis added). CS is concerned with this semantic structure of linguistic elements and the interrelationships of such conceptual structures. These interrelationships include metaphoric and metonymic mapping, prototypes and their extensions, those between text and context, and those in the formation of abstract image schemas (Talmy, 2011).

This chapter discusses two main streams of research under CS that have been observed to have a high relevance for pedagogy: Langacker's (1987, 1991, 2008) cognitive grammar; and Lakoff's (Lakoff & Johnson, 1980; Lakoff 1987) conceptual metaphor and categorization.

Cognitive Grammar

One of the fundamental claims of cognitive grammar (CG) is that 'grammar is meaningful' and that there is no dichotomy between vocabulary items on one hand and grammatical categories and structures on the other (see Langacker, 2008, among others). In other words, grammatical elements (e.g., prepositions) and structures (e.g., passives), which have long been thought to serve the purpose of binding together vocabulary items, have meaning in their own right. What is the nature of this meaning? In CG, meaning is conceptualization, a mental phenomenon. Language is grounded in cognition and draws on general cognitive systems (e.g., perception, memory) and processes (e.g., categorization, schematization). This is why the theory is called 'cognitive grammar'. However, language is not an abstract mental phenomenon; it is rooted in the physical reality around us which includes but is not limited to social interaction, cultural beliefs, conventions and practices. As a functionalist framework, CG argues that grammatical structures, vocabulary and other linguistic elements neither exist in isolation nor are innately acquired. Instead, all linguistic elements (which includes vocabulary and grammar) are acquired from actual instances of language use (e.g., a conversation between two friends at a party). When a particular structure or a word occurs repeatedly in several contexts, the users form an abstract generalization about that particular form —called a 'schema'—and store it for future uses. When they encounter a similar situation, the form already stored is retrieved to 'construe' that particular situation in a specific way. Thus, there is no direct correspondence between the real event and the reported event; the reported event is just a 'construal' of the real event. Sometimes, there may be several options to report the same event, and the speakers choose one way over the others depending on what they are focusing on and what meaning they want to convey. This is where discourse becomes significant because linguistic units have meaning only in a particular discourse context.[2]

---

[2]A discourse can be spoken or written. Since the focus here is on reading, 'discourse' here particularly refers to written texts such as essays, letters, stories, etc.

It is clear that discourse has been accorded an important place in CG. It is the platform where linguistic elements are observed, acquired and offered explanation. A discourse, just like individual linguistic elements, has a definite structure and is rooted in physical reality. Structurally, a discourse is "a series of conceptions associated with forms" (Langacker, 2008: 486). This means every usage event has an expressive and a conceptual dimension. A written discourse is viewed as having multiple layers of organization. Individual linguistic units form phrases which then lead to clauses, paragraphs, sections, a chapter and ultimately a book. In order to understand a discourse as a whole, the reader has to interpret component expressions in relation to what has come earlier and what will come later. Such retrospective and prospective connections can be established mainly through two kinds of coherence: referential and relational coherence (Sanders & Spooren, 2010). The former includes means of introducing individuals and key ideas/topics and tracking them throughout to establish a sense of connectivity across different parts of a text by means of full noun phrases, pronouns, etc. The latter refers to coherence established through relations such as cause–consequence, list, problem–solution, etc., which closely follow the natural order of non-linguistic concepts (Sanders & Spooren, 2010). The second dimension is the usage-based nature of discourse. The writer construes meaning in a particular way and encodes it in linguistic elements for an actual or an imagined reader to decode. This meaning, of course, is not just what is said explicitly; it encompasses all aspects of social interaction (physical setting, social norms, cultural beliefs, etc.). During reading, there is an interaction between the reader and the writer and if there is a substantial overlap between them in meaning making, the communication may be considered successful (Langacker, 2008). One can identify different kinds of written discourses. These genres include diary entries, restaurant menus, scientific articles, newspaper reports, notices, letters and e-mails, narratives, descriptions, etc. Each genre is a schema abstracted from several usage events. This schema is like a template and includes assumed commonalities, some features which occur repeatedly. These include but are not limited to global organization, local structural properties, typical content, specific expressions employed, and matters of style and register (Langacker, 2008).

Theories of Conceptual Metaphor and Categorization

Lakoff and Johnson (1980) argue that "our conceptual system is metaphorical in nature" and that metaphors structure "how we perceive, how we think, and what we do" (p. 3). In other words, we try to "understand and experience one kind of thing in terms of another" (p. 5). For instance, we often talk about arguments in terms of war as the following examples illustrate:

(1)
- (a) The argument *escalated* from there before coming to an end.
- (b) The radio host had a *heated* argument with his co-worker.
- (c) The senator then *demolished* the CEO's argument.
- (d) *Attacking* the character of the person making argument rather than the argument itself is a logical fallacy.

It is further argued that most of these metaphors have a basis in our physical and cultural experience. Space is considered one of the most fundamental domains of experience upon which other experiences are based (Lakoff & Johnson, 1980: 57). For instance, membership of a group, time or an emotional state is construed as being in a container, a three-dimensional space:

(2)
- (a) John is *in* the garage.   (*actual physical experience*)
- (b) Sharma is *in* Mumbai Indians. (*membership of a group/team*)
- (c) The wedding is *in* April.   (*a unit of time*)
- (d) Stella is *in* distress.   (*emotional state*)

Socio-cultural values also influence how we conceptualize the world. For instance, one of the popular values of Western culture is 'The future will be better'. This is reflected in the metaphor 'the future is up; good is up' (e.g. "Keep looking up! I learn from the past, dream about the future and look up"—Rachel Boston) (see Lakoff & Johnson, 1980: 22 for details).

Another important aspect of our world is metonymic concepts—conceptualizing the whole in terms of its parts or vice versa. The following examples illustrate this:

(3)
- (a) The Supreme Court dismissed a PIL on fundamental duties. (*an institution stands for its members, here judges*)
- (b) The latest newspaper reports have upset the Crown. (*an object stands for an institution*)

Lakoff's other major contribution has been the categorization theory. He argues that human beings categorize the world around them and this categorization can be explained in terms of a prototype and radial categories extending from it based on perceived schematic commonalities. For instance, in the category of 'mother', the prototypical would be the biological model, 'one who is married to the father and has given birth and one who nurtures'. There are extensions from this prototype to other categories, such as 'stepmother', 'foster mother', 'surrogate mother', etc. (Lakoff, 1987: 83).[3]

---

[3]'Prototype(s)' or 'prototypical member(s)' refers to the best example of a particular category. 'Radial categories' emerge as extensions from this prototype based on some common features. The extended categories may not share any common feature(s). See Lakoff (1987) for details.

Pedagogic Applications of Cognitive Semantics

The principles that meaning and not syntax is central to language and that meaning is based on actual usage contexts have made CS a favourite for applied linguists. There have been attempts to explain the meaning of grammatical categories and structures and integrate them into language teaching. An area which has been extensively studied is prepositions. Studies have proposed frameworks to teach prepositions based on schematic pictures or icons (e.g., Lindstromberg, 1996); metaphoric extensions (Boers, 2004; Boers & Demecheleer, 1998); and figurative uses, idioms and phrasal verbs as motivated extensions from the prototypical uses of prepositions (e.g., Tyler & Evans 2004, Lindstromberg, 2010). Other areas of grammar which have been studied include modal verbs (e.g., Tyler, 2008), tense/aspect, and definite and indefinite articles as part of a larger referencing system (e.g., Radden & Dirven, 2007), among others. See Boers and Lindstromberg (2006) and Putz (2007) for a detailed survey of studies in applied cognitive semantics.

There have been some attempts to enhance reading comprehension skills based on the theory of conceptual metaphor (Lakoff & Johnson, 1980). These are discussed in detail below.

Cognitive Semantics and Reading in ESL Contexts

Reading comprehension is said to be the result of several psycholinguistic processes happening concurrently. When the reader approaches a text, the first level of processing is at linguistic level. The reader decodes graphic symbols, recognizes words and begins parsing from word level to individual sentence level. The next level is semantic analysis, where the reader combines word and sentence meanings to form propositions and (re)construct the meaning of a text. The reader first builds a microstructure working through coherence and coreference, then organize microstructures into macrostructures (global topics and interrelationships). The final stage is constructing a situation model, where the reader syncs the given information with previous knowledge and with the goal of the reading (Kintsch & Rawson, 2011).

In the following sections, along with the conceptual metaphor theory other implications of CS for reading are discussed. We show how CS can contribute to more effective linguistic decoding, enhanced structure awareness and a critical reading of the text.

Awareness of Conceptual Metaphor in Texts

One of the revolutionary claims within the CS paradigm has been that 'we live by metaphors'. Metaphor here is not just used in its limited interpretation of figure of speech, but as a concept overarching the entire human thought process. Lakoff and

Johnson (1980) term it 'conceptual metaphor' because it structures "how we perceive, how we think, and what we do" (p. 3). It has been claimed that abstract thought is not possible without thinking something in concrete and the concrete domain chosen determines how one looks at the abstract (Littlemore, 2004). For instance, 'time' is usually talked about in terms of 'money' as in the examples below:

(4)
- (a) *Spending* quality family time together is always important.
- (b) To create a meaningful relationship, we need to *invest* the time it takes to understand someone.
- (c) The security won't *waste* time checking entry passes for students.

Similarly, computer-related problems are talked about in terms of human diseases, for example the thing which affects computers is called a 'virus'. This is just one example. The following extracts from a newspaper indicate the pervasiveness of this metaphor:

(5)
- (a) Governments, companies and security experts from China to Britain on Saturday raced to *contain* the fallout.
- (b) While most cyber-attacks are inherently global, this one, experts say, is more *virulent* than most.
- (c) Despite people's best efforts, this *vulnerability* still exists.
- (d) … users' tales of how their computers had been *infected* and tips on how to avoid the *virus*.
- (e) … 45 of its hospitals, doctors' offices and ambulance companies had been *crippled*.

(Scott, 2017)

Studies on enhancing the metaphoric awareness of ESL readers observe that such awareness can lead to more effective retention of keywords and ultimately a coherent text representation in readers' minds. Boers (2000), for instance, investigated whether making metaphoric connections explicit would lead to better in-depth comprehension and vocabulary retention among a group of business studies students. A text on an economic issue with several conventional figurative expressions (e.g., 'overcoming a hurdle', 'bailing out the firms', 'weeding out discrepancies') was chosen. While the control group was taught through the traditional method of explaining word meanings, the experimental group was made aware of metaphoric connections (e.g., weed out: pull out unwanted wild plants). The experimental group performed significantly better than the control group on a test based on inferences and value judgements, and a gap-filling test on keywords used in the text. See also Allbritton, McKoon and Gerrig (1995), Littlemore (2004), among others.

By extension, conceptual metaphors in a written text represent the writer's view of the world. Readers need to understand the underlying conceptual metaphors at the initial level to understand the text and then question the writer's assumptions and arguments critically. This is more relevant in persuasive texts where the validity of underlying arguments is crucial for accepting or rejecting the writer's viewpoints. A related area of research has been critical metaphor analysis, which claims that "metaphorical expressions in text reflect and effect underlying construal operations which are ideological in nature" (Hart, 2011: 270). For instance, Charteris-Black (2006), in an analysis of political speech in Britain, observes the use of the verb 'swamp' in relation to immigration (e.g. "...local schools were being swamped by the children of asylum seekers", p. 570) which "evokes strong emotions and creates a myth that immigration is excessive and communicates the ideological political argument that it should be stopped—or even be reversed" (p. 567). These studies indicate that raising awareness about conceptual metaphor can enhance reading comprehension and also help in evaluating the text.

Significance of Cognitive Processes in Meaning Making

CS claims that meaning making as part of reading comprehension is cognitive in nature. What does this mean? It has been generally assumed that readers approach a text with some background knowledge (known as 'schema') from linguistic, world and socio-cultural domains. On the other hand, any given text has information encoded in words, clauses, paragraphs, chapters and so on. Successful comprehension is said to happen when both these resources interact and readers 'understand' what the writer actually intended. CS approaches argue that the text may have encoded some information, but its processing is essentially mental in nature. Several cognitive faculties such as memory, general cognition and cognitive processes are active in the process of reading and meaning making. In other words, readers employ several cognitive processes and reconstruct the text in their minds.

One of the related claims is that "...connectedness of discourse is a characteristic of the mental representation of the text rather than of the text itself" (Sanders & Maat, 2006: 592). Note here that in Halliday's traditional account, text connectedness or 'coherence' results when "...the interpretation of some element in the discourse is dependent on that of another" (Halliday & Hasan, 1976: 4). This relationship between elements could be reference, ellipsis, substitution, conjunction or collocation.[4]

However, there may not always be overt linguistic signals and readers would still interpret a set of sentences as connected. CS argues that this is made possible through deployment of several strategies such as inference, establishment of metaphoric and metonymic links, propositional links, etc. Sanders and Spooren (2010) discuss this in detail. Let's look at an example.

---

[4]In Halliday's framework (Halliday & Hasan, 1976) 'reference' is a linguistic element (such as pronouns or demonstratives) which makes "reference to something else for their interpretation" (p. 31); 'ellipsis' refers to leaving some linguistic elements "unsaid but understood nevertheless" (p. 142) (e.g., John bought books and Mary bags); 'substitution' is "replacement of one item by another" (p. 88) (e.g., I don't have a cat but my brother has one); 'collocation' is "cohesion that is achieved through the association of lexical items that regularly co-occur" (e.g., 'boy' and 'girl' are cohesive because they have opposite meanings and are used often together) (p. 284).

(6) Greenpeace has impeded a nuclear transportation in the Southern German state of Bavaria. Demonstrators chained themselves to the rails.

(p. 916)

In order to understand this extract from a newspaper as a connected text, as Sanders and Spooren (2010) observe, readers do not just depend on the given textual information but also infer many details based on world or discourse structure characteristics. For instance, readers know that 'Greenpeace' stands for members of that organization and not the organization itself (a metonymic interpretation), that 'demonstrators' in the second sentence refers to members of Greenpeace referred to earlier (an instance of referential coherence), that the nuclear equipment was being transported by train and the protestors chained themselves to the rails on the route this train took (inference based on the world knowledge using the clue 'rails'), and finally that this act made the train stop and the transportation could not take place (inferred from the word 'impede') (Sanders & Spooren, 2010: 916–917). While most of these inferences are based on world knowledge (propositional, metonymic, etc.), discourse structural characteristics such as referential coherence and relational coherence also play a crucial role. The former refers to creating a sense of continuity through repeated references to the key objects and/or themes, whereas the latter refers to connectedness brought about by discourse relations such as cause–effect, problem–solution often instantiated through linguistic markers such as connectives and lexical cue phrases (Sanders & Spooren, 2010). Here the readers infer that there is a cause–effect relationship between the two clauses though the order of the sentences is the other way round.

This analysis implies that in the ESL reading class, teachers need to focus on drawing inferences and interpreting referential and relational coherence markers. This will help to connect sentences, paragraphs, sections and chapters and ultimately to view the text as a whole.

Understanding Discourse Structure and Forming Genre Templates

It has been observed that an awareness of discourse structure can enhance reading comprehension (Grabe, 2009). The CS perspectives on discourse which are of relevance to pedagogy are that discourse, just like individual linguistic elements, is highly structured and is usage based (see Langacker, 2001, 2008). Discourse is structured in the sense that it consists of a series of connected usage events, each having an expressive and a conceptual side. The conceptual content is organized at multiple layers: individual linguistic units form phrases which then lead to clauses, paragraphs, sections, a chapter and ultimately a book. In order to understand a discourse as a whole, the reader has to interpret component expressions in relation to what has come earlier and what will come later. Prior and later connections with each clause-level expression are emphasized since each successive one is related to the previous ones: "building on it, reacting to it, or just by changing the subject—and sets the stage for what will follow" (Langacker, 2008: 460). Langacker (2008) observes that a well-structured discourse adheres to some basic principles: (i) it builds on what has already been established through clear links across the text; (ii) it presents new information at a rate easy for processing; (iii) each clause is self-contained and the need for backtracking is minimal; and (iv) the order of presentation of details conforms to a natural order of non-linguistic conceptualization (e.g., first cause and then consequence). These principles could actually guide selection of level-appropriate texts in ESL contexts.

The second important characteristic of discourse is that it is usage based. Langacker (2008) observes that repeated occurrences of a particular set of structural features in a context lead to formation of a genre (e.g., letters, e-mails, manuals). Each genre is identifiable in terms of "global organisation, more local structural properties, typical content, specific expressions employed, matters of style and register, etc." (p. 478). For instance, the phrase 'Once upon a time' usually induces an expectation that what follows is a story (Langacker, 2008).

In a pedagogic context, it follows from this analysis, it is essential to focus on the structure of a text and help learners build information bit by bit. Also, if learners are exposed to several texts of the same genre, they may form a template and this in turn will help them read more effectively. In this context, a "pedagogic corpus" (Willis & Willis, 2007), a collection of reading texts for use in ESL classrooms, may be an effective tool. A detailed example of structure analysis of a text is presented in Section "Cognitive Semantics and Reading in ESL Contexts".

Encyclopaedic Nature of Meaning: Going Beyond Dictionary Definitions

Traditionally, words are thought to have two 'levels' of meaning: 'linguistic meaning' and 'fuller meaning based on extralinguistic resources'. For instance, the word 'rose' is said to mean a flower literally and in the famous line of Robert Burns 'My love is like a red, red rose', it is said to have a figurative and symbolic meaning. It is literal meaning(s) of a word that is/are listed in a typical dictionary, whereas the extended meaning is said to depend on the context. CS refutes any such dichotomy. It is argued that a word or a sentence is used in a context and its meaning encompasses several domains such as linguistic, socio-cultural, physical setting and discourse context among others. Langacker (2008: 463–465) illustrates this with an example. Let's imagine a reader comes across the following sentence:

(7) The cat is on the mat!

If this sentence is used as a warning, readers/listeners are most likely to imagine a typical domestic cat mounting an expensive decorative mat on the wall. In addition to 'literal' meanings of the words used, we know that there is only one cat and that a particular mat is being referred to (article 'the' denotes definiteness). The preposition 'on' encodes the relationship of support against gravity and it implies that either the cat or the mat or both may fall down. It is because of shared cultural knowledge that we know that cats are kept as pets, that valuable things are mounted on a wall, and that valuable things are protected and hence an alarm needs to be raised. The warning also denotes a kind of amicable relationship between the users. If it were uttered by a subordinate to a superior officer it would be more appropriate to say: "Sir! The cat is on the mat."

This illustrates that dichotomy between 'linguistic' and 'extralinguistic' is completely artificial, as an expression's meaning encompasses several domains. Most often, the other cues are largely implicit and readers need to *interpret* each element in context. Let's look at another example.

(8) No more red beacons for dignitaries

Sentence (8) is a newspaper headline. When a person begins to read this newspaper headline, the linguistic decoding starts. This sentence has six words and if the reader knows all these words, can he/she claim to have understood the sentence? The complete understanding needs a lot more than just dictionary meanings of these words. Readers need to understand the concepts of 'VIPs' and 'red light as status symbol' among others. They need to be aware of the problematic situation—rampant misuse, development of unhealthy VIP culture—which led to this ban on the use of red lights on top of cars by such VIPs.

What does this mean for pedagogy? Teachers need to emphasize that interpreting a word draws resources from multiple domains and not just the literal meaning listed in dictionaries. Teachers may provide an introduction to the given text describing the socio-cultural context in which it was written. By extension, it would also mean that teachers need to prefer texts with familiar backgrounds over those with alien contexts.

Meaningfulness of Grammar

As observed earlier, in CS every linguistic element has a meaning associated with it and this meaning derives from its contextual usage. Traditionally, vocabulary items have been considered to have 'meaning', whereas closed class items (such as prepositions or articles) and grammatical categories and structures 'have grammatical functions rather than rich meanings' (Murphy, 2010: 14). As a result, they are not studied under lexical semantics. This is also reflected in pedagogic contexts. One can usually see these two types of linguistic element being studied under separate sections, 'Vocabulary' and 'Grammar', in school textbooks. While 'Vocabulary' focuses on word meanings and the usage contexts, 'Grammar' deals largely with rules and examples with little or no meaning-based explanations. Even during reading comprehension, teachers 'explain the difficult words' with the assumption that if learners have access to word meanings, then their comprehension is successful.

CS, however, argues that there is conceptualization behind every linguistic element and hence 'grammar is meaningful' (Langacker, 2008). This conceptualization is based on its use in specific contexts. Since it is usage based and context specific, a linguistic element is said to 'construe' the reported event in a particular way. This implies that there may be more than one option available for speakers of a language to encode an event. The structure—let's say Structure A—chosen imposes only one particular way of looking at it. When a speaker encounters similar events in future, this particular Structure A imposes a specific viewpoint. This necessarily entails that the actual events in the outside world are not represented objectively through language; rather, they are seen through a particular lens of an element which selects a few aspects, leaves out the rest and perceives the world in a specific way. Therefore, the choice of a word over another, a grammatical category over another or a structure over another indicates different conceptualizations.

Let's look at an example. Imagine there was a robbery at a local bank. This can be reported as in the following:

(9)
   (a) The bank was robbed last night.
   (b) The thieves robbed the bank last night.

The first one sounds more natural in this context—the reason is that the doer of the action is unknown or too general and hence it is more natural to leave it out and opt for a passive structure. Langacker (2008: 493), in fact, observes that the passive structure is used in English with the following clear conceptualization: (i) in a discourse, the focus of the action has been introduced and in order to keep that particular character in focus even though he/she is not the doer of action (e.g., *I met John yesterday. He has been bitten by a mad dog*); (ii) the doer of the action is unknown (e.g., *A student was lynched in a university in Pakistan on charges of blasphemy*); (iii) the doer is inconsequential or is too general (e.g., *The ATM was robbed last night and Rs 10 lakh was stolen*); or (iv) the identity of the doer is purposefully hidden (e.g., *The antique statue was dropped and broken*).

In a text, it must be noted, a writer has at their disposal a variety of options to encode the same content. By choosing a particular structure or word, the writer 'construes' an event in a particular way. Therefore, in order to comprehend a text in detail, the readers need to understand the construal behind a structure.

Let's look at a few more examples. Sentences in each pair appear to denote the same end result, but there is a difference in conceptualization:

(10)
   (a) Sam caused Harry to die.
   (b) Sam killed Harry.

(11)
   (a) John taught Greek to Bill.
   (b) John taught Bill Greek.

(Lakoff, 1987: 131)

Lakoff (1987) observes that the difference in meaning is brought about by whether the modifier and the modified are placed in proximity or not. The second sentences in these pairs seem to indicate a stronger causal link, whereas the first sentences do not.

Let's look at another set of examples where the position of a locative phrase brings about change in focus.

(12)
(a) Diana came across a python in the middle of the street.
(b) In the middle of the street Diana came across a python.

By preposing the locative phrase in 12(b), the new information is withheld till the end and is then presented to create dramatic effects. Such a construction "directs attention to an already accessible location, and then brings a new participant... into the discourse by establishing it in location" (Langacker, 2008: 81).

While reading, teachers need to focus learners' attention towards the choice of structures or words to express thoughts and ideas. Teachers can highlight various other possible options and then arrive at the possible rationale for choosing one particular structure over another. This may help understand the purpose of the writer or any hidden intentions.

Prototypes and Radial Categories: Understanding Figurative Uses

CS argues that the so-called figurative uses of a linguistic element can be explained in terms of meaning connections with the non-figurative uses. This is rooted in Lakoff's theory of categorization (Lakoff, 1987). It is argued that every linguistic unit categorizes worldly experiences in a certain way. This categorization is usually centred around a 'prototypical category' and 'radial structures' which are extensions from it based on perceived commonalities (Lakoff, 1987). Applying this principle, several studies have investigated meaning–meaning connections which show how peripheral uses of a word are meaningfully extended from the core uses. For instance, Tyler and Evans (2004) is a study which investigates the polysemy of the preposition 'over'. Some uses of 'over' are listed in 13(a–d):

(13)
(a) The picture is *over* the mantle.   (*proto-scene*)
(b) The cat jumped *over* the wall.   (*A–B–C trajectory*)
(c) Arlington is *over* the river from Georgetown. (*on the other side of*)
(d) Your article is *over* the page limit.   (*above and beyond*)

(Based on Tyler & Evans, 2004: 271)

While traditional accounts list these uses simply as an instance of polysemy, CS attempts to link the uses. Example 13(a) is the prototype where 'trajector' (the object in focus) (here 'the picture') is vertically higher than 'landmark' (the reference point) (here 'the mantle'); yet they are "within each other's sphere of influence" (Tyler & Evans, 2004: 262). This sense of being stationary in a vertically higher position leads to the usage in (b) where the trajector is under motion from point A to C passing through point B, which is vertically higher than the landmark. The end result in (b) is being located on the other side of the landmark and this is focused in the usage (c) where the trajector's end state is represented. This sense of being beyond the landmark is metaphorically extended to being beyond the prescribed page limit in (d).[5]

Such meaning–meaning connections may be established on propositional models that specify links in knowledge structure (e.g., after an act of jumping the object reaches the other side); image-schematic models (e.g., the trajectory of 'jumping' from A to C via B); metaphoric models (e.g., beyond a physical boundary → beyond an abstract boundary); or metonymic models (e.g., the name of an organization standing for its members in example 6 above) (see Lakoff, 1987: 113–114 for details).

The other kinds of connections investigated are form–form and form–meaning. Form–form connections include rhyme, alliteration and assonance. These patterns can be observed in some common compounds such as ***pick-pocket, playmate, publish or perish*** (Boers & Lindstromberg, 2006: 312). Studies have investigated whether there is any one-to-one correspondence between linguistic forms and meanings they encode. One of the principles postulated is 'sameness of form, sameness of meaning', that is, a particular set of sound sequence may express similar meanings. For instance, the sequence /sp/ in English occurs at the beginning of a large number of monosyllabic words which have a negative connotation (e.g., *spite, spit, spoil*) (Radden & Panther, 2004: 18).

Amritavalli (1999), though not a study in the CS framework, highlights how meaning connections can significantly help in understanding keywords and ultimately a complete text. She reports an incident in which an intermediate-level ESL learner had difficulty in understanding the phrase 'leave an impression on somebody' in a reading text. Even the dictionaries were not very useful. The learner understood the expression only when the researcher linked the given expression with a more concrete expression 'thumb impression'. She observes that the underlying schema remains the same for these two expressions: (i) something having to press on something; and (ii) leaving a mark (p. 266).

The next section presents a unified model of reading comprehension drawing on all these principles with reference to a sample text.

---

[5]'Trajector'—or 'figure' in Talmy's (2000a, 2000b) framework—is an entity under focus in a motion or static event, whereas 'landmark'—or 'ground' in Talmy's (2000a, 2000b) framework—is an entity which serves as a reference point for describing trajector's motion or location. For instance, in the sentence 'The cat jumped over the wall', 'The cat' is trajector while 'the wall' is landmark. See Langacker (1987: 217–220); Talmy (2000a, Chap. 5) for details.

Applying Principles of Cognitive Semantics to a Text

In the previous sections, we discussed some insights CS can offer regarding reading in ESL contexts. We saw that an awareness of conceptual metaphor can enhance reading comprehension and critical reading; exposing learners to various genre formats repeatedly leads to knowledge about the structure of discourse and genre characteristics which in turn lead to effective comprehension; focusing on the fact that meaning making encompasses several domains other than what is stated explicitly and therefore it is mostly a cognitive phenomenon, learners can be trained to interpret each sentence and connections across the text; and principles of meaningfulness of grammar and meaning-based motivations for figurative extensions facilitate interpretation of structures. In this section, we illustrate how a text can be analysed based on these principles.

The text chosen is an extract from Brecht's "Emphasis on Sport". The extract is given below:

> **Box 9.1 An extract from Brecht's 'Emphasis on Sport'**
> We pin our hopes to the sporting public.
>
> Make no bones about it, we have our eye on those huge concrete pans, filled with 15,000 men and women of every variety of class and physiognomy, the fairest and shrewdest audience in the world. There you will find 15,000 persons paying high prices, and working things out on the basis of a sensible weighing of supply and demand. You cannot expect to get fair conduct on a sinking ship. The demoralisation of our theatre audiences springs from the fact that neither theatre nor audience has any idea what is supposed to go on there. When people in sporting establishments buy their tickets they know exactly what is going to take place; and that is exactly what does take place once they are in their seats: viz. highly trained persons developing their peculiar powers in the way most suited to them, with the greatest sense of responsibility yet in such a way as to make one feel that they are doing it primarily for their own fun. *Against that the traditional theatre is nowadays quite lacking in character.*
>
> (Brecht 1926/1957, p. 9, emphasis in original)

Linguistic Analysis

To begin with let's look at some phrases and expressions in the passage and how a cognitive semantic analysis can help readers understand them.

(a) We pin our hopes to the sporting public

The phrase 'pin hope to somebody' can be explained as an extension of a more concrete experience. The core use would be fastening something onto something using a pin (e.g., 'A life-size poster of MJ was *pinned* to the wall of Joe's bedroom'). An immediate extension of this is forcing something to stay in a fixed place by putting weight on him/her (e.g., 'In the bar a bouncer jumped on me and *pinned* me against the wall'). In the phrase 'pin hope to somebody', instead of an object an abstract notion ('hope') is fastened tightly to a person. By linking this abstract use with the more concrete use, the readers understand the emphasis on the 'sporting public' for building and sustaining hope about the revival of theatre.

(b) Make no bones about it

The idiom means 'have no difficulty/hesitation talking about something'. Where did this meaning come from? By delving into the historical origin of the idiom, teachers can explain that it is likely to have originated from a culinary context: if there are no bones in a soup bowl it is easy to drink it and you do not need to struggle at all. By extension, if there are no bones, then there are no problems talking about an issue. Why is the writer using this idiom here? Brecht here urges the public to acknowledge the great love for sport and uses that analogy to drive home his point —that theatre needs to remodel itself along the lines of sport.

(c) We have our eye on those huge concrete pans

Brecht here uses a metaphor, referring to stadiums as 'pans'. The underlying schema common to both is 'container'. Brecht seems to use this to emphasiz the huge number of people who go to stadiums to watch a game.

(d) You cannot expect to get fair conduct on a sinking ship

Brecht uses the analogy of a sinking ship. An interpretation of this expression calls for encyclopaedic knowledge. Learners may be asked to imagine they are cruising on a ship in the middle of the ocean and suddenly the ship starts sinking due to an accident. They may recall scenes from popular movies and fiction (e.g., the movie *Titanic*). The crowd becomes agitated and lawless. All rules and regulations are broken and everybody wants to save themselves first. Is such behaviour wrong? We may not judge it so. Using this analogy, Brecht argues that if people do not come to theatres, then there is a problem with the plays ('sinking ship') and not with the people themselves.

Semantic Analysis

In this section, we look at how conceptual content is organized in the text.

Template of an Argumentative Text

Looking at the structure of the passage, we can infer that it is argumentative in nature. What can we infer about the genre, based on this text? As an argumentative text, its purpose is to persuade readers to form an opinion (that when compared to sport, theatre is suffering and theatre needs to remodel itself) and initiate a specific action (reforming theatre along the lines of sport). The main argument is that theatre is lacking in character in comparison with sport and is failing to attract people; therefore, theatre needs to restructure itself and meet audience expectations as well as uphold the spirit of art. This argument is built using an analogy—a comparison between sport and theatre in terms of number of people who are interested and the underlying motive. Based on the text, the following template could be proposed for argumentative texts:

Box 9.2 Template for argumentative texts

Purpose: Persuade readers to form an opinion or take a specific action or both

Structure: Thesis statement supported by various kinds of arguments (anecdotes, facts, observations, data, etc.). Points could be organized using an extended analogy, expository structure, narrative, etc.

Language: (i) Direct statements with explicit opinions (e.g., 'We pin our hopes to the sporting public', '*Against that the traditional theatre is nowadays quite lacking in character*') and no understatements.[6]

(ii) Modifiers to make arguments stronger (e.g., 'the fairest and shrewdest audience in the world', 'When people in sporting establishments buy their tickets they know exactly what is going to take place')

If learners are encouraged to notice these features and form a template for themselves, it will facilitate reading of similar texts in future.

---

[6]The above statements could have been hedged as in 'We *might* pin our hopes to the sporting public' or '*One might be tempted to conclude* that against that the traditional theatre is nowadays quite lacking in character'.

Progressive Structuring of Content

Let's see how the conceptual content is progressively built in this text. Recall here that CS insists on interpreting prior and later connections across clause-level expressions. The content is structured as follows:

Box 9.3 Content structure
Current situation (not stated explicitly in the passage): people not coming to theatre; theatre suffering
Solution: Remodel theatre on the basis of sport
Why: (i) Sport attracts people of all classes in huge numbers
    (ii) People ready to play high price for tickets—'sensible weighing of supply and demand'—in contrast, 'demoralised theatre audience'

Is it something wrong with the people then? No—theatre is sinking ship and audience cannot be expected to 'behave' well

What is wrong with theatre then?: (i) In stadiums people have expectations and those expectations are met; in theatre no expectations
(ii) Sportspeople develop their own peculiar powers/talent (means they play for their own sake) yet it appears as if they are doing it to entertain audience; theatre lacks it.

Learners may first be asked to look at the title of the given text and guess what the main thesis could be. Later, starting from the first paragraph connections need to be established across paragraphs and the common underlying thread (the main thesis of the text) needs to be highlighted. Learners may also be encouraged to discuss the rationale for composing each paragraph. The concluding paragraph needs to be examined in relation to all the previous paragraphs and the title of the text.

It must be noted that this simplified discussion is for illustrative purposes only. Not all argumentative texts will have a similar structure or a linear content development. Nevertheless, CS resources can help learners understand text in a more effective way through detailed interpretation of linguistic elements and a careful analysis of text structure.

Conclusion

This chapter has looked at some implications of CS for reading in ESL contexts. We observed that CS can lead to more effective linguistic analysis because it offers meaning explanations not just for vocabulary but also for grammatical structures, and it helps link more abstract and figurative uses with concrete uses. By focusing on the encyclopaedic nature of meaning and the cognitive nature of meaning making based on actual usage contexts, CS emphasizes more comprehensive semantic analysis and text-base formation based on linguistic and non-linguistic domains. At the macro structure level, CS emphasizes cohesion and coherence as a mental phenomenon, and recurring structural commonalities. An awareness of the metaphoric structure of text leads to more coherent analysis and a critical interpretation of author intentions.

However, some challenges remain. One of the biggest challenges for applied cognitive semantics has been arriving at pedagogical versions of meaning motivations. Though several studies have offered meaning-based explanations for grammatical phenomena, they still remain technical and therefore inaccessible to practising teachers and ESL learners. In this regard, more studies bridging the gap between CS and ESL pedagogy are needed. In this chapter it has been proposed that making learners aware of text structure in terms of genre template may result in better comprehension. Experimental studies on text-structure awareness and its effect on reading comprehension from the CS perspective are needed to throw more light on this aspect. Regarding metaphor awareness, a majority of studies are related to reading in ESP contexts and show that such awareness leads to better comprehension. Extending on this, studies in pedagogic contexts on critical metaphor awareness would open a new dimension for applying CS to pedagogy.

References

Allbritton, D. W., McKoon, G., & Gerrig, R. J. (1995). Metaphor-based schemas and text representations: Making connections through conceptual metaphors. *Journal of Experimental Psychology: Learning, Memory, and Cognition, 21*(3), 612–625.
Amritavalli, R. (1999). Dictionaries are unpredictable. *ELT Journal, 53*(4), 262–269.
Boers, F. (2000). Enhancing metaphoric awareness in specialised reading. *English for Specific Purposes, 19*, 137–147.
Boers, F. (2004). Expanding learners' vocabulary through metaphor awareness: What expansion, what learners, what vocabulary? In M. Achard & S. Niemeier (Eds.), *Cognitive linguistics, second language acquisition, and foreign language teaching* (pp. 211–232). Berlin: Mouton de Gruyter.
Boers, F., & Demecheleer, M. (1998). A cognitive semantic approach to teaching prepositions. *ELT Journal, 52*(3), 197–204.
Boers, F., & Lindstromberg, S. (2006). Cognitive linguistic applications in second or foreign language instruction: Rationale, proposals and evaluation. In G. Kristiansen, M. Achard, R. Dirven, & F. J. R. Ibanez (Eds.), *Cognitive linguistics: Current applications and future perspectives* (pp. 305–355). Berlin and New York: Mouton de Gruyter.
Brecht, B. (1957). Emphasis on sport. In J. Willet (Trans.), *Brecht on theatre: Development of an aesthetic* (pp. 6–9.) (Indian ed.,) Radha Krishna: New Delhi. Retrieved from https://ia601601.us.archive.org/14/items/in.ernet.dli.2015.150164/2015.150164.Brecht-On-Theatre.pdf. Original work published 1926.
Charteris-Black, J. (2006). Britain as a container: Immigration metaphors in the 2005 election campaign. *Discourse & Society, 17*(5), 563–581.
Croft, W., & Cruse, D. A. (2004). *Cognitive linguistics*. Cambridge: Cambridge University Press.
Ellis, R. (2003). *Task-based language learning and teaching*. Oxford: Oxford University Press.

Ellis, R. (2010). *SLA research and language teaching* (Indian ed.). New Delhi: Oxford University Press.

Goldberg, A. (1995). *Constructions: A construction grammar approach to argument structure*. Chicago: University of Chicago Press.

Grabe, W. (2009). *Reading in a second language: Moving from theory to practice*. New York: Cambridge University Press.

Halliday, M. A. K., & Hasan, R. (1976). *Cohesion in English*. London: Longman.

Hart, C. (2011). Force-interactive patterns in immigration discourse: A cognitive linguistic approach to CDA. *Discourse & Society, 22*(3), 269–286.

Kintsch, W., & Rawson, K. A. (2011). Comprehension. In M. J. Snowling & C. Hulme (Eds.), *The science of reading: A handbook* (pp. 209–226). Oxford: Blackwell Publishing.

Lakoff, G. (1987). *Women, fire, and dangerous things: What categories reveal about the mind*. Chicago and London: University of Chicago Press.

Lakoff, G., & Johnson, M. (1980). *Metaphors we live by*. Chicago and London: University of Chicago Press.

Langacker, R. W. (1987). *Foundations of cognitive grammar—Vol. 1: Theoretical prerequisites*. Stanford: Stanford University Press.

Langacker, R. W. (1991). *Foundations of cognitive grammar—Vol. 2: Descriptive application*. Stanford: Stanford University Press.

Langacker, R. W. (2001). Discourse in cognitive grammar. *Cognitive. Linguistics, 12*(2), 143–188.

Langacker, R. W. (2008). *Cognitive grammar: A basic introduction*. Oxford: Oxford University Press.

Lindstromberg, S. (1996). Prepositions: Meaning and method. *ELT Journal, 50*(3), 225–236.

Lindstromberg, S. (2010). *English prepositions explained*. Amsterdam and Philadelphia: John Benjamins Publishing Company.

Littlemore, J. (2004). Conceptual metaphor as a vehicle for promoting critical thinking skills amongst international students. In L. E. Sheldon (Ed.), *Directions for the future: Directions in English for academic purposes* (pp. 43–50). Oxford: Peter Lang.

Murphy, M. L. (2010). *Lexical meaning*. New York: Cambridge University Press.

Nation, I. S. P. (2009). *Teaching ESL/EFL reading and writing*. New York: Routledge.

Putz, M. (2007). Cognitive linguistics and applied linguistics. In D. Geeraerts & H. Cuyckens (Eds.), *The Oxford handbook of cognitive linguistics* (pp. 1139–1159). New York: Oxford University Press.

Radden, G., & Dirven, R. (2007). *Cognitive English grammar*. Amsterdam and Philadelphia: John Benjamins Publishing Company.

Radden, G., & Panther, K. (2004). Introduction: Reflections on motivation. In G. Radden & K. Panther (Eds.), *Studies on linguistic motivation* (pp. 1–46). Berlin and New York: Mouton de Gruyter.

Sanders, T. & Maat, H. P. (2006). Cohesion and coherence: Linguistic approaches. In K. Brown (Ed.), *Encyclopedia of language and linguistics: Vol. 2* (2nd ed., pp. 591–595). Amsterdam: Elsevier.

Sanders, T., & Spooren, W. (2010). Discourse and text structure. In D. Geeraerts & H. Cuyckens (Eds.), *The Oxford handbook of cognitive linguistics* (pp. 916–944). New York: Oxford University Press.

Scott, M. (2017, May 13). Hacking attack has security experts scrambling to contain fallout. *The New York Times*. Retrieved from https://www.nytimes.com/.

Talmy, L. (2000a). *Toward a Cognitive semantics—Vol. 1: Concept structuring systems*. Cambridge, MA: MIT Press.

Talmy, L. (2000b). *Toward a Cognitive semantics—Vol. 2: Typology and process in concept structuring*. Cambridge, MA: MIT Press.

Talmy, L. (2011). Cognitive semantics: An overview. In C. Maienborn, K. Heusinger, & P. Portner (Eds.), *Handbook of semantics* (Vol. 1, pp. 622–642). Berlin: Mouton de Gruyter.

Tyler, A. (2008). Cognitive linguistics and second language instruction. In P. Robinson, & N. C. Ellis (Eds.), *Handbook of cognitive linguistics and second language acquisition* (pp. 456–488). New York and London: Routledge.

Tyler, A., & Evans, V. (2004). Applying cognitive linguistics to pedagogical grammar: The case of *over*. In M. Achard & S. Niemeier (Eds.), *Cognitive linguistics, second language acquisition and foreign language teaching* (pp. 257–280). Berlin and New York: Mouton de Gruyter.

Willis, D., & Willis, J. (2007). *Doing task-based language teaching*. Oxford: Oxford University Press.

Chapter 10
Perspectives from the Art and Science of Reading

C. E. Veni Madhavan and C. N. Ajit

Abstract We develop our essay on reading from two principal directions: (a) the art of reading to cover 'subjective' perspectives on reading; and (b) the science of reading to analyse and discuss all that is considered 'objective'. We develop theoretical and empirical arguments towards a principal hypothesis that reading collateral or side-stream material accentuates the understanding of subsequent reading of mainstream material. This intuitively plausible hypothesis is examined from various perspectives drawing upon extant theories from linguistics, cognitive psychology, cognitive neuroscience and computational modelling. In our discourse, we consider the input text material to belong to the dichotomous classes of 'general material' and 'academic (or specialized) material'. We discuss the potential of certain reading experiments with participants from a student population.

Keywords Psycho-linguistics · Cognitive models of reading · Psycho-physics of reading · Readability · Understandability

Background

Reading is an activity of immense value to the human spirit. Reading is one of those human pursuits that does not appear to contribute directly any evolutionary advantage to our species. Yet, this delightful activity seems to contribute greatly to long-term cognitive and emotional balance.

C. E. Veni Madhavan (✉)
Department of Computer Science and Automation, Indian Institute of Science, Bangalore, India
e-mail: cevm@csa.iisc.ernet.in

C. N. Ajit
Society for Innovation and Development, Indian Institute of Science, Bangalore, India
e-mail: ajit@sid.iisc.ernet.in

© Springer Nature Singapore Pte Ltd. 2018
R. Joseph Ponniah and S. Venkatesan (eds.), *The Idea and Practice of Reading*,
https://doi.org/10.1007/978-981-10-8572-7_10

Most of the first two decades of the intellectual development of a person is spent in some form of goal-oriented, directed reading. In the remaining lifespan of a person reading is generally pursued as a pastime with no real tangible goal. In this essay, we examine these two seemingly dichotomous aspects of reading, based on viewpoints from the arts and sciences. We propose a few working hypotheses and present arguments to establish them. A broad theme of this collection of essays is the synergistic roles of reading general material versus specialized (or academic) reading. We also put forward a few hypotheses in this direction. We argue that both the content and the reader are important to the success of the enterprise of reading.

We develop our essay on reading from two principal directions: (a) the art of reading to cover all that is considered 'subjective' about reading; and (b) the science of reading to analyse and discuss all that is considered 'objective'. Further, in our discourse from both directions, we consider the input domain under the dichotomous classes of 'general material' versus 'academic (or specialized) material'.

The Art of Reading

One of our putative hypotheses is that the act of reading is akin to an artistic indulgence. Litterateurs have talked and written about the pleasures of reading in scholarly tones. The pleasures and fruits of reading and understanding have also been referred to in literary or clichéd statements. Many features of the written form, such as genre, style, depth, succinctness, raciness and precision, leave an indelible cognitive imprint on the reader. The higher the aesthetic values of these features, the higher the level of understanding. The process of reading involves feedback—a process of cognitive amplification that occurs due to the interplay between the written (textual) stimulus and the active mind of the reader. We refer to this facet as the art of reading. In this essay, we will consider the expression of 'thought' to be reflected as the content.

In keeping with discussions on analysis of reading of 'text', we deal with 'thought' expressed in a textual form. Renderings in forms like prose or poetry are considered to be at the 'presentation of the thought' level only. To clarify, when we say 'text', the form could be prose, poetry or drama, but we are interested in analysing the nature of the thought expressed in that piece of text.

While content is central, the rendering of the content provides the necessary cognitive strengthening. In the process of reading both the content and the reader are important. In the context of general reading and academic reading, the art aspect is tied to the linguistic, semantic and pragmatic structures. This aspect can be further broken into sub-classes based on genre, style and other features as mentioned above. In the case of the perceptual process of reading, appreciation of read matter is in the mind of the reader. We attempt to model this in an objective manner.

The Science of Reading

We study the process of reading from a variety of objective methodologies, ranging broadly from psycho-linguistics and neuro-physiological processes on the one hand to the computational processes of efficient encoding, tagging and retrieval on the other. One hears of many day-to-day allusions to reading-related activities such as 'casual reading', 'careful reading', 'reading between the lines', 'silent reading', 'thinking aloud' and 'photographic memory'. It is our contention that these phenomena lend themselves to scientific exploration.

We have proposed computational methodologies for the analysis of certain linguistic devices such as sarcasm (Nagwanshi & Veni Madhavan, 2014: 25). We have proposed a generic theory of 'cognitive parsing', which is an overlay on the extant theories of syntactic and semantic parsing. These theories, models and computational results fall into the realm of machine processing of natural languages.

In the course of experiments using an eye-tracker for different stimuli, we identified certain requirements of scan-path analysis. The first author has developed certain methodologies for the analysis of the visual scan paths from an eye-tracker, on text stimuli and for the comparison of the scan paths of several participants. These were done as a part of courses taught by him at the Indian Institute of Science during 2007–2013. Calibrated studies with a variety of input textual stimuli are planned with a view to understanding different types of reading activities mentioned above.

The process of reading does not end with mere scanning of the text. A large amount of post-processing continues, in the form of representation, tagging, encoding, storing followed by recalling, re-iterating, narrating and interacting. These provide what we term 'cognitive amplification'. Cognitive strengthening is a meta-framework of the neuro-biological framework of 'synaptic strengthening'. Representation, retention, recall and re-representation are vital mental processes that accompany reading as with other human perceptual activities.

Notions and Notations

We introduce some notions and set up some notations that will be used in our exposition. First, we address the notion of *readability*.

Classically readability has been measured based on surface-level, structural, statistical characteristics. Readability measures are primarily based on factors such as the number of words in the sentences and the number of letters or syllables per word (i.e., as a reflection of word frequency). Two of the most commonly used measures are the Flesch Reading Ease formula and the Flesch–Kincaid Grade Level.

The output of the Flesch Reading Ease formula is a number from 0 to 100, with a higher score indicating easier reading. For a text input T, the formula gives a score $s(T) = 206.835 - (1.015 * ASL) - (84.6 * ASW)$. Here, ASL denotes the average sentence length (the number of words in T divided by the number of sentences in T) and ASW denotes the average number of syllables per word (the number of syllables in T divided by the number of words in T).

The more common Flesch–Kincaid Grade Level formula converts the Reading Ease Score to a US school-grade level as follows. For a text input T, the formula gives a score $s(T) = 0.39 * ASL + 11.8 * ASW\ 15.59$. Here, the quantities ASL and ASW are as defined above. The scaling weights and the translation parameter values have been arrived at based on experimental statistics.

Readability measures guide the construction of textbooks to conform to the intended student grade level. However, there are at least three major problems with surface structural readability formulas.

1. Comprehension and learning depend to a great extent on processing at the text-base and situation levels. Discourse processing and other computational linguistics measures need to be used to model comprehension and learning.
2. Readers' cognitive aptitudes such as predicting, knowledge and language skills need to be taken into account.
3. Readability formulas as such do not capture the cohesion or coherence of a text. Quantitative and qualitative factors like named entities, anaphora, overlapping text segments, clausal entities, extent of vocabulary, sentence and text structure, concreteness and abstractness of terms, are also needed.

A judicious exploitation of these features is expected to cover readability of general material from the genres of fiction, prose and poetry. It is the combined effect of these factors that constitutes cohesion. The comprehensive Wikipedia article on readability (Wikipedia: 1) covers all these aspects and provides a large set of references. We have used readability measures and certain other statistical metrics in our work on automatic text simplification (Banerjee, Kumar, & Veni Madhavan, 2013: 1).

Readability quality (or quality of readability) has a great bearing on the hypothesis that collateral reading improves mainstream reading. By mainstream reading, we mean the main reading material under consideration. This could be an academic text for a student or a book under study for a reviewer. We merely use 'mainstream' to stand for mainline and with no other connotation. We measure the overall readability with a parameter called QoR measure. Intuitively, this is a measure of the fidelity of the printed, or equivalently the electronic file, version with respect to the intended expression. That is, has the word captured the intent?

This measure has a direct correlation with the reader's understanding. The reader's understanding of the collateral material enhances or sharpens his cognitive abilities to understand the mainstream material better. In principle the nature of the two materials does not play a significant role. Of course this is an intuitive remark, except that this statement is often heard in the world.

We contend that there must be some underlying psycho-physical process that contributes to this cognitive strengthening. In later sections we explore the possibility of putting this and similar hypotheses to the test in the laboratory based on eye-tracker studies.

Let the QoR of a certain piece of text T be denoted $\rho(T)$. To denote the level of understanding by a person on reading a piece of text T, we introduce the parameter $\mu(T)$. We adopt a normalized range between 0 and 1 for these two parameters. The natural numerical order in the range corresponds to the degree of readability or the degree of understanding. We use *SST* and *MST* to denote the side-stream (collateral) and mainstream text material, respectively. For example, *SST* could be thriller fiction and *MST* could be a chapter in a mathematical text.

It would be of great interest to obtain both qualitative and quantitative models that yield a comparison of $\rho(T_1)$ and $\rho(T_2)$ between two pieces of text T_1 and T_2. Similarly, it would be interesting to obtain both qualitative and quantitative models that yield a comparison of $\mu(T_3)$ and $\mu(T_4)$ between two pieces of text T_3 and T_4.

A tantalizing theoretical and applicable goal would be to obtain both qualitative and quantitative models that yield a comparison of $\rho(T)$ and $\mu(T)$ reflecting the correlation between readability and *degree of understanding* of a piece of text T. Also to address the central hypothesis of this work, namely that collateral side-stream reading aids mainstream reading, we impute a correlation between $\rho(T_1)$ and $\mu(T_2)$ via the correlation between between $\rho(T_1)$ and $\mu(T_1)$. In other words it is of interest to obtain qualitative and quantitative arguments supporting the statement,

$$\rho(T_1) \to \mu(T_1) \to \mu(T_2).$$

Notice that *readability* is a linguistic phenomenon, and *degree of understanding* (or by an abuse of terminology, *understandability*) is in general a person-dependent psychological phenomenon. A simplifying assumption can be that understandability of a piece of text T is invariant with respect to the reader. We note that this assumption is reasonable in two situations: (i) a homogeneous group of readers (for example, a set of students in the same class and course); and (ii) in the context where T belongs in particular, to the exact sciences. Also this assumption is quite reasonable when we consider T from the genre of pedagogical text such as school or college textbooks. We relax completely such an assumption on the nature of the sidestream material S.

In short, our central hypothesis reduces to

$$\rho(S) \to \mu(S) \to \mu(T).$$

Here we let S come from any genre such as fiction, non-fiction, prose, poetry, technical material or pedagogic material. We restrict attention to the case of T coming from the pedagogic or instructional material.

A principal thesis of linguistic theories is the existence of universal semantic primes (qtd. in Malt 73). At first sight, one may think that a certain terminological bias due to cultural roots and fixations (called 'terminological ethnocentrism') creeps in during analysis of words that describe mental states (qtd. in Malt 72). However, linguistics research has established that this is not the case. There are about 63 universal semantic primes identified in the *natural semantic metalanguage*.

Language processing by both humans and machine algorithms carry out a sequence of operations involving syntactical, lexical, semantic and usage rules. Many of these rules are dictated by systematic structures which are organized into systems of grammars, dictionaries, thesauri, logic forms, agreement constraints and usage patterns such as idioms. A *cognitive strengthening*, or equivalently in neuro-biological terms a *synaptic strengthening* takes place when the reader is exposed to the read material. In this chapter we consider the textual rendition of language material and focus our attention on reading. The textual input provides the reader with the facility to read, retrace, regress and refine the mental representation.

The text-reading act enables the reader to parse, analysing the input at different scales. Reading is carried out at word/phrase levels, single-sentence levels, multiple-sentence levels and paragraphs and higher aggregations. The diligent reader makes a running model of the worldview offered by the word-view. He performs several linguistic tasks and sub-tasks such as syntactic and lexical checks, resolves agreement rules (with respect to gender, number, tense, mood), gathers the salient semantic categories and develops the meanings from word and phrase levels to the meaning at the whole-sentence level. He further revises, augmenting meaning from successive sentences. During this step he carries out various resolution tasks with respect to named entities, anaphora, referents, semantic categories and cross-cultural linguistic idiosyncrasies based on usage patterns. He builds a loosely structured, inter-linked *concept association network* for an internal representation (Sudarshan Iyengar, Veni Madhavan, Zweig, & Natarajan, 2012: 121). In a sense he builds a *cognitive model* with appropriate *cognitive tags* or *cognitive handles* for eventual retrieval or recall. Many contemporary neuro-psychological theories offer experimental evidence of the anatomical and physiological mechanisms involved in these processes of language recognition and organization (qtd. in Reed, 2007: 248).

We develop arguments in support of the central hypothesis of this chapter, namely that *collateral or side-stream reading* empowers *mainstream or academic reading*. Our principal tenet is that the cognitive models based on the material used for collateral reading provide a framework, test-bed or practice-ground for use during subsequent mainstream reading. This contention is at the abstract level where it does not depend significantly on the nature of *SST* and on *MST* at a macroscopic level. We presume that in the process of understanding a given *MST* the reader has already involved himself in reading-related *MST*. For example, the reader may use one or more books or explanations of a particular technical topic for understanding a particular topic of *MST*. This act certainly provides some amount of cognitive resolution and consequent strengthening. We assert that further cognitive amplification is generated by the simple act of reading a collateral material *SST* from any genre (prose, poetry, etc.) and returning to the *MST*.

The Modelling Mind

Man is said to be a model-making animal. This attribution of physical model-making ability can be extended to mental model-making ability. The human mind has a remarkable propensity to model the external world together with a model of the model. By this we refer to the mind's ability to tag and generate what is termed 'metadata' in computer science. It is a philosophical conundrum as to how deep this recursive internalization can go. The mind captures a worldview and internalizes this view by a representational mechanism. In general, such an internalization consists of the raw information and the metadata about various types of spatio-temporal and contextual information. A compact encoding of both types of information (raw data and metadata) would appear to be in the form of *verbal tags*.

It is possible that auditory and visual (symbolic, pictorial) stimuli have some direct form (i.e., acoustic spectral form and pixellated mosaic form) in the respective anatomical areas of the brain. Such representations are bound to be more voluminous or expensive in terms of hard resources such as neuronal elements. In terms of information theory, the binary encoding of verbal and literal information leads to a more compact representation than equivalent acoustic and graphic representations. Typical human allusions such as 'rings a bell', 'have heard it somewhere, sometime', 'read between the lines', 'tip of the tongue' and 'at one's fingertips' are annotations of such mental models.

These arguments indicate that a reader who is 'reading' text to gather information (reading for knowledge acquisition) or to trigger imagination (fiction reading) (Adler & Doren, 1940 [2014]: 1) makes an internal model of the read material. Our contention is that this model is rich and broad enough to lend itself to an extrapolation to another episode of reading. Many theories on reading draw upon the close interaction between the linguistic aspects of the content and the neuro-psychological aspects pertaining to the reader.

Classical theories were based on a bottom-up view (qtd. in Malt & Wolff, 2010: 72), in which reading was considered a process of decoding a series of written symbols. This view was also said to be an 'outside-in' view, in that meaning existed in the printed text and was interpreted and assimilated by the reader. A cognitive view was introduced to counteract over-reliance on the content. Reading was construed as a psycho-linguistic guessing game. Here an emphasis was placed on the reader's role in making a hypothesis and revising the hypothesis. The 'schema theory' of reading introduced by Rumelhart (Reed, 2007: 233) describes schemata as "building blocks of cognition" used in the process of interpreting acquired input data, organizing goals, allocating resources and guiding the processing system. This view, a more prevalent one, is akin to the computational view of building information systems.

Reading and re-reading activate the synaptic strengthening of the neuronal networks. This process aids the formation and long-term potentiation of neuronal networks responsible for memory formation. Further, every recall of stored fact or associated factoids augments the indelibility of information in the human brain.

A compact, customized linguist coding, or a scheme of mental referents, is worked out by a diligent reader for ease of retrieval. Often, this scheme tends to be based on a clever and intuitive combination of several linguistic devices, such as homophone–homonym substitution, modification of morphological inflections. The reader does not need to exercise any special effort to construct such mnemonic devices, if he utilizes natural linguistic parallels between hard mainstream technical material and light side-stream non-technical material. For example, he may map the details of the working of an electrical machine to a lighter science-fiction description of an alien machine. An astute reader can thus derive the concrete benefit of forming strong mental imagery of the technical reading material with more enjoyable collateral reading material.

Our Models

To build a putative model we need to analyse the two measures ρ and μ. The input (the read material) T can be typified or classified or categorized in socio-psycho-lingusitic terms to obtain a certain 'figure of merit'. We term this figure of merit a readability metric $\rho(T)$. The quantity $\rho(T)$ would be an indicative, quantitative index that captures features such as readability, stylistics, artistry, word-play, socio-cultural milieu, attention holding, raciness. Thus $\rho(T)$ depends on various aspects of the rendering of the read material. The textual content exhibits the interplay of various features consisting of linguistic, semantic, pragmatic, stylistic and emotional categories.

Now we address the issue of readers. Most of the popular texts in the world meant for universal readership cater to the class of first-time readers. Such readers can be said to come with an unprepared mind. They do not have any preparation for receiving the given input. In contrast, specific categories of text, for example, academic, are designed to cater to the prepared mind or the class of minds that have had prior preparation to receive such inputs. Here we will be discussing how reading general or popular literature texts basically meant for the unprepared mind aids a reader in reading categories of text for which they have a prepared mind.

Let π_i, $i = 1, \ldots, N$ denote the preparedness coefficient corresponding to N individuals. We may use carefully calibrated data on these coefficients based on factual information (scholastic performance) or based on self-declarations. We plan to con- duct a reading experiment by presenting the same text T to N individuals. We measure the efficacy of reading by administering an objective test and/or by collecting verbal responses from the participants. Let the normalized performance score be denoted by η_i. We postulate that the readability of text T is correlated with average performance, i.e.,

$$\rho(T) \to \sigma(T) = \sum_{i=1}^{N}, \pi_i * \eta_i(T).$$

As a consequence, a graded sequence of reading material T_j, $j = 1, \ldots, M$, with $\rho(T_1) < \cdots < \rho(T_M)$ should imply that the average performance also varies in the same monotonic manner, namely $\sigma(T_1) < \cdots < \sigma(T_M)$. If this happens, then we have sufficient ground to estimate the correlations when we consider the T_i to come from different genres and establish empirical arguments in support of our main hypothesis, that $\rho(SST)$ aids $\mu(MST)$. Note that $\mu(T)$ refers to an individual performance and $\sigma(T)$ to a group average performance.

Mnemonization

It is known that mnemonic devices are used by humans to represent and store information about places, events, dates and names of objects. Individuals show great inventiveness in coining mnemonic tags. They use numbers and words as tags to describe a variety of categories. This inventive ingenuity often manifests in typical human emotional qualities of humour, wit, surprise, concise meaningful acronyms or alphabetization. Numbers and words, coming from two different information types, are invoked along with their idiosyncratic and special properties, to great effect. Humans extend such cross-modal relationships to bilingual and multilingual situations. This gives them more degrees of freedom in their choice of mnemonic tags. Our contention is that human beings adopt conceptual generalizations to build their personalized schema and encode them with memorable tags to enhance their levels of understanding of a given textual input. This argument is in favour of the hypothesis that collateral reading and the concomitant mnemonic devices and abstractions strengthen the consequent reading experience of the mainstream input text. We give some examples.

- *amma, poochi kandein, nee po* (in Tamil) meaning, 'Mother, I saw an insect, you go away' standing for 'Hamoi, Fucho, Canton, Ningpo', a mnemonic in a geography lesson.
- 'All Silver Tea Cups' as a mnemonic for positive signs of 'all, sine, cos, tan' in quadrants 1, 2, 3, 4, in a geometry lesson.
- our research project, titled DIAMETERS, an acronym standing for 'dialogues, metaphors, translation, expansion, rewriting and summarization'. This project is on the unified study of a proposed cognitive parsing model built over linguistic models of syntax parse trees and dependency grammars for handling various natural language processing (NLP) tasks.

Catchphrases

The human mind is very adept at inventing verbal tags of many forms. Single words convey many meanings—some literal and some metaphorical. The same words can be used in different senses, different grammatical parts of speech and in different homophonic manners. Further, a combination of homophonic syllables and words carrying different meanings from different tongues (languages) gives rise to quirky effects leading to humour and mirth. In addition, the operations of verbing a noun, adjectivizing a noun or converting verb forms to nouns give additional powerful ways of creating many meaningful expressions. Words can be juxtaposed into bigram, trigram and longer formations, giving rise to rich collections of compound nouns, phrasal verbs and catchphrases. All these combinatorial constructs provide the user of a language with many handles and many rules to represent, retain, retrieve and refine complex ideas about the world. In this sense man has thus evolved into a linguistic rule-making animal from a simple tool-making animal.

We contend that such a linguistic rule-making capability gives a human the power of being able to transfer the abstractions he makes from active reading of text matter to subsequent active reading of another text. Intuitively, an independent coinage or a 'nice coinage' of a verbal construct seen for the first time by a reader evokes a sense of wonder followed by a sense of appreciation or 'feel-goodness'. These psychological states generate powerful mental activations in the brain's internal reward centres.

This phenomenon is called the act of mnemonization. Some examples of catchphrases are 'divide and rue', 'high moss power', 'sins of the soil', 'chef-preneur', 'it is very punny', 'kill morbid thoughts'.

Figures of Speech

The active reader strives to capture both the knowledge information and the imaginative depictions from read material in his own personalized, internal representation. Clearly, such active reading depends a lot on the *readability measure* of the text and the *understandability measure* of the reader. Assuming a non-weighted, neutral, typical reader, the process of model making can be cast in an analytic framework. Such a model will consider issues such as questions raised by the reader, satisfactory resolution of doubts and ambiguities, and appreciation of the nuances of the language.

Consider the scheme of reading mainstream material after being primed by reading auxiliary material of a different genre. The priming material is likely to trigger certain thought processes, imagination and questions. These are expected to sharpen the mind so that subsequent reading of the mainstream material clarifies the understanding. In a way, this phenomenon contributes positively to our proposed theory of augmentation of mainstream reading.

The human mind loves challenges. It likes to be constantly stoked. One of the many linguistic theories that characterize humour, which is closely related to novelty or surprise, in a piece of text is that of *incongruity* (Mulder & Nijholt, 2002: 4). This incongruity applies over different granularities—from word/phrase level to sentence to paragraph to chapter to whole-book levels. In general, incongruity is generated by means of non-standard, surprising usage. Such non-standard linguistic usage forms are referred to as figures of speech to contrast them with the syntactically systematized forms called parts of speech. The term 'figures of speech' alludes to the many indirect forms in language use, in contrast with literal or direct ways of using language for communication. The many indirect forms include satire, sarcasm, metaphors, similes, wit, pun, double-entendre, jokes, gags, quotes, aphorisms, sayings, proverbs and memorable lines.

From a psycho-linguistic perspective, these language traits enable the model-making mind to cleverly capture and exploit linguistic constructs for its internal representation. For example, often the ludicrousness of the verbal tags of a mnemonic device leaves an indelible impression (or strong long-term memory association). Such mnemonic codes range from personal to universal forms. Some of the examples above reflect the universal nature of such devices.

Our contention is that collateral reading material provides opportunities for conjuring catchy, mnemonic tags for use while reading the mainstream material, thereby enhancing ability to build models of the mainstream reading material. This observation implies that additional reading material provides the ability to build *cognitive cues* at a basic, functional level.

Analogic Augmenters

The idea of synaptic strengthening enunciated in the colourful phrase 'fire and wire' or the 'Hebbian learning' (Shatz, 1992: 60), is at the core of our hypothesis of collateral strengthening of reading success. Synaptic strengthening happens at the neuronal junctions through increased flow of certain neuro-transmitter molecules such as glutamate, referred to as a "mnemonic glue" (LeDoux, 1996: 218). This chemical mediation occurs with augmented levels of cognitive or emotional activity accompanied by enhanced levels of electrical activity in the neuronal assemblies of many neuro-anatomical tissues in the cortical and sub-cortical areas. Such pronounced neuronal activity happens during elevated psychological states of intense cognitive engagement—in deep study or thought, and during emotional immersion. This phenomenon is also noted during the process of long-term potentiation (LTP) (Churchland & Sejnowski, 1999: 255) during short-term memory to long-term memory commitment phases.

Synaptic strengthening at the neuronal level leads to a cognitive strengthening at a phenomenological level. The complex system of memory formation, conceptualization and establishment of the associative memory retrieval mechanism is activated in this phase. In computer science this phase would cover the indexing and creation of pertinent metadata tables for subsequent information retrieval and processing. Our putative model attempts to capture this idea of the transference of the abstraction information and the prescriptions for generating the mnemonic tags, built from reading a collateral material, in order to easily encode information from the mainstream reading material.

We assert that at the cognitive level every individual has the ability and innovative skill required to build, refine and draw upon previously constructed cerebral models of information gathered from reading. The cognitive percepts would be similar to the *wh* parts-of-speech tags—who, what, whom, where, when, which, why, how. We call these 'cognitive tags' and plan to develop a cognitive mark-up language (CML) (Nagwanshi & Veni Madhavan, 2014: 1) to reason about these in a formal model of language processing at the cognitive level. We build our cognitive model of language processing with a view to using it for various NLP tasks. This is part of the composite DIAMETERS programme mentioned earlier. In our proposal, the information structures representing this cognitive layer would rest over the information structures of parse trees (based on Chomsky's constituency grammar theory) and on dependency relations (based on Tesniere's dependency grammar theory).

The Potential of Reading Experiments

Reading experiments can be carried out with human participants to elicit numerical data on readers' performance by correlating the readability measures of text inputs with the nature of responses. This methodology is akin to the reading comprehension tests given to students taking multiple-choice aptitude tests. In addition such experiments can be conducted using an eye-tracker system to measure and correlate participant performance with the visual response features of *fixations, saccades, blinks and eye dilations,* and *scan paths*. Such psycho-physical experiments have been conducted to study the foveation pattern responses to visual input stimuli (Reichle, Erik, Rayner, & Pollatsek, 1998: 5). Our plans for experimentation are under way. It has not yet been possible to produce quantitative data and inferences. However, there is potential for such experiments to provide an objective strengthening of our intuitive hypotheses.

As regards the linguistic aspects of the input text stimuli, we comment as follows. There is classic, well-known material in every genre of text and we can prepare a compendium of paired samples (side-stream with mainstream). For a first set of experiments we could use the same genre of text for both the side-stream and the mainstream. For example, we could draw a sample from an article in the *Economist* magazine for a side-stream input followed by a mainstream input from Paul Samuelson's textbook on economics. We could set up the input in a similar manner for other genres.

Thus responses to the input text stimuli will take two forms: (i) a question/answer form; and (ii) scan-path data from an eye-tracker. A large number of papers (e.g., Reichle et al., 1998: 1) address the issue of correlation between the scan-path features of fixations, saccades, regressions, blinks and eye-ball dilations and the text being read. A model (Reichle et al., 1998: 10) EZ reader is a prominent example. We have developed (unpublished) nascent models to represent scan-path data in the form of normalized, aggregated sequence data from spatio-temporal eye-tracking information. The eye-tracker data on text stimuli is a source of much valuable parametric information. For example, it is possible to assess the difficulty level of a word or a phrase by means of the total fixation time in the corresponding area of interest on the console. A similar assessment can be made using the regressions or rapid return saccades to identified areas of interest during reading.

Conclusions

We study the phenomenon of reading from the perspectives of art and science. We propose a few theories and models connecting different pertinent aspects of the content and the reader. The discussion on content is mainly based on linguistic and literary typology. The discussion on the reader is based on neuro-biological, psycho-physical, cognitive and formal mathematical terms. Our endeavour is to utilize all these techniques and tools to establish by heuristic and empirical argument that collateral or general side-stream reading augments the comprehension and understanding of academic reading material.

References

Adler, M. J., & Doren, C. V. (1940 [2014]). *How to read a book*. New York: Touchstone.
Banerjee, S., Kumar, S., & Veni Madhavan, C. E. (2013). Text simplification for enhanced readability. In *INSTIC Conference on Knowledge Discovery and Information Retrieval*, Vilamoura, September 2013.
Churchland, P. S., & Sejnowski, T. J. (1999). *The computational brain*. Cambridge: MIT Press.
LeDoux, J. (1996). *The emotional brain*. New York: Touchstone.
Malt, B., & Wolff, P. (Eds.). (2010). *Words and the mind*. New York: Oxford University Press.
Mulder, M. P., & Nijholt, A. (2002). *Humour research: State of the art* (pp. 1–24). Technical Report, University of Twente, The Netherlands.
Nagwanshi, P., & Veni Madhavan, C. E. (2014, October). Sarcasm detection using sentiment and semantic features. In *INSTIC Conference on Knowledge Discovery and Information Retrieval*. Rome.
Reed, S. K. (2007). *Cognition theory and applications*. Belmont: Thomson Wadsworth.
Reichle, E. D., Rayner, K., Pollatsek, A. (1998). *Comparing the E-Z model to other models of eye movement control in reading* (pp. 1–57). Technical Report, University of Pittsburgh, USA.
Shatz, C. J. (1992). The developing brain. *Scientific American, 1992*, 60–67.
Sudarshan Iyengar, S. R., Veni Madhavan, C. E., Zweig, K. A., & Natarajan, A. (2012). Understanding human navigation using network analysis. *Topics in Cognitive Science, 4*(1), 121–134.
Wikipedia. https://en.wikipedia.org/wiki/Readability.

Chapter 11
Cognitive Load Theory, Redundancy Effect and Language Learning

Carlos Machado and Pedro Luis Luchini

Abstract When learners read a text they turn to an array of cognitive procedures to process information, mainly retrieving and storing new input which is often associated and connected with previous knowledge. To be able to process this information, they need to deploy and make use of a number of reading strategies to make sense of what they read. This chapter aims to investigate the extent to which the so-called redundancy effect influences the L2 reading comprehension skills of two groups of young learners with different proficiency levels in a middle school in Argentina. Both groups completed a reading comprehension task. The first group was exposed to a single mode of instruction—reading—while the other was presented with a twofold format which combined reading with listening. Results showed that the group which worked with the single mode of instruction obtained better scores than the other group. Based on these findings, the extent to which language proficiency compensates for or reduces the redundancy effect is analysed. Finally, some pedagogical implications for the teaching of L2 reading comprehension are discussed.

Keywords Reading comprehension · Cognition · Redundancy effect
Instruction

Introduction

ESL (English as a second) and EFL (English as a foreign) language instructors know that reading comprehension is a very important predictor for successful language learning. The process of comprehension involves the construction of a mental representation of a text (Kintsch, 1998; Zwaan & Radvansky, 1998). In this chapter, we do not intend to provide a model of the entire reading process, starting off with the focusing of the eye on the printed page and ending with the encoding of

---

C. Machado (✉) · P. L. Luchini
Universidad Nacional de Mar del Plata, Mar del Plata, Argentina
e-mail: carlosmach@gmail.com

© Springer Nature Singapore Pte Ltd. 2018
R. Joseph Ponniah and S. Venkatesan (eds.), *The Idea and Practice of Reading*,
https://doi.org/10.1007/978-981-10-8572-7_11

information into long-term semantic memory or its subsequent retrieval for purposes of demonstrating comprehension. However, we mean to focus on one specific aspect of comprehension relevant to reading comprehension. This aspect is related to how the reader's schemata, or knowledge already stored in memory, operates in the process of interpreting new information and allowing it to enter and become part of the knowledge store. Indeed, it is the interaction of new information with old knowledge that we mean when we use the term 'comprehension'. To lay fair claim to have comprehended a text means to say that we have found a mental storage for the information in the text, or worded differently, that we have altered an existing mental storage to provide room in our minds for that new information (Anderson & Pearson, 1984). As was said earlier, several simultaneous operations are involved in the comprehension process; lexical processes are required to access word meanings, memory retrieval is required to elaborate on the text and thus form connections to prior knowledge, and inference processes are crucial when it comes to integrating a sentence with prior ones and background knowledge (Moss, Schunn, Schneider, McNamara, & VanLehn, 2011).

Most human cognitive activity is driven by the contents of a huge long-term memory that functions as an information store. Some activities such as perceiving and identifying input and determining familiar problem-solving situations depend greatly on the contents of such long-term memory. Information is obtained from the long-term stores of other people by emulating what they do, listening to what they say, or reading what they write. Working memory, on the other hand, processes new information, and only a few elements of novel information can be processed in working memory simultaneously, resulting in a limited-capacity working memory (Diao, Chandler, & Sweller, 2007).

Cognitive load theory (henceforth, CLT) is concerned with relationships between working and long-term memory and the effects of those relationships on learning and problem solving. CLT has been used to generate many instructional procedures (Sweller, 2004; Sweller, Ayres, & Kalyuga, 2011) and has analysed phenomena like the redundancy effect (henceforth, RE) (Sweller et al., 2011). This effect occurs when the same information is presented to learners in different forms simultaneously (for example: read and listen). The act of having to pay attention to and match up spoken and written text at once slows down comprehension and turns out to be counterproductive if learning English is the ultimate goal (Diao et al., 2007; Machado & Luchini, 2013; Luchini, 2015; Luchini, Ferreiro, & González, 2016; Sweller et al., 2011; Tuero & Luchini, 2012a, b).

Contrary to these research findings, it is often the case that many ESL/EFL instructors use an explicit dual mode of presenting a text to teach L2 reading comprehension. In many reading comprehension lessons, most of the work teachers do implicitly assumes that spoken and written text should be presented jointly when students are learning to read comprehensibly. In cases like this, multiple instructional resources are often encouraged in language teaching to provide learners with rich linguistic knowledge. The belief underlying this common teaching practice is that the more integrative the presentation modes are, the more beneficial for learning they will be. However, CLT suggests otherwise. Instructional design that pushes learners to divide their attention between multiple sources of information is ineffective for learning to happen. It follows then that information should be presented to students in ways that do not impose on them a heavy extraneous cognitive load; for example, presenting reading alone (Diao et al., 2007; Sweller et al., 2011).

Along these lines, the purpose of this chapter is to investigate and compare the effect of simultaneous presentations (read and listen) and single presentations (read only) on reading comprehension in L2 with two groups of young learners with different English proficiency levels. In the light of the results obtained, the extent to which language proficiency compensates for the so-called RE will be analysed and some of its pedagogical implications will be discussed.

Extensive Review

In recent decades there has been growing interest in the field of reading comprehension in a second/foreign language. In this scenario, comprehension cannot be reduced to a mere process of accessing word meanings and combining them; it is an undeniably more active and complex process as there are a number of interactive variables involved in it. When learners tackle a comprehension task, they must resort to several cognitive procedures to select information from discourse clues, and connect it to their existing knowledge located in long-term memory (Gao, 2012).

As we have seen, comprehension is not a simple process of accessing word meanings and then combining them. It involves the construction of a mental representation of a text as a result of intricate cognitive processes (Kintsch, 1998; Zwaan & Radvansky, 1998). Given this complexity, reading comprehension becomes a very important predictor for successful language learning because it subsumes the mental processes of learning, memory and problem solving (Graves, Juel, & Graves, 1998). And this complexity becomes ever greater when students have to read in L2 because of the interactive nature of variables and factors involved. Although many studies have been conducted to examine and illustrate the L2 reading strategies used by different learners in diverse contexts (Hosenfeld, 1977; Block, 1986, 1992; Sarig, 1987; Barnett, 1988; Carrell, 1989; Pritchard, 1990; Anderson, 1991; Raymond, 1993; Liontas, 1999; Young & Oxford, 1997; Schueller, 1999; Brantmeier, 2000), there has been some disparity in the research methods utilized across them, a fact that has made it difficult to formulate generalizations. Given this situation, there are still a certain number of limitations in their instructional implications.

As a whole, learner strategies are the cognitive steps learners follow to process L2 input. In general terms, these cognitive procedures include retrieving and storing new input (Brown, 1994). More specifically, reading strategies are the comprehension processes that readers use in order to make sense of what they read. This process may entail skimming, scanning, guessing, recognizing cognates and word families, reading for meaning, predicting, activating general knowledge, making inferences, following references, and separating main ideas from secondary ideas (Barnett, 1988).

As was mentioned above, a plethora of studies have been conducted to investigate the comprehension strategies that L2 readers use to process a text. Disregarding the variety of research method used in the process of collecting data, all researchers engaged in similar tasks. The research processes generally involved some type of mental process of learning, memory and problem solving, and the tasks used to elicit and examine strategy type and frequency of strategy use were mostly think-aloud verbal protocols, interviews, questionnaires, observations and written recalls. The reading passages used to collect data often varied in content or topic, difficulty level, and text type or genre. In all, the studies varied in both text type and test type. Given the wide range of variability of participants, tasks and reading materials employed in them, it has thus become difficult to compare their results and make some generalizations (Brantmeier, 2002). It is evident, therefore, that much important research remains to be done in this area. Subsequently, generalizations could be made based on the synthesis of research done at different levels of instruction. We could directly model and teach the strategies that good readers use to comprehend their L2 reading materials grounded in empirical research. We could also teach students how to be active L2 readers by providing them with effective instructional materials that facilitate learning by directing cognitive resources towards activities that are relevant to learning rather than toward preliminaries to learning. Ineffective instruction, however, takes place when learners are required to mentally divide their attention to mutually referring information such as reading and listening to the same text simultaneously. This split-source information often generates a heavy cognitive load, because material must be mentally integrated before learning can start to happen (Chandler & Sweller, 1991).

Cognitive load can be understood as the burden that a task imposes on an individual's working memory (Gao, 2012). Cognitive load may be classified into two different types: *intrinsic* and *extrinsic*. Chandler and Sweller (1991) first defined intrinsic cognitive load as the inherent difficulty of learning material. It is important to highlight that it cannot be altered by any instructional means other than changing the task or the levels of knowledge held by learners (Sweller, 1994). On the other hand, extrinsic cognitive load is defined as an unproductive burden imposed on the cognitive system which results from learners investing cognitive resources on activities which are irrelevant to learning. Unlike intrinsic cognitive load, the extraneous one typically results from an inappropriate mode of instruction and can therefore be altered and even reduced if a more effective instructional procedure is employed (Gao, 2012).

CLT (Sweller, 2003, 2004; Sweller et al., 2011) has contributed to shedding some light on some phenomena known as the RE. The RE occurs when one source of presentation is redundant and should be eliminated to free working memory for efficient learning. That is, the RE takes place when the same information is presented to learners in different forms, requiring them to mentally coordinate multiple forms. On some occasions, the learners may need to translate one form into the other to check that the two forms contain the same information (Diao et al., 2007). Presenting information to learners using a dual format forces them to synchronize psychologically the multiple forms and inflicts an extraneous cognitive load on them that may obstruct learning (Chandler & Sweller, 1991; Sweller, 2005; Sweller & Chandler, 1994).

In the ESL/EFL class, this effect may take place when the same information is presented to learners simultaneously through different modes of instruction (e.g. spoken and written). Sweller (2004) states that learning is inhibited when a written and spoken text containing the same information is presented concurrently rather than in written or spoken form alone. When learners are presented with the same information in a dual mode, they are required to mentally bring together the multiple forms. This manifold operation generates, as was said earlier, an extraneous cognitive load that impedes learning (Chandler & Sweller, 1991; Sweller, 2005; Sweller & Chandler, 1994).

Background to the Study

When learning to read in a foreign language, it is a common practice among EFL teachers and instructors to use an explicit dual mode to present a text. Indeed, many textbooks include the phrase "listen and read" every time there is a text. In many cases, it seems to be the 'textbook advice' to expose students to the same information using a dual format. However, as stated before, the effects of this manifold operation do not seem to be conducive to learning. Many studies based on CLT suggest that multiple forms of presenting information turn out to be counterproductive for comprehension purposes. In fact, it has been demonstrated that simultaneous reading and listening is less effective than just reading (Luchini, 2015; Luchini, Ferreiro, & González, 2016).

In a study carried out with a group of 30 students preparing to take the TOEFL (Test of English as a Foreign Language) exam at a private middle school in Mar del Plata, Argentina, Machado (2014) showed that there were significant differences in gain scores in a reading comprehension task across the two presentation modes of instruction. Examination of text comprehension scores indicated that learners exposed to the reading-only mode (group A) obtained better results than those in group B, exposed to the redundant mode of instruction (read and listen). That is, the students who only read the text were able to retrieve more main ideas than the other group which read and listened to the same material at the same time. In a similar study conducted with EFL trainees on a teacher training programme at a university in Mar del Plata, Argentina, similar results were obtained. In this investigation, two groups of university students were exposed to two different reading treatments: read only, and read and listen, and the group exposed to the reading-only treatment outperformed the other one.

In another experimental study, and using the CLT as the theoretical framework, Luchini, Ferreiro, and González (2016) also analysed the extent to which the RE influenced the L2 reading comprehension skills of a group of young learners in a private school in Mar del Plata, Argentina. A group of 24 Spanish-L1 speakers participated in the study. They were divided into two groups, A and B, and both completed the same reading comprehension task separately, but each used a different mode of presentation. Group A was exposed to a single mode of instruction, reading, while group B was presented with a dual format which integrated reading with listening. Both groups had the same amount of time on task. Results revealed that group A (non-redundant group) outperformed group B (redundant group). Once more these findings were consistent with the ones deployed by other investigations in similar contexts.

On similar grounds, Luchini and Ferreiro (2014) carried out another study in which they explored the effect of the RE on the L2 reading comprehension skills of another group of young learners taking a low-intermediate course in English in a local middle school in Mar del Plata, Argentina. The students were divided into two groups: A & B. Group A was exposed to a single mode of instruction (reading) and group B was given a multiple-format presentation (reading + listening). Data were gathered using a text that was carefully chosen to meet the students' age and English language proficiency level. After completing the reading task, both groups filled out a questionnaire, and five students from each group were interviewed separately. Using a mixed research design, qualitative and quantitative information coming from different instruments of data collection was cross-checked. Findings showed that group A scored better results than group B. Therefore, anchored in the CLT and based on results from previous experimental research and our own professional experience, the present research study was designed to analyse the effect of simultaneous presentations (read and listen) and single presentations (read only) on reading comprehension with learners who have different proficiency levels: students preparing to take the PET (preliminary English test, Cambridge Certificate Exams) and the FCE (First Certificate in English exam, Cambridge Certificate Exams), both international examinations administered by the University of Cambridge.

Purpose

The purpose of this study is twofold. On the one hand, we aim to determine whether dual modes of presenting the same information generate an RE when reading in English. On the other hand, we set out to determine the extent to which language proficiency can reduce or compensate for the possible RE. Finally, based on these results some recommendations will be given for the teaching of reading comprehension in the foreign language class.

Research Question

In this study, we will explore and compare the effects of simultaneous presentations with those coming from single modes of instruction. To do this, we will have two groups of students (divided into two subgroups) complete the same reading comprehension task, working under the two different treatments. The research question that will guide this study is as follows:

- In the case of EFL reading comprehension, does language proficiency reduce or compensate for the extraneous cognitive load generated when dual modes of presentation are used in the reading class?

Methodology and Materials

Participants

Participants were two groups of students preparing to take PET and FCE exams. The total number of students from both groups was 50. The PET group included 24 students aged 14–15. In the FCE group, there were 26 participants, ranging in age from 16 to 18. Both groups were divided into two equal subgroups: PET, group A and B; FCE, group A and B. The students were randomly selected. Each group completed a task separately and at different times. Group A was exposed to a single mode of instruction (reading), while group B was asked to read and listen to the same scripted text simultaneously.

Procedure

Data were gathered employing a full text of about 500 words. This text was drawn from a students' course book used for preparation for the PET test (Baker, 2010). This passage was deliberately selected from this source to guarantee that its linguistic complexity and its length would not become an internal factor that would eventually threaten the validity of the study.

Three evaluators segmented the text into main and secondary ideas. Initially, two evaluators worked together to spot the main ideas. Then, a third intervened to cross-check their findings. Inter-marker rating and agreement was used. In cases of discrepancy between the raters, the three evaluators, working jointly, discussed them until they reached a common consensus. A total of nine main ideas were identified.

The text was broken into five different paragraphs, each similar in length (approximately 100 words). These paragraphs were shown to the learners on five

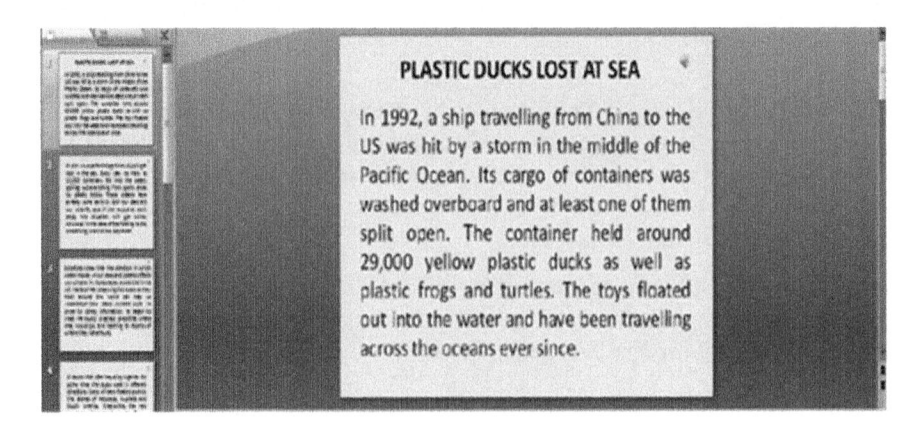

Fig. 11.1 First slide shown to both groups

successive PowerPoint slides. Each slide was held on display for about 30 s. Learners were not allowed to control the pacing of the slides. The time allotted for learners to read each slide was calculated taking into account a pilot experience carried out by their teacher, prior to data collection, in which the average time it took learners to read and understand excerpts of a similar linguistic complexity and length was measured.

Group A was asked to read the narration on slides, while group B was presented with the audio narration along with a synchronized redundant on-screen text. The slide presentation was shown to both groups individually in two consecutive turns. Right after the reading/listening tasks, the learners were asked to write a summary of what they had read, containing as much information as they could retrieve. They could choose to write their ideas in L1 or L2, to facilitate the expression of their ideas.

Figure 11.1 shows the first slide shown to the learners, containing the opening fragment.

Results

The ideas included in students' free recall procedures (A: read; B: read and listen) were then analysed following the set of nine main ideas selected by raters. These ideas were used as 'master ratings' to analyse the students' written texts and evaluate their productions.

In the PET group, the students exposed to the reading-only treatment (group A) identified 51 main ideas out of a total number of 108, whereas group B spotted a total number of 32 main ideas. In the FCE group the students exposed to the reading-only treatment identified 78 main ideas, whereas the learners presented with the dual mode of instruction spotted a total number of 54 main ideas. Table 11.1

11 Cognitive Load Theory, Redundancy Effect and Language Learning

Table 11.1 Students and main ideas retrieved

Group A: reading only		Group B: read and listen	
Participants	Main ideas	Participants	Main ideas
Student 1	6	Student 1	6
Student 2	2	Student 2	6
Student 3	6	Student 3	1
Student 4	4	Student 4	5
Student 5	4	Student 5	2
Student 6	4	Student 6	4
Student 7	3	Student 7	0
Student 8	7	Student 8	0
Student 9	6	Student 9	2
Student 10	5	Student 10	1
Student 11	2	Student 11	3
Student 12	2	Student 12	2
Total	51	Total	32

shows the number of students in each group and main ideas retrieved by each student in each group.

Examination of text comprehension scores indicated that those learners who were exposed to the reading-only treatment obtained better results than those exposed to the redundant mode of instruction. On applying the ratio suggested (9 main ideas, 12 and 13 students per group), the analysis of media indicates that, in both groups, the ones exposed to the reading-only treatment (subgroups A) were able to retrieve more main ideas than the students in subgroups B (exposed to a dual format) (see Table 11.1).

Although looking at media scores may show a difference, that information does not tell us if the difference is reliable. To check whether the average of the two means is reliably different from each other, we decided to run an unpaired T-test. The value for p (two tails) is 0.06. Because the p value is greater than 0.05, we can then say that the average of these two means is statistically significant (see Table 11.2).

Table 11.2 also reveals a difference between means when comparing scores between the FCE subgroups A and B. Results show that this difference favours considerably group A, which was exposed to the single mode of instruction. In much the same was as we did with the PET group, we also ran an unpaired T-test to verify the reliability of this difference (see Table 11.3).

The T-test showed that the p value is 2.53. Once more, as this value is much higher than 0.05, we may claim that the difference between the means for these subgroups is statistically significant.

Table 11.2 *T*-test for the PET group

	Group A	Group B
Media	4.25	2.66
Variance	3.11	4.6
Number of participants	12	12
Hypothetic diff. between means	0	
Degree of freedom	21	
Statistic 1	1.97	
$P(T \leq t)$ one tail	0.03	
Critical value of T (one tail)	1.72	
$P(T \leq t)$ two tails	**0.06**	
Critical value of T (two tails)	2.07	

Table 11.3 *T*-test for the FCE group

	Group A	Group B
Media	6	3.92
Variance	1.16	0.91
Number of participants	13	13
Hypothetic diff. between means	0	
Degree of freedom	24	
Statistic 1	5.19	
$P(T \leq t)$ one tail	1.26	
Critical value of T (one tail)	1.71	
$P(T \leq t)$ two tails	**2.53**	
Critical value of T (two tails)	2.06	

Conclusions

In our research question, we wondered whether English language proficiency could reduce or compensate for the extraneous cognitive load generated when dual modes of presentation were used in the reading comprehension class. The results of this experiment revealed that those learners who were exposed to the reading-only treatment obtained better results than those who read and listened to the same text at the same time. In both groups, a single mode of instruction decreased the RE and seemed to facilitate reading comprehension skills.

In the FCE group, where all students read a text which was not highly challenging for them as it was relatively below their proficiency level, the students from group A (read only) outperformed the students from group B (read and listen). Once again, it seems that an instructional design that integrates a dual mode of instruction imposes an extraneous cognitive load that manifestly obstructs reading comprehension, regardless of students' linguistic proficiency level.

This last claim may contradict some SLA (second language acquisition) theories which foster the use of multiple presentations. When, with the aim of fostering overall comprehension, the same text is presented using two different modes of instruction, learners are pushed to activate two different channels simultaneously to process the same information and to build up referential network connections (Sweller, 2005).

Decoding an L2 text using one sole mode of instruction already implies a demanding cognitive load over working memory. It is very unlikely that L2 learners will have sufficient working memory capacity to be able to handle a dual mode of instruction that involves reading and listening simultaneously, as this implies competition between resources in working memory. As experts in the field of CLT have pointed out, when a text containing the same information is presented simultaneously in written and spoken form, students are immersed in a manifold operation which generates an extraneous cognitive load that hinders comprehension (Sweller et al., 2011; Sweller, 2005; Sweller & Chandler, 1994).

Some Pedagogical Implications

Although small-scale, the present study has some practical pedagogical implications. It suggests, first, that teachers and material designers should appraise their work in ways that reduce learners' extraneous or unnecessary cognitive load, so as to facilitate comprehension. Along these lines, a set of numerous steps could be taken in the foreign language reading comprehension class to foster learning. Teachers should reconsider the impact of the RE on the reading aloud of instructions.

A popular belief among language teachers points out that reading instructions aloud, along with their students, will facilitate reading comprehension. Another common practice that reinforces the RE consists in teachers reading out loud a passage along with their students who are later required to explain, in their own words, what they have understood. In some other cases, teachers often appoint one student to read aloud a text while the rest of the class does it silently. Once the reading stage is over, one of them is asked to reconstruct what they have understood. Certainly such practice is not conducive to learning (Luchini, 2015).

As shown in this and in previous studies, the RE affects EFL learners no matter what their command of the language may be. It is not a question of how each individual student tackles the reading task at hand, but rather of the extent to which a dual mode of instruction may thwart the reading comprehension process, imposing on students a heavy cognitive load.

We are confident that this study, along with some others in the area, will serve as a trigger to open new doors and raise ESL/EFL teachers' and researchers' motivation and interest to keep on investigating the impact that the RE has in their students' reading comprehension process.

References

Anderson, N. J. (1991). Individual differences in strategy use in second language reading and testing. *Modern Language Journal, 75,* 460–472.

Anderson, N., & Pearson, D. (1984). A schema-theoretic view of basic processes in reading comprehension. In D. Pearson, R. Barr, & M. Kamil (Eds.), *Handbook of reading research.* London, Mahwah, New Jersey: Lawrence Erlbaum Associates, Publishers.

Baker, D. (2010). *PET result.* Oxford: Oxford University Press.

Barnett, M. A. (1988). Reading through context: How real and perceived strategy use affects L2 comprehension. *Modern Language Journal, 72,* 150–160.

Block, E. (1986). The comprehension strategies of second language readers. *TESOL Quarterly, 20,* 463–494.

Block, E. (1992). See how they read: Comprehension monitoring of L1 and L2 readers. *TESOL Quarterly, 26*(2), 319–341.

Brantmeier, C. (2000). *The relationship between readers' gender, passage content, comprehension and strategy use in reading Spanish as a second language* (Unpublished doctoral dissertation). Indiana University at Bloomington, IN.

Brantmeier, C. (2002). Second language reading strategy research at the secondary and university levels: Variations, disparities and generalizability. *The Reading Matrix, 2*(3), 1–14.

Brown, H. D. (1994). *Principles of language learning and teaching.* Upper Saddle River, NJ: Prentice Hall.

Carrell, P. L. (1989). Metacognitive awareness and second language reading. *Modern Language Journal, 73,* 121–133.

Chandler, P., & Sweller, J. (1991). Cognitive load theory and the format of instruction. *Cognition and Instruction, 8,* 293–332.

Cooper, G. (1998). *Research into cognitive load theory and instructional design at UNSW.* School of Education Studies: The University of New South Wales, Sydney.

Craig, S. D., Gholson, B., & Driscoll, D. M. (2002). Animated pedagogical agents in multimedia educational environments: Effects of agent properties, picture features, and redundancy. *Journal of Educational Psychology, 94,* 428–434.

Diao, Y., Chandler, P., & Sweller, J. (2007). The effect of written text on comprehension of spoken English as a foreign language. *American Journal of Psychology, 120*(3), 237–261.

Fayer, J. M., & Krasinski, E. (1987). Native and nonnative judgments of intelligibility and irritation. *Language Learning, 37,* 313–326.

Gao, Y. (2012). *Effects of speaker variability on learning spoken English for EFL learners.* A thesis in fulfillment of the requirements for the degree of Doctor of Philosophy.

Graves, M. F., Juel, C., & Graves, B. B. (1998). *Teaching reading in the 21st century: Order processing.* Des Moines: Allyn and Bacon.

Hosenfeld, C. (1977). A preliminary investigation of the reading strategies of successful and unsuccessful second language learners. *System, 5,* 11–123.

Johnson, P. (1981). Effects on reading comprehension of language complexity and cultural background of a text. *TESOL Quarterly, 15,* 169–181.

Kalyuga, S., Chandler, P., & Sweller, J. (2000). Incorporating learner experience into the design of multimedia instruction. *Journal of Educational Psychology, 92,* 126–136.

Kalyuga, S., Chandler, P., & Sweller, J. (2004). When redundant on-screen text in multi-media technical instruction can interfere with learning. *Human Factors, 46,* 567–581.

Kintsch, W. (1988). The role of knowledge in discourse comprehension: A construction-integrated model. *Psychological Review, 95,* 163–182.

Kintsch, W. (1998). *Comprehension: A paradigm for cognition.* Cambridge: Cambridge University Press.

Lee, J. F., & Ballman, T. L. (1987). Learners' ability to recall and rate important ideas of an expository text. In B. Van Patten, T. R. Dvorack, & J. F. Lee (Eds.), *Foreing language learning: A research perspective* (pp. 108–117). Rowley, MA: Newbury House.

Lightbown, P. (2000). Classroom SLA research and second language acquisition. *Applied Linguistics, 21,* 431–462.
Lightbown, P. M., Spada, N., & White, L. (Eds.). (1993). The role of instruction in second language acquisition. [Thematic issue] *Studies in second language acquisition, 15*(2).
Liontas, J. I. (1999). *Developing a pragmatic methodology of idiomaticity: The comprehension and interpretation of SL vivid phrasal idioms during reading* (Unpublished doctoral dissertation). The University of Arizona, Tucson, AZ.
Luchini, P. (2015). Simultaneous reading and listening is less effective than reading alone: A study based on cognitive load theory. In E. Piechurska-Kuciel & M. Szyszka (Eds.), *The ecosystem of the foreign language learner: Selected issues* (pp. 71–81). New York, Dordrecht, London: Springer Cham Heidelberg.
Luchini, P., & Ferreiro, G. (2014). La interface entre la Teoría de la Carga Cognitiva y habilidades de lectura comprensiva en L2: Un estudio experimental mixto. *DILL (Didáctica Lengua y Literatura), 26,* 241–262.
Luchini, P., Ferreiro, G., & González, M. P. (2016). Effects generated by cognitive load theory: An experiment with young learners' reading comprehension skills. *COPAL (Concordia Working Papers in Applied Linguistics) 6*: 46–61 (Concordia University, Montreal, Canada). http://doe.concordia.ca/copal/volumes/.
Machado, C., & Luchini, P. (2013). *Effects generated by cognitive load theory: Does language proficiency reduce the redundancy effect?* V Jornadas de Actualización de la Enseñanza de Inglés: Facultad de Humanidades, Universidad Nacional de San Juan, Argentina.
Mayer, R. E., Heiser, J., & Lonn, S. (2001). Cognitive constraints on multimedia learning: When presenting more material results in less understanding. *Journal of Educational Psychology, 93,* 187–198.
McNamara, D. S., & Magliano, J. (2009). Towards a comprehensive model of comprehension. In B. H. Ross (Ed.), *The psychology of learning and motivation* (pp. 297–384). New York: Academic Press.
Miller, G. A. (1956). The magical number seven, plus or minus two: Some limits on our capacity for processing information. *Psychological Review, 63,* 81–97.
Moss, J., Schunn, C., Schneider, W., McNamara, D., & VanLehn, K. (2011). The neural correlates of strategic reading comprehension: Cognitive control and discourse comprehension. *NeuroImage, 58,* 675–686.
Munro, M. J., & Derwing, T. M. (1999). Foreign accent, comprehensibility and intelligibility in the speech of second language learners. *Language Learning, 49*(1), 285–310.
Pritchard, R. (1990). The effects of cultural schemata on reading processing strategies. *Reading Research Quarterly, 25,* 273–295.
Raymond, T. M. (1993). The effects of structure strategy training on the recall of expository prose for university students reading French as a second language. *Modern Language Journal, 77,* 445–458.
Sarig, G. (1987). High-level reading in the first and in the foreign language: Some comparative process data. In J. Devine, P. L. Carrell, & D. E. Eskey (Eds.), *Research in reading in English as a second language* (pp. 105–120). Washington: TESOL.
Schueller, J. (1999). *The effects of two types of strategic training on foreign language reading comprehension: An analysis by gender and proficiency* (Unpublished doctoral dissertation). The University of Wisconsin-Madison, Madison, WI.
Sweller, J. (1994). Cognitive load theory, learning difficulty, and instructional design. *Learning and Instruction, 4,* 295–312.
Sweller, J. (1999). *Instructional design in technical areas.* Camberwell, Victoria: Australian Council for Educational Research.
Sweller, J. (2003). Evolution of human cognitive architecture. In B. Ross (Ed.), *The psychology of learning and motivation* (pp. 215–266). San Diego, CA: Academic Press.
Sweller, J. (2004). Instructional design consequences of an analogy between evolution by natural selection and human cognitive architecture. *Instructional Science, 32,* 9–31.

Sweller, J. (2005). The redundancy principle. In R. E. Mayer (Ed.), *Cambridge handbook of multimedia learning* (pp. 159–167). New York: Cambridge University Press.

Sweller, J., Ayres, P., & Kalyuga, S. (2011). *Cognitive load theory*. New York: Springer.

Sweller, J., & Chandler, P. (1994). Why some material is difficult to learn. *Cognition and Instruction, 12*, 185–233.

Trofimovich, P., & Isaacs, T. (2012). Disentangling accent from comprehensibility. *Bilingualism: Language and Cognition, 15*(4), 905–916.

Tuero, S., & Gómez Laich, M. P. (2012a). Análisis de los efectos de presentaciones en modalidades múltiples en cognición. In *XIII Congreso de Lingüística Sociedad Argentina de Lingüística, IFDC-San Luis*. March 27–30, 2012 Potrero de los Funes, San Luis, Argentina.

Tuero, S., & Gómez Laich, M. P. (2012b). Sobrecarga cognitiva: Relación entre presentaciones múltiples en el proceso de lectura. In Adolfo M. García (Ed.), *Aproximaciones teóricas y empíricas a la lingüística cognitiva* (pp. 335–345). Editorial Martín: Mar del Plata.

Varonis, E. M., & Gass, S. M. (1982). The comprehensibility of nonnative speech. *Studies in Second Language Acquisition, 4*, 114–136.

Yali, D., Chandler, P., & Sweller, J. (2007). The effect of written text on comprehension of spoken English as a foreign language. *American Journal of Psychology, 120*(2), 237–261.

Young, D. J., & Oxford, R. (1997). A gender-related analysis of strategies used to process input in the native language and a foreign language. *Applied Language Learning, 8*, 43–73.

Zwaan, R. A. (1999). Situation models: The mental leap into imagined worlds. *Current Directions. Psychological Science, 8*, 15–18.

Zwaan, R. A., Langston, M. C., & Graesser, A. C. (1995). The construction of situation models in narrative comprehension: An event-indexing model. *Pyschological Science, 6*, 292–297.

Zwaan, R. A., & Radvansky, G. A. (1998). Situation models in language comprehension and memory. *Psychological Bulletin (USA), 123*, 162–185.

Printed by Printforce, the Netherlands